Talks My Father Never Had With Me
Never Had With Me
(Helping The Young Male Make It To Adulthood)

MENTOR'S GUIDE
Volume One
Expanded & Revised 2004

Dr. Harold D. Davis

KJAC PUBLISHING

P.O. Box 111
Champaign, Illinois 61824-111
• 1-800-268-5861 • www.kjac-publishing.com • staff@kjac-publishing.com

©1997 by Dr. Harold D. Davis

About the cover:

The tear-away (heads missing) is the motif of the TALKS Mentoring Curriculum series. It symbolizes how wisdom is not being shared between mature men and today's young men. Mentors serve to partially bridge this gap and fill this void.

The models on the front of the book are: Left: Greg Bunch and son Lawson Right: Johnnie Lee Harris and son Kevin

Cover Design by Carlton Bruett

Drawings by Chris Evans

Training videos, mentor handbooks and other materials are available from the author. You may contact Dr. Harold Davis or order additional books by writing or calling
1-800-268-5861
217-352-1098 fax

Contents

A Call To Action

We believe that when future generations assess our culture, they will discover that we were guilty of allowing communication between adults and youth to slip dangerously below acceptable levels. As parents and youth workers, we're surrounded by kids, and at times we forget that our experience is not the norm.

An unacceptably high percentage of today's men and women don't interact with adolescents or children at all. When mature, empowered adults neglect to spend time with the next generation, their society will soon disintegrate because of the loss of core values to sustain it. No society survives long when young people must learn the basic principles of that society without the instruction, influence, and guidance of mature men and women.

Our nation is facing a crisis: many young people have no concept of the principles that have **made our** nation great. The struggles of past generations are being lost; most of our young **people have no** historical appreciation or perspective. This lack of understanding will doom **them** to repeat the mistakes of the past.

As adults, we are very much in touch with our childhoods and empathize with children, or feel what they feel. When we look into the eyes of a child, the child inside us challenges the adult we are now to do something to make a difference.

The TALKS Program contributes to the solution by providing a tool that any adult can use to impact the lives of boys or girls. It has been our experience that when parameters are given to busy adults, they find that it is possible to fit mentoring into their busy schedule. The TALKS Structure provides the parameters and the Curriculum provides the "what to do."

The mentoring curriculum includes:
Talks My Father Never Had With Me: Helping the Young Male Make It to Adulthood, Dr. Harold Davis, author in three editions (Church, public elementary school, public middle or high school); and *Talks My Mother Never Had With Me: Helping the Young Female Transition to Womanhood,* Dr. Ollie Watts Davis, author (also in three editions).

These and other books, training videos, and additional materials for young people are available from: KJAC Publishing
P.O. Box 111
Champaign, IL 61824
1-800-268-5861
Web page: http://www.kjac-publishing.com Email: staff@kjac-publishing.com

About the TALKS Mentoring Curriculum

TALKS is both an approach and a curriculum.

- **T**RANSFERRING
- **A**
- **L**ITTLE
- **K**NOWLEDGE
- **S**YSTEMATICALLY

The Vision of TALKS is to share wisdom between generations.

The Purpose of TALKS is to lead young men and women to make personal commitments to integrity and excellence.

The Goal of TALKS is to structure opportunities for constructive dialogue between mature, adult role models and youth, by creating networks between schools, communities and churches that will provide instruction in moral, ethical and responsible living.

The Approach TALKS uses is to coordinate short, weekly, content-based meetings between one adult and three youth at the school, during school hours, while providing all of the necessary materials for successful mentoring.

Unique Features of This Approach Include:

A minimal time commitment:
The average session lasts 25-45 minutes. For mentoring in the schools, mentors can budget about one hour per week for the lesson, preparation, and travel time.

A content-based curriculum:
The TALKS curricula discuss many topics such as academics, self-esteem, peers, family, relationships, and life skills. The curricula is designed to make a pre-emptive strike on the pressing adult issues of our time.

A one-to-three approach:
Mentoring three students at a time reduces many of the common pitfalls associated with mentoring such as: student manipulation, the mother/father-replacement syndrome, unhealthy dependence on the mentor, and the risk of false accusations against the mentor.

Adaptability to a variety of settings:
Mentoring can happen in public or private schools, homes, juvenile facilities, religious or community youth organizations, and long-distance (particularly by relatives).

Design of the Curriculum
*   Structured, practical, and pragmatic.
*   Addresses topics that are often hard to discuss.
*   Allows the public schools to partner with the community in a pro-active position to remedy moral disintegration and decline.
*   Creates the opportunity for mature men and women to share wisdom regarding positive, ethical, and responsible living.

The Varied Uses of the Curriculum
The TALKS Curriculum is being used in a variety of settings by individuals, youth clubs, schools, juvenile facilities, churches and men's groups. There are many viable ways to use the curriculum. Let's consider a few:

*   **One Mature Adult With Three Young People**

In this setting, three diverse children are placed in a group with a mentor. This grouping creates a positive peer environment for the boys. Because of the large number of boys who need mentoring and the small number of men available to mentor, the one-to-three approach serves more children.

*   **The Large Group Setting**

In this setting, one or two men are grouped with a whole group of boys. The author of this curriculum mentors seven boys in a local middle school. Other appropriate large group uses are: a sports team, classroom, summer camp and any setting where a group of boys are gathered.

*   **One With One: A Father With His Son**

Very few men talk to their sons as much as they should. Reading this or any other book would be a great way for a father and son to approach the difficult subjects that need to be discussed.

*   **Long-Distance Mentoring**

This curriculum is often used as a correspondence course for children, grandchildren and those in penal institutions.

One primary benefit of the TALKS Curriculum is that the mentor can let the book be the villain as he deals with sensitive subjects.

How to Use the Curriculum

1. Let the book be the villain as you deal with sensitive subjects.
- From the start, establish that you will discuss one subject until you complete it.
- Don't change the order of topics, but deal with them as they come.
- Feel free to repeat chapters or spend several weeks on them as the need dictates.
- Let the curriculum assist you when participation is slow by having the boys read.

2. The Order of a Lesson.
Read the mentor's page (first page of every chapter) before you meet your boys (about 10 minutes of preparation time).

Introduce the lesson by saying, "Last week we talked about_____." After a brief review, state, "Today we will read and discuss Chapter __. Turn to page __ and I would like for someone to start reading" or, "Today we will continue to discuss Chapter __." If they draw a blank on last week's lesson, repeat it. Please note: We are not interested in finishing the book or chapter. It is possible to spend up to six weeks on one chapter if it is done correctly.

Read the lesson. Have the students take turns reading a paragraph. As the student reads, stop to emphasize certain points or to share personal experience. Never allow boys to kick themselves when they make a mistake reading. This happens when a boy makes a mistake, cringes in pain and makes self deprecating statements. At this point you must encourage him and let him know that everybody makes mistakes and that it is OK.

Once the reading begins, you are the reading teacher and encourager. Compliment each boy after they read and always note every major and minor success. Remember, boys in our society are rarely complimented by men on academic issues.

The use of a dictionary is suggested. We suggest you use a small dictionary, not the big red one that is available in the classroom. Our preference is "Webster's Pocket English Dictionary," Revised Edition, ISBN 0-7607-2720-1. One way to use the dictionary is to assign words to each boy. Let everyone know that this word is (David's word). Ask David to look the word up, help him read the word, put his initials in the margin beside his word. The next week ask him what was his word. Then give him the dictionary and ask him to look it up. His initials in the margin will help him find it quickly. Do this with all the boys and try to challenge each boy with five or six words per year.

Read the questions. When the chapter is concluded, read each question at the end of the chapter or state them in your own words and encourage discussion. Please note: You may see a question repeated or worded differently. The repetition is designed to aid retention.

Read the quotes. Quotes (hereafter referred to as wisdom) are peppered throughout the chapter and a collection of wisdom is found at the end of each chapter. Please do not rush through this section of the chapter. Learn to take your time and savor the wisdom found here. **It is very important that the boys memorize at least two quotes per chapter.** Your attitude about wisdom and the importance of memorizing it will be picked up by the young people so show some excitement about the wisdom and take your time as you discuss it.

The questions after each quote are designed to promote discussion. Be sure to read all of the quotes. Consider requiring the young men to memorize two quotes for each chapter and as a group compose a quote that compliments the chapter. Feel free to share with the boys that you are truly wrestling with the truth found in a quote. When you do this you will breathe life into the activity.

Feel free to spend as much time as necessary on a subject if the mentees remain excited about the subject matter. **There are *no* time limits.** Do not be concerned with the amount of time spent on a lesson. Some lessons will make a tremendous impact and others will only be moderate in their effect. When you consider interruptions, distractions, and time spent in unrelated conversation, it is necessary to prolong some chapters in order to adequately address the subject matter. It is not unusual to only do four or five chapters per year. This is fine.

You will not be able to do more than five or six chapters per school year if you do the following:
- Read the chapter taking time to look up words in the dictionary
- Read and discuss all of the questions
- Read all of the wisdom, questions and memorizing two quotes per chapter, you will not be able to do more than five chapters during a school year.

Each chapter in the book is important and can generate discussion that will lead you to examine many other related issues. Because the TALKS Curriculum is designed to be a pre-emptive strike on adult problems, some issues may not seem important to the young people right now. Explain to them that our goal is to help them with the issues they are dealing with now and prepare them to meet the challenges of the future.

It is important to always remember that in order to take the first step in healing, one must first identify the problem. When young men are quiet, reflective or frustrated it may be because you are addressing a subject that is sensitive to them.

3. The Mentor's page (lesson plan) includes:
- A Definition of the subject matter.
- A challenge for the mentor to connect with his past on the subject. When a mentor teaches and shares with his past in mind his teaching will be very powerful because it will come from his heart.
- A Caution (alerts you to sensitive issues, actions and attitudes that should be avoided).
- A Charge (a point that needs to be repeated often).

Wisdom is presented in three waves:
(The Lesson, Questions and Wisdom)

4. The Lesson (First Wave of Wisdom)

This is the chapter that is included in the student's book. It is designed to open the door of discussion. Share your world and try to get into their world as you read the lesson. Since each chapter is included in the mentor's guide, it is not necessary for the mentor to have a copy of the textbook. If you find redundancy in several chapters, this is by design. Our goal is to reinforce basic principles by stating them in various ways.

5. The Questions (Second Wave of Wisdom)

These may be discussed verbally or used as a written assignment. If the students are slow to start discussing, remind them of the contract they signed promising to answer the questions. Some of the questions say, "Find and complete this sentence." In these cases, the mentor reads the first part of the sentence and asks the boys to find the rest of the sentence in the text. This is to stimulate their interest in the printed page. The student will eventually realize the need to become familiar with the text. Remember, the questions may be answered orally, in writing or both. If you use the questions as a written assignment, xerox the questions, and instruct the students to use a separate sheet of paper to write the answers. Don't rush through this section of the lesson.

6. Wisdom From The Elders (Third Wave of Wisdom)

These will broaden the discussion and give the mentor an opportunity to share. The quotes deal directly with the subject and also touch on a variety of related subjects, coming from individuals representing many periods in World and American history. **Help the young men memorize at lest two quotes per chapter.**

Read the quote and explain what it means to you. Use a dictionary to look up words that are not familiar to you. Occasionally take the time to discuss the personality of the person who is credited with the quote and why, in your opinion, they said it.

Quotes and/or their authors may be used as subjects for further research. Each student should do at least I report per semester. Have the students compose their own quotes for the chapter using the principles you have discussed. Try to help them as little as possible. **The quotes should be kept handy and referred to often.**

> *Listen carefully to what the country people call mother wit. In those homely sayings are couched the collective wisdom of generations.* MAYA ANGELO

Using the TALKS Thesis Statement

The TALKS Leadership Thesis Statement is the Foundation and Guiding Principle for the Mentor/Mentee Relationship. Make a copy of the thesis statement from the back of the book and distribute to the boys. Please feel free to substitute the words "young man" for "boy" when appropriate. For best results have the boys recite the thesis statement as the second thing you do each time you meet. The first thing you do is the standard greeting (Why am I here etc.)

The TALKS Leadership male thesis statement should be recited and memorized. I suggest that you recite it at the beginning of each session. This thesis statement is followed by an explanation. By the end of the year, the young men should memorize both the statement and the explanation. Have the young men memorize all of the Thesis Statement. Be sure to break it up into sections to make it easier for them. This activity is designed to help the boys now but also later in life when there is a natural tendency to rebel against authority.

The TALKS Leadership Male Thesis Statement:

> *Every boy needs a man in his face challenging him with wisdom regarding critical issues and decisions in his life.*

Explanation: Every boy needs a man who will firmly, unflinchingly and lovingly correct him with wisdom when he has made a bad decision. Our prisons are full of young men who had no one to get in their face, tell them that they were wrong, and then provide them with a solution.

Make the point with the boys that not only do boys need men who will challenge them, but men need men who will challenge them with wisdom too. Consider the President of the United States, who meets with smart men who challenge him with wisdom each day. All successful businessmen have other men who challenge them with wisdom. Share with the boys the fact that you listen to older men.

Responding to the challenge.

Make this point with the young men: Wise men respond to wise challenges from wise people. Fools respond to foolish challenges. We have all responded to foolish challenges in the past, that is called being young. But as you mature, you learn to ignore the foolish challenges and respond to wise challenges. The thesis statement is all about responding to wise challenges. Challenge the young men to learn to ignore foolish challenges and respond to wise challenges.

Copy the thesis statement from the back of the book, divide it and give it to the boys to memorize. Memorization of this quote will help the young men see the benefit of dialogue with older men. Feel free to change the word "boy" to "young man" if they find the word "boy" offensive.

How to Set Up The TALKS Structure in Schools

1. Identify a school coordinator who will.
- Identify the children who need mentors.
- Secure student applications and permission slips
- Match mentors with mentees.
- Make arrangements with teachers as necessary.
- Oversee the practical details of the program.

2. Recruit mentors.
- Recruit through personal references. I don't recommend advertising for mentors. Look for consistency, trustworthiness, and morality.
- Have prospective mentors fill out an application. If the program is to be conducted through local schools, ask the school district for a volunteer application. Most schools require background checks and have a system for this.
- Schedule an orientation meeting to give mentors basic training (about one hour long). Training videos for mentors are available, contact publisher.

This meeting is a time for mentors, site coordinator, administrator (principal or dean) to connect. At this time, the men will be introduced to the physical building and given detailed instructions on how to implement the curriculum. Any and all incomplete paperwork will be finalized at this time. These meetings go well during the lunch hour with brown bag lunches provided for those present. Following are some of the basic expectations that should be shared with the mentors. Please adapt this to meet your specific needs.

Share the expectations of mentors
- Mentor 3 boys for approximately 30 minutes per week.
- Mentor during school hours.
- Be punctual. This is part of the instruction to the boys.
- Check in the office upon arriving at the school.
- Please observe all school rules, i.e. (no hats, smoking, cursing, etc.)
- Please contact the office if you will not be able to be there.
- Be timely (start and stop on time).
- Respect your employer by leaving and returning on time.
- Be patient with the school personnel because they are usually understaffed
- You are required by law to report signs of abuse. Contact the site coordinator, dean or principal if you detect physical abuse.

Some characteristics of elementary school boys
- Impressed with your manhood.
- May act uninterested, but will listen to what you have to say.

- They are masters at manipulating and diverting the conversation, keep the lesson focused.
- Remember that you are the oldest and have a vast life experience to share.
- They love to hear stories from your childhood. Feel free to juice them up a bit.
- Be sensitive to a possible fear of reading. Some boys may read below their level.

3. Identify the mentees.

- Choose three young men of similar age and grade. Ideally, the group should include one at-risk child, one median child and one well-adjusted, high-achieving child.
- Try to break up cliques and put related children in different groups.
- Get parental permission to enroll the youth in the program. Generally, sending a permission slip home is sufficient, but may require a home visit. It is worth the extra effort.
- Invite the mentors, mentees, and parents to the contract signing.
- Give young men an overview of the mentoring effort and answer questions.

4. Have the mentors and mentees sign contracts.

- The contracts spell out the terms of the relationship. Both parties are held to the same standards. The students appreciate that the mentor must also be committed to the same terms. Everyone promises to participate with good intentions, read, answer questions, and maintain privacy when necessary. The third clause of the contract gives the mentees permission to disagree with their mentor. The mentee should disagree by saying, "Mr. Smith, I would like to respectfully disagree with you." Have the young men memorize that sentence and use it when they must disagree with an adult.
- Make a big deal out of the contract signing ceremony. Invite witnesses and have someone (coordinator, principal, counselor, etc.) read the contract aloud. After each sentence, have the parties respond, "yes" to agree that they will follow the conditions outlined. Have each group agree to the contract in the presence of each other. Copy the contracts using resume paper for a professional look.
- The contract will usually last for one school year, but may be adapted to fit the needs of individual situations.
- The TALKS Mentoring Thesis Statement and explanation should be discussed and the memorization process started at the contract signing. The thesis statement is very important because it serves as a philosophy of life. It is a philosophy that wise men live by. Wise men know that they benefit when they have older wise men challenge them with wisdom. When discussing the thesis statement break it down into sections. For example take the first section of the thesis statement:

Every boy needs a man in his face - explain to the boys that because of the nature of men, we often need confrontation in order for us to hear what is being said. Boys often need someone who is physically more powerful than they are to get their attention. It is implied that a man being in a boy's face is in his face in the context of love. In other words, "young man, I am telling you this because I love you and I don't want anything bad to happen to you." It is a healthy thing when a man gets in a boy's face. As a matter of fact, it is a powerful thing when a mature man gets in a young man's face.

Challenging him with wisdom - Explain to the young men that when adults care about young people, they challenge inappropriate behavior. Impress upon them that it is a sign of caring concern when adults challenge you. Tell the young men that successful men are challenged daily with wisdom from other men. In every board room, laboratory, factory or plant, men challenge other men with wisdom everyday and that is good for everyone involved.

Regarding critical issues - Please note, the wisdom that is shared pertains to important issues. Wise men do not fool around with the foolishness of young men but will rise up and speak when critical issues are involved. It is a fact that one wrong decision on a critical issue can alter your life's course. Knowing this will help young men listen when they are challenged with wisdom regarding critical issues.

And decisions in life - As adults we know the importance of the decisions we make. While talking about this, share with the young men some decisions you made and the role those decisions had in charting your life's course.

Orientation Meeting for Mentors

This meeting is a time for mentors, site coordinator, administrator (principal or dean) to connect. At this time, the men will be introduced to the physical building and given detailed instructions on how to implement the curriculum. Any and all incomplete paperwork will be finalized at this time. These meetings go well during the lunch hour with brown bag lunches provided for those present. Following are some of the basic expectations that should be shared with the mentors. Please adapt this to meet your specific needs.

Expectations Of Mentors

- Mentor 3 boys for approximately 30 minutes per week.
- Mentor during school hours only.
- Be punctual. This is part of the instruction to them.
- Upon arrival in the building, check in with the office.
- Observe all school rules, i.e. (no hats, smoking, cursing, etc.)
- Contact the office if you will not be able to be there.
- Be timely (start and stop on time).
- Respect your employer by leaving and returning on time.
- You are required by law to report signs of abuse. Contact the site coordinator, dean or principal if you detect physical abuse.

Characteristics of Elementary School Boys

- Impressed with your manhood.
- May act uninterested, but will listen to what you have to say.
- They are masters at manipulating and diverting the conversation, keep the lesson focused.
- They love to hear stories from your childhood. Feel free to juice them up a bit.
- Be sensitive to a possible fear of reading. Some boys may read below their level.

Preparing To Teach The Lesson

- Read the introductory pages of the guide to view the big picture.
- Before you teach the lesson, read the preparatory page for that chapter in the Mentor's guide. This first page will stimulate thought and prepare you to interact with the boys.
- Always discuss the photo at the beginning of the chapter before you read the chapter. Ask questions like: What does that photo say to you? Have you ever felt like that before?
- When you feel that it is appropriate, assign a work sheet for that chapter.
- Always feel free to repeat any lesson that you did not complete or when you feel the boys need more time on a lesson.
- Be sure to use the wisdom of the elders as springboards for discussion.
- At the end of the lesson, as a group activity, compose your own quote.
- Remember that your life and presence, gives credibility to the lesson for the day.

Approach Your Interaction As A Business Appointment

Approaching this mentoring effort as a business appointment is a safety net for the emotions and self-esteem of the man and the boy. When two men meet for a business appointment, it is not necessary that they connect emotionally to successfully conduct business. Business can be successfully conducted between two men without any mutual admiration, general interests or plans for future fellowship. This type of relationship with the boys would be the entry level relationship upon which mutuality can be built. In the event that there is no interest on the part of the men or boys to deepen the relationship, do not be discouraged. The information that is shared between the generations even in a bland emotional environment will be profitable to the young men. It is the responsibility of mature men to share with young men, regardless of their interest in the subject matter. So, keep your business appointments with the boys and do not be discouraged if they are less than excited to share with you, press on!

Encouraging Mentors

Even the best and most motivated mentors can become discouraged. Keeping mentors focused and energized is vital to the success of a mentoring effort. Failure to provide this support is equivalent to neglect! Use these ideas to encourage mentors:

Hold meetings for mutual encouragement.
Mentors can trade stories and encourage each other. The coordinator may invite motivational speakers to make presentations. All mentors should share victory reports with their fellows.

Mentors need mentors too!
Regular conversations with people more experienced than they are will help mentors put problems into perspective and see the big picture. Encourage mentors to seek wise counsel from pastors, child specialists, successful parents or older, wise adults.

Remind mentors that seeds take time to grow.
Often the benefits of mentoring can't be seen early in the mentoring process. Don't become discouraged by this. Often young people don't realize until later how they've benefitted from the experience.

Get the support of the mentors' spouse.
The mentoring effort may be misunderstood by the mentor's spouse. The time spent mentoring could be seen as time stolen from the mentor's own family. As a man or woman sows good seed into the life of a child, that same seed will multiply and come back to benefit his house.

Short-term benefits that signal success
- Men and boys can dialogue freely.
- Men are spending regular time with boys.
- Young men can repeat many of the principles shared with them.
- Adults become familiar with the school environment.

Long term benefits—a road to reconciliation
A strong mentoring program can contribute to reconciliation between races, generations, and social classes. Each community has it's own set of problems and difficulties. Mentoring will help break down barriers and bring solutions to your community.

Sometimes the benefits of mentoring aren't obvious for years.

Tips for Mentors

You are a rich resource for the kids.
You may feel nervous or inadequate when it comes to discussing serious issues with young people. I assure you that you don't need to be an educator, have a college degree, or even be a good talker. If you are willing to share with youth stories about your past and the lessons you have learned, you are in a position of great influence! It is very important that you feel free to reach into your past to retrieve memories regarding the subject matter. The sharing of these memories, situations and problems (using discretion) will greatly encourage the mentees. They love to hear stories about your past struggles, victories and failures. Allow the wisdom in the book to challenge you and feel free to share with the boys when you find yourself wrestling with the truth found in a quote.

Remember that you are impressive!
Most adults have forgotten how impressive they are to young people. Once you develop a track record of meeting with them, your influence will increase with each meeting. Youth are impressed by our cars, our credit cards, our clothes, our spouses, our mobility, and many other factors.

Let the book be the villain.
The TALKS curriculum is an off-with-the-gloves approach to mentoring. It doesn't beat around the bush or dance around sensitive issues! For the most part, the youth know more than we think they know, and can handle more than we may think. When the discussion becomes difficult, find a passage in the book, say "the book says," then quote from the book. This also serves to bring the conversation back to the subject at hand.

Review the lesson plan again.
The mentor's guide is designed to take away fears of inadequacy and help the mentor enjoy the process. The guide provides a one-page reading to prepare the mentor for each session. This introduction connects the mentor with his past and encourages him to let his experience talk. You may want to read the lesson plan more than once to keep your goals fresh in your mind.

Don't rush!
As a mentor, never rush through a lesson; take your time. Don't let the faces of the young men discourage you. Each lesson will be different, and each will hit home with a different person or in a different way. When you come upon a sensitive area, don't rush to conclude. When the young men get quiet, it is a good sign. You may be in a sensitive area for them. This is a good time to tell a related personal story. This will further drive home the point. *Please remember that you are often most effective on those occasions when you feel the least effective.* When in doubt, keep talking and teaching.

Use a vocabulary of praise.
I suggest that you choose several statements to be used with each of your boys. They love praise just as adults do. Use a corresponding smile to go with your words.

Statements of General Praise: Way To Go! - You're Jammin' - Nice Work - Good Job - Beautiful - You're Catching On! - How Nice - You Are On Top Of Things - Bravo - That's The Best! - Hurray For You! - You're Spectacular! - Crucial! (Ask the boys for the latest slang words to use when complementing them)

Statements of Praise For A Particular Accomplishment Like Getting The Right Answer:
I Told You That You Were Smart - Magnificent! - You Figured it Out! - Fantastic Job! - Phenomenal - Great Insight - Beautiful Work - You Learned it Right! - Now You've Got It - Awesome! - Encore! Pick one or more to use during each session.

Statements of Personal Praise to Encourage: You Tried Hard - You've Discovered The Secret - You Are Responsible - What An Imagination - What A Good Listener - You're Perfect! - You Made My Day - That's The Best - You're Important - You Are A Treasure - I Respect You Man. Remember, young men are rarely praised for academic excellence by men. When they perform well academically, pour on the praise! Pick one or more statements to use with each session.

Time Management.
It is important that you share wisdom with the young people in each session before your time is gone. Youth are master manipulators and can direct your attention and the lesson to a more comfortable subject. It is OK to move slowly when the students are internalizing important concepts or when you are dealing with critical issues, but don't let any one person be a "TW" or time waster. The students are required to think, not socialize while they are with you. Get down to the business of the day. If the chapter is long and the reading is moving along slowly, step in and say, "I'll read for awhile." You teach them that time is important by not letting them waste yours.

Maintain a Business Environment.

The following ritual will promote success as you interact with your students.

We have learned that maintaining a business relationship with the young people enhances your chances for long term success. What we suggest is that each time you greet your young men, exchange pleasantries and then ritualistically ask the following questions.

Mentor: Why am I here?
Mentee: To take care of business
Mentor: What is the business?
Mentee: Wisdom
Mentor: Let's get busy . . . Turn to page__ or what did we talk about last week.

It is very important that you do this at the beginning of each session. This practice accomplishes many things, several of which are:

- Reminds the young men of the business nature of your relationship.
- Reestablishes wisdom as the focal point for your meeting.
- Sets the tone for the serious nature of your meeting.

Use the contract as a motivational tool.

When students are slow to participate, remind them of their promise (in writing) to participate. Keep the contracts handy and occasionally read them to the students to remind them of what they have committed themselves to.

The use of a contract teaches responsible behavior and the need to keep commitments. It teaches the youth what their future adult life will be like. Tell them how many contracts you are currently obligated to keep (bank notes, credit card, insurance, etc.)

Use Creative Ways to Further Stimulate the Students.

- Share a book from your personal library.
- Write to the students. The letters could be about a newspaper article that is relevant to your efforts to help the youth. Have them write back to you. Inform their teacher of the letter writing activities and they may give official or unofficial credit for the effort.
- Spend part of a lesson discussing the life of a person who impacted you.
- A quarterly or semi-annual trip to McDonald's is a great motivator. (Be sure to secure permission slips)

Don't Neglect The Importance of Reading.

You may encounter situations where young people will be unable to read and comprehend at their grade level. Please approach these instances carefully. Establish a comfortable, non-threatening environment for the young person. Coax them to read or follow along with you as you read. Urge them to participate even if they are uncomfortable with the idea.

This will accomplish several things:

- Enhance their reading ability and endear the book to them (possibly their first book).
- Aid in retention of the principles shared.
- Reinforce what you are telling them.
- Stimulate them academically.

When reading the book, be careful to take your time. Words and phrases that are familiar to you may be quite foreign to the students. Refrain from glossing over the quotations as if on automatic pilot. Give the students time to digest what is being said and read. Quiz their comprehension with open-ended questions.

Below are some ice-breaking statements to encourage discussion:
- "Look at what that says right there on page 32."
- "If I hadn't read this for myself, I would not have believed it."
- "I wish page 97 was not written because it really challenged me and now I must do better."
- What do you feel the author was thinking when he wrote that?

The goal is to communicate principles, not just to get through the book. I repeat again, don't rush through the chapter.

Getting The Most Out of The Wisdom (quotes)
Review, Repeat, Rehearse

Are you spending enough time on the quotes? Consider taking a whole lesson to discuss one quote—a whole session digging the wisdom out of the quote. One of my favorite quotes is found in the first chapter of the volume one book:

> *"If a man be gracious and courteous to strangers it shows that he is a citizen of the world and that his heart is no island cut off from other lands but a continent that joins them."*

My favorite words in this quote are:
- gracious
- courteous

Consider this: When a leader extends grace (kindness) to a stranger, it places the leader in charge of the conversation. Extending grace to a stranger forces (a reasonable) stranger to respond to your leadership. It is like being able to make the first move in a game of checkers.

When a person is courteous to a stranger, the stranger is challenged to respond. His response will give you some idea of what type of human being your are dealing with. There are definite advantages to being gracious and courteous to strangers. When children memorize this quote it should positively impact the way they conduct themselves in all of their future relationships.

Consider going back to a previous chapter and revisiting the quotes for the purpose of review. **If your children are not using the quotes and talking about them in general conversation, you may want to go back and review them.** Consider the following approaches, they have worked for me.

1. Read the quote as a group.
2. Have your best reader read it alone.
3. Proceed to have each child read the quote. Take time with the slow readers and encourage them.
4. As the leader, expound on the quote and tell what it means to you. Tell stories from your personal experience to highlight the truth found in the quote. Take time to identify new words and their meanings. Use a dictionary if needed.
5. Have your best reader read the quote, close the book, stand up and say the verse from memory.
6. Proceed to have all of your kids read the quote, close the book, stand up and say it from memory.
7. The desired goal is to memorize two quotes per chapter and compose one quote as a group. Be sure go back and review all quotes that you have learned. Our goal is to have the children live the words in each quote. Remember, if you are excited about the quotes, the children will pick up on your excitement. The quotes "if repeated often enough" can become part of the fabric of their thought life. Have fun in the process.

Weekly Check List
(to remind us)

It is very easy to forget the fundamentals. One of the challenges of the TALKS Mentoring Program is to remember to maintain that discipline of reading, remembering and reciting. It is easy and often fun to sit and talk with your boys. You should do this occasionally but your goal is to stay on task share wisdom and make progress through the curriculum.

After a mentoring session, take a moment and check yourself to confirm that you are staying on task. Ask yourself the following questions and see how well you do.

___Did I use the standard introduction?
    Mentor: Why am I here?
    Mentees: To take care of business.
    Mentor: What is the business.
    Mentees: Wisdom.
    Mentor: Let's get busy.

___Did I work on the Thesis Statement?

___Did we read the book together?

___Did we use the dictionary?

___Have we memorized at least two quotes per chapter?

___Did tell some personal stories from my past?

___Did I Compliment my mentees?

___Did I Sign in at the office?

How did you do?
Please remember, you are the man!

Every boy needs a man in his face challenging him with wisdom regarding critical issues and decisions in his life.

Use Code Words or Phrases

Code words are critical. You should actually develop your own language with the boys based on a quote or favorite portion of a chapter. For example, in chapter three, you find the story about the Harrison boys. This is a favorite of mine because it teaches the benefit of hard work even when you do not understand the logic of it all. When I want to compliment one of my boys for their diligence and hard work I compare them to the Harrison boys. They take it as a compliment and the Harrison boys have become a code word that I use with the boys and they use with each other. It is our personal secret phrase that we use when we want to stress excellence.

Work to develop code words around the thesis statement and other wisdom that you study. Simply choose a word and use it in your general conversation. One of my favorites is "challenging him with wisdom."
I often say to a young man:
"I am challenging you with wisdom, how are you going to respond?"

DR. HAROLD DAVIS

Chapter 1

How To Meet Strangers

Definition of a stranger: Any person (young or old) that you are not familiar with. You have not met them before and you have no knowledge of their character and conduct.

Connecting With And Learning From Your Rich, Personal, Painful, Productive Past: Before meeting with your boys, reflect on some of the meetings that you have had with strangers. Recall several things that were real eye-openers to you. Think of some meetings that went well and others that went poorly. Share with the boys how accurate or inaccurate some of your first impressions were. This lesson is a perfect time to share some of the dangers of allowing older strangers to get too close too soon.

CAUTION: Be careful to help the young men see the need for balance. For example, not all strangers are bad people. We must meet new people as we progress through life. It is important to have a cautious openness as we meet new people. One of the worst things that can happen is to develop a stand-offish attitude about all strangers.

CHARGE: Charge the young men to present themselves well when they meet a stranger. The first impression is the one that will be remembered the longest and have the greatest impact. Challenge them to always remember to be impressive on the first impression.

ACTIVITY: Role-play having the boys take turns introducing themselves to each other. Have them look each other in the eye and clearly speak a greeting and their name. This activity can be given as an assignment for them to introduce themselves to others in the school setting. Make it fun.

TIP: When dealing with young people it is very important to establish the tone of your relationship in the beginning. The formal business relationship may seem plastic, cold and uninviting but it is easier to loosen control that you have than it is to gain control that you do not have.

Mentor: Why am I here?

Mentee: To take care of business

Mentor: What is the business?

Mentee: Wisdom

Mentor: Let's get busy . . . Turn to page__ or what did we talk about last week.

Lesson 1

How To Meet Strangers

You are beginning a relationship with a man who has agreed to spend some time with you and share some of his wisdom with you. You are making a first impression today. The first impression is what people think about you the first time they meet you. First impressions are important because they cannot be repeated. You do not know this man, who has agreed to mentor you and just like all men you meet you will need to make a good first impression and get to know him. How do you learn something about a man when you first meet him? Well, the first thing you should do when you meet a stranger is introduce yourself. This is done by shaking the man's hand and looking him in the eye. It has been said that to look into a man's eye is to look into his soul.

When you shake a man's hand, you can learn a little bit about him based on how hard he squeezes your hand, how fast he shakes it and how long he holds on. In our American culture, you should be concerned when a man will not look you in the eye. This is a sign that either he has something to hide or he does not feel good about himself. Another reason you should look him in the eye is that only really good liars can look you in the eye and lie to you.

You can also learn about a man by the clothes he wears. Some men wear suits and ties, and other men wear blue jeans. Our society gives a lot of respect to men who wear suits and ties. Some days I wear a suit and tie and some days I wear blue jeans. When I go in a store with a suit on, the people give me more respect than when I go in a store with blue jeans on. Some men wear suits to impress others and other men wear suits because they like them. It is a fact that the clothes we wear affect how others view us.

Another thing to consider when meeting a stranger is the manner in which he speaks to you. For example, if you meet a stranger and he just says "hi," you can tell that he may not be very excited about meeting you or that he is not much of a talker. On the other hand if you meet him and he says "Hello, my name is David. What is your name?," you can see that he is showing an interest in getting to know you.

I suggest that when you meet a new person, you take the lead. Shake the person's hand, look the person in the eye and say "Hello, my name is ___. It is a pleasure to meet you." This makes a good first impression. The person that you are meeting thinks that you are a smart person and a nice person. This is good for you.

Some men are "people people" and they love meeting strangers and getting to know them. Usually they will give you a good greeting when you meet them. Other people are not very interested in meeting new people, they prefer to be alone and work with machines. These men will say "hello" to you and never really look at you very much. How would you like to present yourself when you meet new people? Would you like them to see you as a "people person" who likes to meet new people, or would you like for them to see you as a "non-people person" who prefers machines and not people?

What do you think about your mentor, this man that you have just met? How do you see him? What have you figured out about him in this short time since you have met him? Do you feel that he is a "people person" or would he work well with machines? Does he wear a suit or does he dress casually? Have you shaken his hand? If so, how did he do? I want to challenge you to analyze your first impression of him and remember it. Later on after you get to know him better you can go back and see if you were right in your analysis of him. If you learn how to do this well, it will help you in the future as you meet new people.

Questions
(to discuss and think about or to serve as a written assignment)

1. Do you think about making a good first impression when you meet someone new?

2. In the first paragraph of this chapter, the author tells us what to do first when we meet a stranger. What did he say you should do?

3. It has been said that to look into a man's eye is to look into his soul. In your opinion, what does this mean?

4. What is a first impression?_____

5. How do you stand when you meet a new person?

6. Have you ever met a famous person? Yes__ No__ If yes, who was it?

7. Find this sentence and complete it: "When you shake a man's hand, you_____

8. Do you look people in the eye when you shake their hands? Yes__ No__

9. What could it mean when a man does not look you in the eye?_____

10. There are many different things you can say when you meet a person. You can say: hi, hello, ola, whad's up, greetings, yo, pleasure meeting you, my pleasure. Which of these do you think you would use?

11. On page 4. the author states how we can tell when a person is showing an interest in getting to know us. What did he say would happen?

12. Do you take the lead when you meet someone new? Yes__ No__

13. Explain how to take the lead when you meet someone new._____

14. Some men have difficulty looking other men in the eye. Is this difficult for you? Yes__ No__

15. When men do not feel good about themselves or do not feel secure they may have difficulty looking another man in the eye. Have you ever had that problem?

16. Are you a "people person" or should you work with machines? _____

17. Can you name some jobs that do not require interaction with people?

18. Can you name some jobs that require a lot of interaction with people?

19. Why is it important to make a good impression?_____

20. What are some of the pros and cons to being social or nonsocial?_____

21. Does it matter to you what other people think about you? Yes__ No__ In reality, it is important what other people think about us because we all live in a world where we depend on other people for the necessities of life. Other people will be your teacher, boss, girlfriend, etc. It is important to develop a balance between being a people pleaser and a person who is not overly concerned about what other people think. Where do you fall between the two?

22. Learning how to analyze people when you meet them is a very important skill that you need to develop. You will use it in your business dealings and personal relationships. Now that you are aware of how important first impressions are and the need to evaluate new people that you meet, what do you plan to do in the future?

23. Learning how to meet new people is a skill that will really help you in life. Are you ready to work on this skill and try to improve it? Yes__ No__

Wisdom From The Elders

Read the quotes and explain them to the boys. Use the questions to begin the discussion. Be sure to work with the boys to compose your own quote that relates to this chapter.

If a man be gracious and courteous to strangers, it shows he is a citizen of the world, and that his heart is no island cut off from other lands, but a continent that joins them.
ESSAYS 1625, OF GOODNESS AND GOODNESS OF NATURE

1. Do you want to be a citizen of the world and relate well to strangers or do you want to be cut off from meeting new people?
2. How do you treat someone who is different from you the first time you meet him/her?
3. If you went to Japan how do you think the people would treat you the first time they met you?
4. According to this quote, what must you do to show that you are a citizen of the world?
5. What does gracious mean?
6. What does courteous mean?
7. Is your heart (the person you are inside) willing to meet strangers or would you rather be alone?
8. This quote discusses two types of hearts. What are they? Which heart do you have?

When one is a stranger to oneself then one is estranged from others too.
ANNE MORROW LINDBERGH

1. In your opinion, how can a person be a stranger to him/herself?
2. How well do you feel you know yourself: Not well, Well, Very Well?
3. Sometimes people who do not feel good about themselves take their frustration out on strangers. Do you feel good about yourself?
4. What are you doing to get to know yourself better?
5. How is having a mentor helping you to get to know yourself better?

Ants and savages put strangers to death. BERTRAND RUSSELL

1. When you meet new young people your age, do you put them to death or are you friendly toward them?
2. In your opinion, why do you feel ants kill other ants that they do not know?
3. What do ants and savages have in common?____ In your experience, have you met any savages in your neighborhood or school?

There are...two kinds of people in this world, those who long to be understood and those who long to be misunderstood. It is the irony of life that neither is gratified.
CARL VAN VECHTEN

1. Do you like to be understood by new people that you meet?
2. Why do you feel that some people want to be misunderstood?
3. What does it mean to be gratified?
4. What gratifies you most, to be understood or to remain mysterious and be misunderstood?

Whoever lives at a different end of town from me, I look upon as persons out of the world, and only myself and the scene about me to be in it. JONATHAN SWIFT

1. Do you consider people that you don't know to be as important as you are?
2. Do you have any negative opinions of people who live in certain parts of town?
3. Is your world big enough to include people who speak a different language?
4. How big is your world? At what point do you stop including people? Family, Cousins, Neighbors, Church friends, School friends, People in your city, People of the same race, People in a different country?
5. If you were lost in a different town, how would you want to be treated?

You have only one chance to make a first impression. Make it count.
MARKITA ANDREWS, GIRL SCOUT WHO HOLDS RECORD FOR COOKIE SALES

1. Before reading this chapter, did you ever think about how to make a first impression?
2. Why is it impossible to get a second chance at making a first impression?
3. Have you ever made a bad first impression and wished you had another chance?
4. In your opinion, why are first impressions more important than second impressions?

The only justification for ever looking down on somebody is to pick them up. JESSE JACKSON

1. What do you think when you meet someone and he/she is different or they have a problem? Do you look down on them?
2. Do you believe that tomorrow everything in your life could change and you could be the person who needs help?
3. What does the word "justification" mean?
4. When was the last time you helped someone in your school who was having a difficult time?
5. What is the first thought that goes through your mind when you see someone having a problem: Do you want to laugh at him/her or help them?

When you face a crisis, you know who your true friends are. EARVIN "MAGIC" JOHNSON

1. Have you ever had a crisis?
2. Have you ever had a friend to let you down when you needed help?
3. Have you ever had a stranger to help you when you needed help?
4. Do you think it is a good way to make new friends when you help someone who is having a difficult time?

Compose a quote and write it here:_____

_____

Chapter 2

Expectations With An Example

Definition of an example: a person or thing to be imitated and followed.

CONNECTING WITH AND LEARNING FROM YOUR RICH, PERSONAL, PAINFUL, PRODUCTIVE PAST: Before meeting with your boys, reflect on some of the goals that you have had in life and how having an example has helped you meet those goals. Think of the earliest examples and goals that you embraced on up to your current examples and goals. Try to be specific and share examples with the boys.

CAUTION: Explain to the young men that not all people who are in the limelight are good examples. You can use specific athletes and discuss the non-sports related example that they set for young people. You can ask the boys if they feel that certain athletes set an example to follow and see what their responses are. Also consider the use of music stars for discussing purposes. This may require some research on your part.

CHARGE: Charge the young men to be discerning when they choose to follow the example set by an older person. When in doubt, go to a wise person and ask his advice about his choice. Be sure to challenge the boys to choose their examples carefully. Discuss the common mistakes young people make because of the absence of an example in their lives. Let them know that we have all gone through that stage of life, and experience has taught us that the way to avoid common youthful mistakes is to grow in wisdom.

ACTIVITY: Discuss several occupations and lifestyles. Then name some individuals who live that way and discuss if you and the boys agree that it would be good to follow that person.

TIP: It is important that the mentor model patience in learning and memorization. It is easy to cover the material in a chapter and move on. We would rather you linger on important words, phrases, quotes and points of wisdom that will help the boys. Did you do this in the last chapter? Develop the habit of reaching back to the previous chapter to review some point of interest. Frequently review the quotes that have been memorized to keep them fresh as you progress through the book.

Lesson 2

Expectations With An Example

My mother has always encouraged me to be my best. She always told me that I could do whatever I wanted to do. My mom had high expectations of me. I have learned that it is easier to reach your goals when you have an example to follow. All of my life I have looked for men to be good examples for me. We all do better when we have an example. An example is someone that we can imitate and copy. Children are great imitators; they can do almost anything that they see other children or adults do.

Not too long ago, there was a famous basketball player who stuck his tongue out when he played. I don't know why he stuck his tongue out, he just did it. Before too long, kids from all across America were playing basketball and sticking their tongues out. I guess the kids stuck their tongues out because of the example that had been set.

Our society have expectations of you and all young people, especially boys. The adults expect you to talk politely, be considerate, work very hard and prepare yourselves to be the future rulers of this country. Those are the expectations. We must remember that, expectations need an example. In other words, it is easier to do what is expected of you when you watch someone else do it. If the adults have these expectations of you, then the adults must be prepared to provide examples for you to follow.

When I take a minute to think about my youth, I remember that there were always adults who had expectations of me. My mother had great expectations of me. She would often tell me: "You can do it son, you can do it!" It didn't matter what it was. She would tell me that I could do it. Now that I am grown I realize that my mom's expectations encouraged me. Let me ask you a question: When someone tells you that they believe that you can do it, whatever "it" is, how does that make you feel? For me, it motivated me and made me really want to accomplish what they believed that I could do. A very important thing to remember when someone has high expectations of you is to immediately find someone to watch who has already accomplished what you are trying to do.

My mom was not my example for a businessman, musician or baseball player. Other people served as those examples. I had to find someone to be an example in every area that I wanted to excel in. So, it is possible that your mom, dad or friend can have high expectations of you, but another person can be your example to help you reach those goals.

31

My dad also had high expectations of me and he was the example for me in many areas, but there were other men who knew more about certain things than my dad did. In those areas I listened to them and learned from them. It is important to remember that all men have areas where they are strong and areas where they are weak. All men have areas where they know a lot and other areas where they don't know anything.

I think that because of your age, you should work very hard on meeting the expectations of your parents, teachers and mentors. Studying hard in school is the number one job for young people. The lessons that you learn in school will help you meet the challenges of the future. Remember, when you are challenged to learn something new that may be difficult and challenging, find an example to follow. Learn to ask for help when you need help finding an example. Remember that healthy adults enjoy helping young people who are serious about improving themselves.

Questions
(to discuss and think about or to serve as a written assignment)

1. Many people criticize today's young men because many of them have low expectations of themselves. In your own words, explain your expectations of yourself. How would you rate your expectations of yourself? High__ Medium__ Low__

2. What man is your main example?_____

3. The author stated that his mother encouraged him to do his best. Tell the truth and not a lie: Who encourages you to do your best?_____

4. Find and complete this sentence: "I have learned that it is_____"

5. In your opinion, is it easier to follow bad examples or good examples?

6. How many men do you watch to learn new things from? _____

7. Are you working hard to live up to the expectations of the adults in your life? Yes___ No___

8. Do you feel that the expectations that some adults have of you are unreasonable?

9. Find and complete this sentence: "Children are great_____"

10. Can you name one positive behavior you are imitating today? Yes__ No__

11. What do you want to learn to do well in life?_____

12. Who are your examples in that area?_____

13. Are you careful not to use negative people as examples? Yes___ No___

15. Who is your favorite athlete?_____

16. Does he set a good non-sports related example? Yes___ No___

17. What kind of shoes do you wear and why do you wear them?_____

18. Read the sentence that comes after this one: "Adults in our society have expectations of you and all young people, especially boys."

19. In your opinion are these reasonable expectations? Yes__ No__

20. If there are no doctors, teachers or lawyers in your family, does it mean that you cannot be a doctor, teacher or lawyer? Yes__ No__ Maybe__ Don't know__

21. Find and complete this sentence: "A very important thing to remember . . . "

22. It is important for young men to have men who have high expectations of them. How many men can you name who have high expectations of you?

23. Tell the truth and not a lie: Does it bug you when adults have high expectations of you? Yes__ No__ Please note: When you are grown and your bridge of wisdom is complete, you will be thankful for the adults that challenged you with wisdom.

24. Complete this last sentence in the lesson: Remember, when you are challenged to learn something new_____

25. What are some characteristics that you like in your role models?_____

26. How would you go about picking a good role model?_____

Wisdom From The Elders

Read the quotes and explain them to the boys. Use the questions to begin the discussion. Be sure to work with the boys to compose your own quote that relates to this chapter.

People seldom improve when they have no model but themselves to copy after.
  OLIVER GOLDSMITH

1. As great as you are, you need someone to challenge you and model for you. Who challenges you in the area of Grades?
2. Do you feel you have improved since last year this time?
3. In your opinion, why do you think people seldom improve when they have no model but themselves?
4. Tell the truth and not a lie: Do you see yourself as your best role model?
5. What would America be like if everyone was just like you?
6. We copy some people on purpose and we unknowingly copy other people. If you stopped to think about it, could you come up with any people that you have unknowingly copied?

Example is the school of mankind, and they will learn at no other. EDMUND BURKE

1. Name three men whose examples you learn from.
2. Every person goes to school. Life is a school because you are always learning. What do you think the author means when he says: "The school of mankind?"
3. Do you agree with the author of this quote when he says that people only learn from examples?

A good example is the best sermon. THOMAS FULLER

1. Can you name one thing that you have seen a man do that really sticks out in your mind?
2. What is a sermon?
3. Do your parents/teachers ever preach to you? . . . Do you learn more from what they say or from what they do?

It is the true nature of mankind to learn from mistakes, not from example. FRED HOYLE

1. In your opinion, what does the author mean by learning from mistakes?
2. Why do you think such a large number of human beings are so hard headed?
3. Would you rather learn from mistakes or example?
4. When you see another young person do something dumb and get hurt, do you think that you can do it smarter, slicker and not get caught? If you do then you will have to learn from your own mistakes and not the mistakes of others.

There is a difference between imitating a good man and counterfeiting him.
  BENJAMIN FRANKLIN

1. What do you think it means to counterfeit a man?
2. What do you think it means to imitate a man?

3. Name one man of character and high quality that you are trying to imitate.

We are all too quick to imitate depraved examples. JUVENAL
1. Take a minute to look up the word "depraved."
2. Tell the truth and not a lie: Do you sometimes imitate poor or unhealthy examples?
3. In your opinion, why is it that the wrong things look like so much fun?
4. What bad thing have you seen someone do that looked like fun?
5. What do you do to stop yourself when you want to do bad things?

Lives of great men all remind us, We can make our lives sublime, And, departing, leave behind us Footprints on the sands of time. LONGFELLOW, A Psalm of Life
1. How many great men can you name who have left foot prints for you to follow in?
2. Although you may now know these men, they walked on planet earth before you and in that sense they are related to us. Do you feel like you owe the great men of yesterday anything for what they did?
3. Who was Longfellow?
4. According to Longfellow, what fact does the lives of great men remind us of?
5. What does the term "the sands of time" make you think about?

Success always leaves footprints. BOOKER T. WASHINGTON
1. What successful man's footprints are you trying to walk in?
2. In your opinion, how many young men want to be like the MVP of the NBA right now? . . These young men are trying to walk in the MVP's footsteps. Whose footsteps are you trying to walk in?

People may doubt what you say, but they will always believe what you do.
   NANNIE HELEN BURROUGHS
1. Have you been lied to by a man that you trusted? . . If yes, has this made it difficult for you to trust men? Yes__ No__
2. It has been said that talk is cheap. Are you a talker or a doer?
3. What man do you believe because of what he has done?
4. Do people doubt what you say, or, to say it another way, is your word trustworthy?
5. Is there anything that you have promised to anyone right now that you have not done?

The tragedy of life doesn't lie in not reaching your goal. The tragedy lies in having no goal to reach. BENJAMIN E. MAYS
1. Unfortunately, many young men seem to be going in circles with no real direction in life. Although you are young, you can have some direction in life. Do you have any idea of what direction you want to go in life?

Compose a quote and write it here: _____

Chapter 3

Self-Discipline

Definition: Self-discipline is the ability to do the right thing at the right time, regardless of how you feel.

Connecting With And Learning From Your Rich, Personal, Painful, Productive Past: As men, we have all struggled with self-discipline in one form or another in our past. Try to recall an area where you have struggled and have not yet overcome your lack of discipline. Share other areas where you have had success, and give details of how you were successful. As always, leave out any details that would not be appropriate for young boys.

CAUTION: Remember, some of these boys may be hearing this wisdom for the first time. Be patient, and repeat yourself often. It is possible that they are not getting any support or guidance on how to be disciplined at home.

CHARGE: Focus on positive possibilities. Challenge any boy who feels that a disciplined life is not possible for him. Get in his face with positive, affirming statements like: "You can do it!" "I believe in you," or "anything is possible to the person who believes and works hard."

ACTIVITY: Have each boy make a private list to be kept in secret of three areas where they want to become more disciplined. Promise that you will revisit this list at the end of the school year to assess the progress. Take time along with the boys to create a list of areas that you need to work on. When you join them in this activity you give additional meaning to the project.

TIP: Remember to use the dictionary whenever possible. It is important for boys to see that their mentor refers to and enjoys the dictionary.

TIP: Be encouraged. It is the horizon that gives dignity to the foreground. We can find dignity in our weekly commitments to share wisdom with children when we look at the horizon to see the benefits of our efforts. When you look at your present efforts to find dignity and rewards, you may be disappointed. I can assure you that the fruit from the seeds you are planting will be visible to everyone in the future. Be encouraged.

Lesson 3

Self-Discipline

I have worked hard to have self-discipline in my life. Self-discipline is the ability to do the right thing at the right time, like study, clean up your room or turn your homework in on time. When I was a kid, there was a family in our neighborhood named the Harrisons. They were very different from most of the other families because their kids were very disciplined. Their parents did not let them spend all day at the playground. They made them come in the house before it was dark. We would often tease them and call them babies and momma's boys because they could not hang out like the rest of the boys.

What we did not know was that while these kids were in the house they were working on their homework and learning how to have discipline in their lives. They learned at an early age that there is a time to play and there is a time to work. Many kids and adults never learn the difference between the two. Well, the Harrisons learned at an early age that you must do the right thing at the right time. They did play and have fun, but they did it at the right time and at the right place. They did not horse around in school and get in trouble. They always did their work well and always had their homework in on time.

As we grew older, entered high school and college, we noticed that the Harrisons were always the smartest kids in class. They took all of the hard subjects like algebra, calculus, and advanced English, and they did well in them. Now that they are grown, they are engineers with good jobs and they make good money. So, who is laughing now? Who is having fun now? Who gets to play now?!

It is very unfortunate that many kids spend too much time playing and not enough time preparing for the future. If you plan to grow up, you will need a job, a house to live in and food to eat. Your parents will not be around to take care of you forever. If you are wise, you will do like the Harrisons did. They worked when it was time to work and they played when it was time to play, and in the end they were ready for their future.

When a boy understands that the future is coming, he will see the need to be disciplined. Many stories are designed to teach children about discipline. For example, think of the three little pigs. If you remember, the two lazy pigs were almost eaten by the wolf because they were lazy and not disciplined. Parents work hard to teach their children discipline because parents know that if their children don't learn discipline, they will not be successful in life.

Many boys who do not learn discipline early in life end up in prison or worse. Today, I work with adults who partied all of the time while they were young and they never had discipline. When I was in school, I met people who wanted to party more than they wanted to study. As a result of their choices when there were young, they suffer now. Self-discipline in the life of a child is worth more than a million dollars because **if you have discipline you can always make money.**

One good thing about the Harrison family is that they had parents to make them come inside and work. Many kids today don't have parents to make them do right. What are these kids supposed to do? Well, they are supposed to make themselves do right. It works this way. When you know that it is time for you to be disciplined and there is no one there to discipline you, you should talk to yourself and say something like this: "I know that it is time for me to go in the house and study. I also know that if I don't do this, I will not be prepared for class tomorrow. I am going to do what is right and go to my room and do my homework." I want you to know that it is alright to talk to yourself when you are telling yourself to do something good.

What about you? Are you disciplined? Do you do the right thing at the right time? The results of your discipline will show up when you become an adult, just like in the Harrison family.

Questions
(to be used for discussion or as a written assignment)

1. Read the first sentence of this chapter again. (Ask one student to read) Can you say that you have worked hard to have discipline in your life? Yes__ No__

2. Are you becoming more disciplined as you get older? Yes__ No__

3. Is all of your schoolwork done right now? Yes__ No__

4. If I were to visit your bedroom right now, would your clothes be on the floor or hanging up?

5. What do you tell yourself in order to be disciplined?_____

6. Who is the most disciplined person you know?_____

7. Adults help you develop discipline by MAKING you do the things you need to do. Are you happy when they do this or sad?

8. The author talks about the Harrison family. Do you know any young people like the Harrisons?

9. The Harrison boys had parents in their faces with wisdom. How did this affect them in the long run?

10. Do you ever tease the people in your class who always get their work in on time and make good grades? Yes__ No__ Sometimes__

11. Hanging out is fun, but what do you think will happen if you hang out all of the time?

12. Find and complete this sentence. What we did not know was that_____

13. Tell the truth and not a lie: Do you know when it is time to work and when it is time to play?

14. Before your next meeting with your mentor, interview three teachers and ask them how much discipline it took to make it through college. Be prepared to share your answer with your mentor next session.

15. For our next meeting, ask three teachers who know you if they feel that you have good discipline for a kid your age. If they say yes, then thank them. If they say no, then ask them to give you three things that you can do to improve. Bring the results back to the group next week so we can discuss it.

16. The Harrison boys were under strict discipline when they were young. Find and complete this sentence: "As we grew older_____"

17. In your opinion, why were the Harrison boys the smartest in the class? (Look back at the book if you can't think of anything)

18. As it relates to the Harrisons, the author asks the question "who's laughing now?" Do you realize that if you laugh at kids today that one day they may laugh at you? Yes__ No__

19. Find and complete this sentence. It is very unfortunate that many_____

20. Do you realize today that your parents will not take care of you much longer? Yes__No__ If yes, what are you doing to prepare for your future?

21. According to the author, what did the Harrisons do that was wise? (Check the book)

22. Find and complete this sentence. When a boy understands that the_____

23. The author talks about stories that are designed to teach children about discipline. He uses the three little pigs as an example. Can you think of another story that teaches the importance of being prepared?

24. It is fun to party all the time, but according to the author, what happens to people who party all the time?

25. The author states that not all people have parents to make them do right. What did he say you should do if you are in this situation? (Look in the book)

26. Tell the truth and not a lie: Do you think you could do what the author suggested? In other words, could you go in the house early and study about three hours each day while the other young people played?

27. Do you have the discipline to come inside and do your work even when you are in the middle of a game or having fun? Yes__ No__

28. In what area of your life do you feel that you need more discipline?_____
What are you doing to get more discipline in that area?_____

Wisdom From The Elders

Read the quotes and explain them to the boys. Use the questions to begin the discussion. Be sure to work with the boys to compose your own quote that relates to this chapter.

Take off the strong cord of discipline and morality and you will be an old man before your twenties are past. Preserve these forces. Do not burn them out in idleness or crime.
PRESIDENT GARFIELD

1. Do you know anyone who is undisciplined and getting old really fast? Discipline is pictured as a strong cord or rope that holds you back when you want to do something you shouldn't do. In your opinion, why do you think boys need a strong cord in their lives?
2. Have you ever wanted to do something wrong and there was no one to stop you, so you did it? . . Are you glad you did it or do you wish someone had stopped you?
3. Every Nation, Race or Culture has rules that EVERYBODY knows about. The morals of that nation are based on those rules that everybody knows about. Can you name some of the rules or morals that our country has?
4. What do you think people mean when they say: "Jim is a moral person."
5. In your opinion, what would happen if there were no morals in America or in your school?
6. Discipline and morality are strong cords that protect young men from pain and eventually an early death. Do you know any young men who do things they shouldn't and look older than they are?
7. Idleness and crime will destroy your strong cord of discipline. As you get older, you need to stay busy and stay away from troublemakers. How do you plan to stay away from trouble makers?
8. What will you do today to preserve the forces of discipline and morality in your life?
9. Please memorize this quote by next week.

Discipline is the soul of an army. It makes small numbers formidable; procures success to the weak, and esteem, to all. LETTER OF INSTRUCTIONS TO THE CAPTAINS OF VIRGINIA REGIMENTS (July 29, 1759)

1. Do you feel that learning to live a disciplined life will make you a very powerful man?
2. The author of this quote states that discipline is the soul of an army. What do you think he means by "the soul of an army?"
3. The author uses the word "procures." Look it up in the dictionary.

Perhaps the most valuable result of all education is the ability to make yourself do the thing you have to do, when it ought to be done, whether you like it or not. WALTER BAGEHOT

1. Can you do the thing you have to do when it needs to be done, whether you like it or not?

Children have to be educated, but they have also to be left to educate themselves.
ABBE' DIMNET

1. Your teacher can teach you, but only you can decide to be disciplined. What is your decision?

It is better to be slow-tempered than famous; it is better to have self-control than to control an army. PROVERBS 16:32

1. Would you rather have self-control or be rich?
2. Are you slow to get angry or are you hot tempered?
3. There are a lot of famous rich people who have no self-control. If you could make a choice, which would you choose, to have self-control or to be rich and famous?

He who conquers others is strong; He who conquers himself is mighty. LAO-TZU

1. In your own words, tell me why you feel self-control is so important.
2. Is there any part of your body that is out of control? For example, your mouth, eyes, hands?
3. Do you know any young men who struggle with self-control?
4. Are there any boys in your school who struggle with self-control?
5. Which is easier for you to do, conquer others or conquer yourself?
6. Can you control your temper tantrums, pity parties, and running mouth? If you can, you are a mighty man.

He that would govern others, first should be Master of himself. PHILIP MASSINGER

1. Has it ever dawned on you that in order to rule others you must first rule yourself?

He is most powerful who has power over himself. SENECA

1. Tell the truth and not a lie: Do you want to be a powerful man when you grow up? . . If yes, are you prepared to do the work necessary to bring your anger under control? Yes__ No__

He who is allowed to do as he likes will soon run his head into a brick wall out of sheer frustration. ROBERT MUSIL

1. Are you allowed to do as you please or does someone discipline you?
2. Do you have any knots on your head from running into a brick wall?

You will never develop discipline until you start with small pieces. B. J. TATUM

1. What little thing can you begin doing today that will help you become more disciplined?

Compose a quote and write it here:_____

_____

_____

_____

A Tip For The Mentor
There'll Be Days Like That

Nobody wants to listen. Everyone wants to talk. Nobody wants to read. One word answers or "I don't know," are the extent of the discussion. Nothing seems to be working on this day. Mentors must learn what seasoned teachers already know—there will be days when nothing you do seems to work with the children. There will be days when it seems you are losing ground with the kids. Don't let difficult days discourage you. Difficult days are part of the mentoring landscape. They are no reason to quit. The bottom line is—your effort always improves the situation. And remember, there's always tomorrow.

Dr. Harold Davis

Chapter 4

The Power Of A Positive Attitude

Definition of Positive Attitude: A positive disposition, opinion, mental state of mind.

Connecting With And Learning From Your Rich, Personal, Painful, Productive Past: It takes years to develop the skill and maturity necessary to maintain a positive attitude in spite of the negative influences all around us. I am sure that you have struggled in this area as I have. Recall several situations when you struggled to be positive in the face of negative influences. Recall school experiences where you sought to be positive even when others were negative. Remember, the boys love to hear stories from your past that demonstrate your human struggles. Share with the boys where you are in your struggle to be positive in negative environments.

CAUTION: We do not want to paint the picture that everybody is supposed to be up and positive all of the time. We allow each other to be human, to struggle and grow as we mature in this area. These young men are in the beginning stages of learning emotional discipline and our goal is to challenge them to stay on course to emotional maturity.

CHARGE: We want to get one main point over to these boys and that point is this: Your attitude determines your altitude. In other words, your attitude plays a tremendous role in determining how successful you will be in the future. Press the point that we are in charge of our attitudes. If our attitudes are stinky, we can change them. Please feel free to repeat yourself with these young boys. Seek to say the same thing in different ways so that they leave with the main points of the lesson.

ACTIVITY: Have the boys keep an attitude journal. Have them record their attitude during the day. Have them document when their attitude went sour and when it was sweet. Make the teacher aware of this project and have her confirm his assessment of himself and sign the attitude form. This is especially true for young men who struggle with attitudinal problems. Teachers will welcome this lesson. Ask the office staff to copy the attitude form found in this chapter and give a copy to your mentees. Have them show it to their teacher.

ATTITUDE WORK SHEET   Name_____ Date____/____/____

Dear Teacher: This form is designed to monitor the attitude of your student. It is given in conjunction with the chapter "The Power of a Positive Attitude." He is to document his attitude on a daily and hourly basis by writing "good" or "bad" in the appropriate space. You must verify that his assessment is correct by signing this sheet at the end of the day. He is to return this sheet to his mentor next week.

Time	Monday	Tuesday	Wednesday	Thursday	Friday
8:00					
9:00					
10:00					
11:00					
12:00					
1:00					
2:00					
3:00					

Signature   _____ _____ _____ _____ _____

The Second Week

Time	Monday	Tuesday	Wednesday	Thursday	Friday
8:00					
9:00					
10:00					
11:00					
12:00					
1:00					
2:00					
3:00					

Signature   _____ _____ _____ _____ _____

Lesson 4

The Power Of A Positive Attitude

I never will forget Mrs. Grey's favorite words when a boy was misbehaving in her class. She would walk up to the boy, get very close to his face. and say: "Young man, you need to change your attitude!" This is what she would tell the boys in her class when they would frown, pout, throw things and display bad behavior or a bad attitude. Your attitude is your state of mind. It can be pleasant, good and positive or it can be unpleasant, bad and negative. Adults hate it when kids have bad attitudes. A bad attitude can be very unpleasant to the people around you and it can turn others off.

I had a girlfriend once who had a bad attitude. I thought she was cute and she did look good on the outside, but on the inside she had a stinky attitude. A good attitude can be worth more than a million dollars because people like kids with good attitudes. When I was a kid, my dad would knock me out if my attitude turned stinky. Today, adults do not knock kids out. They just ignore and avoid them. To be ignored is worse than being knocked out. When adults ignore kids with bad attitudes, the attitude becomes the real enemy that needs to be dealt with.

A bad attitude will cause you to be the last one considered when it is time to pick kids for the fun things in life. A bad attitude is when something is stinking on the inside and the person tries to pour it out on everyone around him. Mrs. Grey would show her disgust with us boys when we had a bad attitude and we would miss out on many fun activities. Now that I am grown, I understand why adults hate bad attitudes in kids. I always encourage kids to have good attitudes because a good attitude will open many doors for you. Let's look at some of the reasons you should work on having a good attitude.

1. A bad attitude only hurts you. It is a childish mistake to believe that your bad attitude is punishing someone else. Your bad attitude *always* hurts you more than it hurts other people. Your bad attitude separates you from people who could and would help you. Unfortunately, I have seen young people with attitudes suffer many things and not know why. I can remember when a 5-year-old kid walked up to his mom and said: "If you don't let me go outside and play, I am going to hold my breath until I die!" The kid then held his breath until he turned red and eventually he decided to breathe. The kid was trying to punish the parent by hurting himself. This is the same thing that happens when a older person has a bad attitude. It only hurts you and you look very foolish holding your breath.

2. A bad attitude may indicate that you have other problems. Usually when kids have a bad attitude they are mad at someone about something they did. Many times it is their father or mother that they are mad at. What the child does not realize is that when he has a bad attitude in school because he is mad at someone at home, it is misdirected anger. Misdirected anger is when you are mad at the people who didn't do anything to you. When a kid yells at Jennifer when David is the one who hit him that is misdirected anger. If you must have a bad attitude, have it with the people who hurt you and not with others who are trying to help you. The mature thing to do is to learn not to misdirect your anger.

3. Some kids have bad attitudes because they feel that no one loves them. They have a bad attitude because they don't want anyone to get close enough to show them love. Some kids have been hurt by adults who should have loved them, so they now are mean to all adults who would be kind to them because they fear that another adult will hurt them. This defensive tactic actually makes it hard for adults to get close to them and be their friend.

4. Some kids have bad attitudes because their family and friends have bad attitudes. It is hard to be loving and kind when everyone around you is bitter and negative. It is hard to do, but it can be done. I have met some wonderful young people who have come out of bitter homes. They made up their minds that they were not going to be bitter but work on getting better.

There is an old saying that your attitude will determine your altitude. I believe that this is true because life must be lived around other people. Other people will pick up on your attitude very quickly, so a good attitude will do wonders to help you get ahead in life and a bad attitude will really hold you back. I believe that the choice is yours. You can choose to work toward having a good attitude or you can just have a stinky attitude and live with the results. What will it be?

Questions
(to discuss and think about or to serve as a written assignment)

1. Have you ever been told by an adult that you need to change your attitude? Yes__ No__

2. What adult challenges you the most about your attitude?_____

3. If you had a girlfriend, which would be more important: a good attitude or good looks?__

4. What did the author say that adults do when kids have bad attitudes?_____
_____

5. Find and complete this sentence: "A bad attitude is when something is_____"

6. Do you agree with the author that good attitudes will open doors for you? Yes__ No__
If you said yes to that question, how do you feel good attitudes will open doors for you?

7. Who does a bad attitude hurt the most?_____

8. Complete this sentence found under point number one: It is a childish mistake_____
_____

9. Complete this sentence found under point number one: Your bad attitude *always*_____
_____

10. Tell the truth and not a lie: Have you ever tried to punish your parents or other adults by hurting yourself like the kid in the book? Yes__ No__

11. According to point number two, what may a bad attitude indicate?_____
_____

12. How does your teacher show his/her disgust when you have a bad attitude?_____

13. What is misdirected anger?_____

14. Tell the truth and not a lie: Have you ever been mad about something and yelled at someone although they did not do anything to you? Yes__ No__ According to this lesson, what is that called?_____

15. Now that you know what misdirected anger is, you should be patient when people misdirect their anger toward you. Do you think that you will be able to do this? Yes__ No__

16. Under number three, the reason given why some people have bad attitudes is because they feel unloved. How many people love you? Name them._____

17. Name one person you know who has a positive attitude._____

18. How do you feel their positive attitude helps them?_____

19. People who feel unloved act strange. When you act strange, is it because you feel unloved? Yes__ No__ When you act strange, do you work hard trying to figure out why you are acting strange or do you not think about it?_____

20. Under point number 4, find this sentence: "It is hard to be loving and kind when everyone around you is bitter and negative." Do you agree with it? Yes__ No__ Do you agree with the next sentence that says: "It is hard to do, but it can be done." Yes__ No__

21. It is a fact that the attitudes of those around us rub off on us. Do you hang around people with bad attitudes? Yes__ No__

22. Peer pressure is a very powerful force. Young men who are weak are often influenced by the pressure of their peers. Tell the truth and not a lie: Are you a peer follower or a peer leader?

23. Most people are looking for someone to follow. It is hard work to be a peer leader. In your opinion, what things do you have to do in order to be a peer leader?

24. Complete this sentence found in the last paragraph found in this chapter: There is an old saying that:_____

25. If you have a stinky attitude in class, how long do you think your teacher should put up with it?_____

26. Find and complete this sentence: "Your attitude will determine_____"

27. In your own words, what does the previous sentence mean?_____

28. Do you believe that the decision to have a good or bad attitude is yours? Yes__ No__

29. If the previous question was yes, what decision have you made regarding your attitude?

Wisdom From The Elders

Read the quotes and explain them to the boys. Use the questions to begin the discussion. Be sure to work with the boys to compose your own quote that relates to this chapter.

A negative attitude is a true handicap. THE IMPOSSIBLE DREAM, 1986
1. What is a handicap?
2. Do you have any handicaps?
3. Which do you feel is the worst handicap, an outside handicap with the body or an inside handicap with the attitude?
4. Do you know any people whose attitude is so bad that they can not function in school?

Persistence and a positive attitude are necessary ingredients for any successful venture. ANONYMOUS
1. What is persistence? (Look it up if you do not know)
2. What is a venture?
3. Do you want to be successful in life?
4. What are you working hard at and having a good attitude about? For example: math, science, reading, writing.
5. Most parents tell their children that at this point in their lives, their job is school. Do you agree with that statement or disagree?
6. Are you currently being successful in school? Before you answer, what I mean is, are you working as hard as you can on your grades and are you working as hard as you can to get along with people? If the answer to those two questions are yes, you are being successful.

It is impossible for a people to rise above their aspirations. If we think we cannot we most certainly cannot. Our greatest enemy is our defeatist attitude. ROBERT WILLIAMS
1. What is an aspiration?
2. Look at the person sitting next to you and say: "What do you aspire to?"
3. In sports, when you are about to make a play, should your mind tell your body that this shot is or is not going to go in? . . . It is defeatist when you tell yourself that it is not going to go in.
4. Is there any area in school where you have developed a defeatist attitude?
5. According to this quote, what role does your mind play in success?
6. According to this quote, what is our greatest enemy?
7. In your opinion, what should you do if you find that you have developed a defeatist attitude in an area of your life?

Only those who dare to fail greatly can ever achieve greatly. ROBERT F. KENNEDY
1. Have you ever failed before?
2. Are you the type of person who is not afraid to try to accomplish anything?
3. It takes guts to succeed. Many people are comfortable with failing and they are terrified at the thought of succeeding. What type of person are you?

4. Who was Robert F. Kennedy and what do you know about him?

The secret to success is to learn to accept the impossible, to do without the indispensable, and to bear the intolerable. NELSON MANDELA

1. Nelson Mandela was in jail for about 23 years and he came out of it with a good attitude. What is your attitude about pain and discomfort?

2. Some people said that it was impossible for Mandela to get out of jail. He accepted the impossible and it happened. Are you facing an impossible situation right now? Is there a problem in your life that is so big that you feel like you will never get over it? If the answer is yes, be like Nelson Mandela and accept the impossible.

3. To be successful, you must learn to do without the indispensable. Many things that we consider to be necessities are really luxuries. There are many people in other countries that do not have the things we take for granted in America. Consider doing without some or all of the following things in order to be successful: TV, computers, video games, lots of clothes, a car, a bicycle, fast food, the mall. Could you do without these things in order to be successful?

4. The last thing Mandela mentions to be successful is to bear the intolerable. Something that is intolerable is something that drives you crazy. Is there anything in your life right now that is intolerable?

No one knows less than the person who knows it all. HUGH GLOSTER

1. Do you feel that you know everything?

I don't understand it. People are always saying that I've got an attitude. WHOOPI GOLDBERG

1. If your teacher, mentor, or best friend told you that you had an attitude, would you believe them or feel that they were picking on you?

I've benefitted from many scholarships. A number of people paid a lot of dues for me to do what I do. I feel it's my responsibility to give back. WYNTON MARSALIS

1. What is your attitude about those who have worked to make your life possible?

2. In Japan teachers are highly respected people. Do you feel that you owe your teacher anything or do you feel that he/she is supposed to help you?

3. Have a lot of people paid dues for you to make it?

4. Based on what you have received from others, what type of responsibility do you have?

Compose a quote and write it here:_____

_____

Chapter 5

Things You Can't Change

Definition of inability to change: The inability to alter, cause to become different or vary in any way.

Connecting With And Learning From Your Rich, Personal, Painful, Productive Past: Age and maturity equips the adult population with a perspective that cannot be obtained any other way. Maturity enables adults to look at situations and realize that there is nothing that can be done to make a significant change. I can remember my youthful days of trying to change everything and everybody. I actually felt that I could make wars cease, force racial strife to go away, solve the monetary problems of the poor and find cures to most major diseases. Well, you and I know that maturity dampens our youthful zeal and the struggle to survive often puts change on the back burner. Share with the young men some of your dreams for change. Share with the boys the changes that you have helped bring to pass, the changes that you still want to see happen and the things that you realize will never change.

CAUTION: Be careful not to dampen the wild dreams that young people have. As adults we often get frustrated with youthful, unrealistic dreams. It is futile to try to talk them out of their dreams for change, no matter how unrealistic they may be. One of my dreams was that the world would be at peace. With age I have learned that there are many complex reasons why this has not happened. Life will challenge their dreams just as it has challenged ours. The strong will persevere and continue to pursue change, while the average will do as many adults have done, which is accept the norm and cease to fight for healthy change.

CHARGE: Charge the young people to never stop seeking to change the broken things in our society. It is through youthful zeal and enthusiasm that our world becomes a better place to live. It is through the dreams and hopes of a fresh new generation of leaders that the changes that can be made will be made. Encourage the young people to dream of making the changes that their parents failed to make.

ACTIVITY: Discuss with the young people what changes need to be made in society. Make a list of items that need to be changed. Discuss the items one by one, listing solutions to the obstacles for change.

Lesson 5

Things You Can't Change

One of the joys of being young is that you have the rest of your life to overcome any problem or struggle that you face. I can remember that as a kid, I did not learn how to swim. I had always wanted to learn how to swim, but I was afraid of water because I almost drowned when I was six years old. Not long ago, I put my mind to it and swam for the first time in my life.

What's exciting about this story is that there was something that I couldn't do, something I was afraid of, but I learned how to do it. I am excited about the things that I can change in my life, but I also realize that there are many things in life that no one can change.

One of the keys to being successful is learning how to deal with the things you can't change. There are two types of problems in life: the kind that you can change and the kind that you can't change. Many people waste many years of their lives trying to change things that will never change. You can't change the color of your skin or your sex. You can't change where you were born or who your parents are or how tall you are. Accepting these unchangeable things as facts of life is very important.

It is also very important to work hard to change the things you can change. Just as I overcame my fear of swimming, there are things you need to overcome. Elementary school is a very important time in life. It is a time when many boys develop the attitude of a winner or a loser. I can remember a boy in my 4th grade class named Clinton. Clinton became a loser in the 4th grade because he failed a geography test and decided that he would never be any good in geography or any other class. From that day on, Clinton never really tried very hard to do well in school.

Clinton's problem was that he did not choose to change the things that he could change. It takes guts to face a problem and decide to work to change it. Let me share some steps to take to challenge and change the problems that you can change:

1. Identify the problem. If you are making poor grades, suffering with behavior problems or forget to take baths, your problem is easy to identify. A simple change of behavior is all that is needed. Listen to other people who care about you. They will identify areas in your life that you need to work on. Even critics can give good advice every now and then.

2. Decide if this is a problem that can be changed or not. Remember that there are some problems that can't be changed for reasons beyond your control. One key thing to remember is that you can't change other people. If you like a girl and she does not like you, you can't change that; but you can change the way you feel about her.

3. Share with an adult that you want to change and get some advice from them. A secret that most adults will not tell you is that they have had many problems that they have tried to change and they found out that some problems they could change and others they could not change. They have experience with problems and a lot of wisdom and advice to share with you as you face the problems in your life.

4. Start doing the things you need to do to bring about the change. Think about this: If you act a certain way, you will begin to think a certain way. You can develop new habits by doing something every day, the same way. Before long, you will have a new habit. Habits are formed by doing something over and over.

5. Always celebrate your success. A reward is always in order when a task is completed successfully. Learn early in life to reward yourself when you accomplish a goal. This reward may simply be telling yourself out loud in private that you did well. The reward may be more significant like a trip to your favorite fast food restaurant.

For the rest of your life, you will be challenged with problems. Decide to face them head on! Remember to seek the advice and encouragement of others as you seek to make changes in your life. Don't forget to celebrate when you successfully eliminate a bad habit.

One of the greatest things that you can *always* change is your attitude. If you have a bad attitude you can choose to change it by deciding to have a good attitude. When we are motivated we can choose to change our attitudes. I know this is true because not too long ago I was with three boys and one of them had a bad attitude. We had planned to go out for a burger on this day and I told him that if he didn't change his attitude he would not go. An amazing thing happened. He immediately took the frown off of his face and began smiling; he chose to change his attitude. Remember that you can change your attitude if you want to, but you can't change the attitude of others.

Are you ready to start changing the things you can change, identifying and dealing wisely with the things you can't change? Good luck.

Questions
(to discuss and think about or to serve as a written assignment)

1. In your opinion, is it difficult to change? Yes___ No___

2. Is there anything that you cannot do right now that you would like to learn to do in the future?

3. The author said that he could not swim and was afraid to swim. What did the author do to overcome that? (Look back at the second paragraph)

4. Name five things in your life that you can change_____

5. Name five things you can't change._____

6. Have you identified something in your life that you want to change? Yes___ No___

7. What bad attitude or behavior do you need to change?_____

8. Find and complete this sentence: "One of the keys to being successful_____"

9. What happened to Clinton in the 4th grade?_____

10. Is there anything that you have failed at that you are now afraid of?_____

11. Do you know any boys who have stopped trying like Clinton?_____

12. What advice would you give Clinton if you could talk to him?_____

13. Find and complete this sentence: "It takes guts to face a problem and_____"

14. Do you have a good attitude about the things you can't change?_____

15. How do you feel about the kid who immediately changed his attitude?_____

16. Ask an adult in your life to name three things he/she would like for you to change.____

17. The chameleon lizard is capable of changing its color to match the color of its surroundings. Do you try to change your behavior or attitude to match the kids around you?_____

18. Can you change your attitude when you want to? Yes___ No___

19. Why is it important to change a bad attitude?_____

20. Why did the kid in the story change his bad attitude?_____

21. What are some of your strengths/weaknesses?_____

22. The author gives five steps to take to challenge and change the problems that you can't change. Under point number one, what does he say that the people who care about you can do?

23. Under point number one, what does he say about critics?_____

24. Are you good at quickly deciding whether a problem can be changed or not? If yes, can you give an example of when you had a problem and you quickly decided that you should or should not worry about it?

25. Do you find it difficult to do what it says in point number three? Yes__ No__
If the answer is yes, what do you plan to do about it?
If the answer is no, who are the adults that you can get advice from?

26. Read the last sentence under point number four_____

27. Under point number four, what does the author say will happen when you begin to act a certain way?

28. How does the author say that habits are formed?_____
Do you have any bad habits that you think should be broken?

29. Do you celebrate when you change something in your life from bad to better? If yes, what do you do?

30. Find and complete this sentence: "Learn early in life to_____"

31. The author states that for the rest of your life, you will be challenged with problems. How do you feel about that statement?

32. Find and complete this sentence: "One of the greatest things that you can_____"

Wisdom From The Elders

Read the quotes and explain them to the boys. Use the questions to begin the discussion. Be sure to work with the boys to compose your own quote that relates to this chapter.

When it comes to changes, people like only those they make themselves. FRENCH PROVERB

1. Whose changes do you like the most, yours or your parents?
2. What changes have been forced on you this school year?
3. What changes are you resisting because you think they are bad for you?
4. What changes are you resisting because you don't like them?
5. When someone (a parent or other adult) forces changes on you, what is the first thing you say to yourself?
6. What is the most recent change that has been requested of you?_____ Who requested it?

None but a fool worries about things he cannot influence. SAMUEL JOHNSON

1. It is a very serious thing to call someone a fool. In your opinion, why do you think such a strong word was used to describe someone who worries about things he cannot change?
2. Have you ever worried about something that you could not get done? Did you just sit there and worry or did you work?
3. What are you worrying about today? Is it something that you can change?
4. What does it mean to influence something?

Change is not made without inconvenience, even from worse to better. RICHARD HOOKER 1. What does it mean to be inconvenienced?
2. What change were you afraid of that turned out to be good for you after it was over?
3. How do you feel about the idea that you often have to be discomforted, hurt or inconvenienced before change can take place?
4. Can you name one bad habit you changed and it was not difficult at all?
5. Do you know any people who smoke but they do not want to change even though we know that smoking kills people?
6. Can you think of a situation where people were given the opportunity to change but refused to change because they were afraid?
7. Kickin' wisdom with your mentor will provide you with many opportunities to change your life for the better. Are you going to take advantage of those opportunities?

All things must change to something new, to something strange.
      HENRY WADSWORTH LONGFELLOW

1. Does change ever seem strange to you?
2. What has been the most difficult change this school year? Pick one: teacher, classes, friends, home life, etc.

Every new adjustment is a crisis in self-esteem. ERIC HOFFER

1. Your self-esteem is how much you think you are worth. It is the value that you put on your life. It is how you feel about yourself. It is unfortunate that many young men do not feel good about themselves. They feel that other people are better than they are. In your opinion, how can an adjustment or change in life affect your self-esteem?

2. Have you ever had a crisis in your self-esteem? **(Note to mentor)** Share the first time you were rejected by a girl or some similar crisis

3. Are you currently going through any adjustments? . .   If yes, how is it affecting your self-esteem?

4. Change frightens kids and adults. What do you tell yourself when you see a change about to take place?

The world hates change, yet it is the only thing that has brought progress.
   CHARLES F. KETTERING

1. What could you change in your life that would really help you and those around you?

Everyone thinks of changing the world, but no one thinks of changing himself.
   LEO TOLSTOY

1. Have you ever asked yourself the question: "What kind of world would it be if everybody was just like me?"

2. What do you feel should be the first step you take in changing the world?

God grant me the serenity to accept the things that can't be changed, the courage to change the things I can and the wisdom to know the difference. REINHOLD NIEBUHR

1. Are you working hard to change the things that you can and having patience with the things that you can't change?

A wise man changes his mind sometimes, a fool never PROVERB

1. Do you ever change your mind once you realize that you are wrong?

It takes twenty-one years to be twenty-one. REGGIE JACKSON

1. Do you wish you were 16 years old and had your drivers license? (Well if you do, it is a stupid wish because it takes 16 years to be 16 years old and you can't change where you are right now.)

Compose a quote and write it here:_____

_____

Note to the mentor/teacher: As a result of this lesson, are there any needs that these young men have that can be met by networking with parents, other teachers, social agencies or religious institutions?

The Best Is Yet To Come

One of the benefits of getting older is that you learn to articulate life. In other words, as you get older you learn how to put life into words. It is for this reason that mature people often have short sayings that are full of wisdom. As you interact with the boys, let them know that life gets better as you get wiser. The reason is that you gain an understanding of what life is about.

When the boys are reluctant to listen to you, ask them are they any wiser now than they were two years ago? Take it a step further and ask them if there is anything they know now that they did not know four years ago? After they respond positively to these two questions, ask them do they think that they will be smarter in four years than they are now? You may have to help them answer "yes"?

Let them know that the best "you" is found in the future. The smarter "you" the wiser "you" the "you" with more resources (money) to work with. The "you" who has a college education etc. It is for this reason that you really need to prepare now to insure that in the future you will be able to live the best life possible. In other words, don't spend all of your time serving the present you, but work to make sure that the future you will have what he needs. The Best Is Yet To Come.

DR. HAROLD DAVIS

Chapter 6

Understanding How I Learn

Definition of learning: Getting knowledge or a skill in a subject.

Connecting With And Learning From Your Rich, Personal, Painful, Productive Past. When we reflect on school days it is easy to recall the difficulty we had with the challenging classes. A limited understanding of how we learn can stifle the learning process. Share with the young men how you learn something new. Share with them how you read, where you read and what you have to do to remember what you read.

My ability to learn was directly affected by my desire to learn. The classes that I considered boring and irrelevant were my most difficult subjects. So, I learned best when I was interested in the subject matter and I also learned well when I read and wrote the material. What about you? Share freely with the boys your strengths and struggles as they relate to learning.

CAUTION: There are some cases where there is a learning disability present in one or more of the boys. This is what we call a special situation. Don't slack off because of his handicap. At the appropriate time encourage the young men to get help. Assure him that it is OK to have a problem and to get help. Each person succeeds when he does his best.

CHARGE: Charge the boys to reach their maximum potential by mastering their learning style. Charge them not to be intimidated by how slowly they learn or how difficult the learning process is for them.

ACTIVITY: Monitor the learning process and progress for a particular subject. Ask the teacher to provide you with material from a future lesson. An ideal situation would be the memorization of a list like the presidents, states, multiplication tables, etc. Have the boys start learning the material using combinations of the three learning styles, (sight, hearing and touch). Have them read, write, recite, and draw pictures of the items or concepts to be memorized. Observe which activity helps them learn the quickest. As you observe them, you must consider their desire to learn. They will not learn well when the motivation of desire is not present.

Lesson 6

Understanding How I Learn

I enjoy being an adult because I now understand why so many subjects really bothered me in elementary school. To tell the truth, I was not the smartest kid in the class. I struggled with math, science, geography and spelling. I really thought that I was just a dumb kid. It was not until I went to college to be a teacher that I learned that there are different ways to learn.

You see, in every classroom there are different learning styles. For example, some people can see something and remember it. If they see it on the board, in a book, or on TV they can remember it. These people are called visual learners. They can see something and the information goes straight to the brain and is stored. Other people can hear something and they have it. If the teacher says it, they hear it on a tape, or they hear it from a friend, they can remember it. These people are called auditory learners (auditory means hearing).

There are still other kids who must touch something to learn it. I believe that this is the kind of kid that I was in school. This kid is called the tactile (touch) learner. Many times tactile learners have difficulty because it is difficult to touch math or a story that you are reading in a book. The teacher may not take enough time to allow every child to touch the subject matter. There are still other kids who learn through a combination of the three. The most important thing is for you to figure out early in life how you learn. Do you understand your learning style? Are you a visual learner, an auditory learner or a tactile learner?

Babies learn about things by putting things in their mouth and tasting them. I hope you don't do that any more. It is very important to discover your learning style so that you can begin to concentrate on using it to get the best possible grades. Remember that we all learn differently and that no one learning style is better than the other. The important thing is to discover how you learn and then become very good at mastering your learning style.

Be sure to eliminate any obstacles that would prohibit you from learning. My son was having trouble getting his assignments in school. We had him tested and learned that he needed glasses. There are other children who have been labeled learning disabled when the only thing wrong was they had a hearing problem. If you feel that there is a physical problem holding you back, please be sure to talk to your teacher about it.

I am excited to understand how I learn and I am working on mastering my learning style. Also it is very important for me to continue to develop the other styles that are not natural to me. For example, I learn better when I read and then write what I have read. If I don't write it, most of the time I don't remember it. I am now working on becoming stronger in just reading the material one time and then knowing it. This is a challenge for me which I am enjoying very much.

You should seek to learn from people who have learning styles that are different than yours. For example, my wife has a learning style that is different than mine. I watch how she works her learning system and I try to imitate her. This has helped me develop in other areas. Never be intimidated by how you learn, because if you really master your learning style you will be able to go on and accomplish many great things.

Very often people around us can tell us a lot about ourselves. Talk to your teacher to see if she understands your learning style. Ask him/her if they would help you master your learning style. Also talk to parents and other adults who have watched you for some time. They can be very helpful. I predict that if you start working to understand your learning style that your grades will improve this year and you will be proud of how smart you really are.

Questions
(to discuss and think about or to serve as a written assignment)

1. Why did the author say he enjoyed being an adult?_____

2. What subjects bother you the most?_____

3. Tell the truth and not a lie: Are you the smartest kid in school? Yes__ No__

4. Before you read this chapter had you thought about how you learn? Yes__ No__

5. What are the three styles of learning?_____

6. Do you know what your learning style is?_____

7. Who do you know that has a different learning style that is different than yours?_____

8. When you don't understand something, do you feel dumb or do you try to learn it a different way?_____

9. Are you excited about mastering your learning style? Yes__ No__

10. Do you feel that you are very smart, smart, average, or below average?_____

11. In the first paragraph, the author states that it was not until he was in college that he discovered his learning style. Are you going to wait until you are that old before you discover your learning style? Yes__ No__

12. The author states that in every classroom there are different learning styles. Have you ever thought about the different learning styles that are in your classroom? Yes__ No__

13. Do you ever feel like the teacher rushes when he/she teaches? Yes__ No__

14. When you don't get what the teacher is saying, do you ask questions or are you afraid that someone may think that you are dumb?_____

15. Nobody is all one learning style. For example, nobody is just auditory (hearing) or visual or tactile (touch), but we are all a combination of the three. How do you rate yourself: visual first, auditory second and touch third or touch first, visual second and hearing third? Think about it and discuss it or write it down.

16. Is there any physical condition, hearing, sight, mental condition that makes it difficult for you to learn? Yes__ No__

17. Did you know that new studies show that too much television and video games will actually make it difficult for you to learn in school? How many hours of televison and video games do you watch daily?_____

18. Attention Deficit Disorder or ADD has been linked to excessive television while children are young. With this new information, how do you think you can help your younger brother/sister or other little kids?

19. In your opinion, why is it important to understand your learning style?_____

20. Find and complete this sentence: "The most important thing is to_____"

21. What did the author discover about his son's learning difficulty?_____

22. According to the author, what should you do when you discover an obstacle that keeps you from learning?

23. Can you think of one bad habit you have that keeps you from learning? Yes__ No__ If yes, are you willing to eliminate that habit from your life? Yes__ No__

24. The author knows a young man who watches one or two movies every day. He spends so much time watching television that he rarely gets his homework done. In your opinion, what should this young man do to fix his problem?

25. Find and complete this sentence: "You should seek to learn_____"

26. The author stated that he watched his wife's learning style and imitated her. Whose learning style are you watching and imitating?_____

27. Do you think your teacher understands your learning style? Are you brave enough to discuss this with your teacher? Yes__ No__

28. Find and complete this sentence: I predict that if you start working_____"

29. As a result of this lesson, are there any things that you need to change in your life? Are there any behaviors or habits that you need to eliminate?_____

30. Are there any subjects that you feel dumb in? Yes__ No__ If yes, what are they?_____

Wisdom From The Elders

Read the quotes and explain them to the boys. Use the questions to begin the discussion. Be sure to work with the boys to compose your own quote that relates to this chapter.

All our talents increase in the using, and every faculty both good and bad, strengthens by exercise. ANNE BRONTE
1. What is your strongest talent?
2. Do you agree that talents increase or get better as we use them more? Yes__ No__
3. Can you read better this year than you did last year? Yes__ No__
4. Do you believe that if you read for at least five hours a day that your reading will improve?
5. Faculty is the ability to perform an action. This quote states that every faculty both good and bad, strengthens by exercise. Do you believe this?
6. Do you believe that people who practice bad things get better at them?
7. Which of your talents have you decided to work at until you perfect it?

What we have to learn to do, we learn by doing. ARISTOTLE
1. In your opinion, is there any way to learn something other than doing it?
2. Can you name the things that you need to learn how to do?
3. In order to learn the hard subjects like math, science and English, you must do all of the assignments that the teacher gives. Are you completing all of your assignments?
4. Tell the truth and not a lie: Are you willing to practice your Math problems until you can do them well or do you just do enough to pass the test?
5. Who was Aristotle? (Look it up)

Learning is by nature curiosity . . . prying into everything, reluctant to leave anything, material or immaterial unexplained. PHILO
1. Are you a curious person? Yes__ No__ If yes, are you curious about subjects that have academic value like Physics, Chemistry, Calculus and English?
2. If learning is prying into everything, what are you prying into right now?
3. How deeply do you dig into subjects? Are you satisfied with a surface knowledge or do you stick with it until you feel you know it?
4. Who was Philo? (Look it up)
5. What are you currently studying in class that really has your attention?

Don't measure yourself by what you have accomplished, but by what you should have accomplished with your ability. BEN CHAVIS
1. Have you ever been told that you could do better in school? Yes__ No__ If yes, do you believe the person who told you was right or wrong?
2. In your opinion, what is your most significant accomplishment in life?
3. Do you feel that you have accomplished as much as you should have accomplished?
4. Do your grades reflect your ability?

5. Do you compare yourself to others or do you compare what you are currently accomplishing with what you could have accomplished?

6. How much smarter are you now than you were this time last year?

Disabilities can sometimes be definitions. You can think of yourself in terms of what you can't do and never realize the possibilities of what you can do.
BONNIE ST. JOHN, ATHLETE AND SCHOLAR

1. Have you been labeled with a learning disability? If you have, are you working hard to overcome it?

2. If you have a disability, do you use it as an excuse not to do your best?

3. Many young people are being labeled with the Attention Deficit Disorder (ADD). Do you think that is an excuse for them to flunk out of school?

4. How do you think of yourself? Each day do you get up thinking about the things you can do or the things you can't do and the reasons you can't do them?

5. Do you know of anyone who has a disability, but is still excellent in all that he/she does?

Start where you are with what you have, knowing that what you have is plenty enough.
BOOKER T. WASHINGTON, EDUCATOR

1. How do you feel about what you have, your brains, looks, and finances?

2. Do you focus on what you have or do you focus on what you don't have?

3. Do you think if you had more money you could do better in school?

4. How do you feel about where you are in life right now?

5. The author of this book was very poor when he was your age. He made up his mind at an early age that he was going to work hard to make sure that he did not stay where he was. Have you made up your mind to do better, and are you prepared to do whatever it takes to improve your life?

6. Do you believe that what you have is plenty enough?

Great opportunities come to those who make the most of small ones. DEMPSEY TRAVIS

1. Your small opportunity is to study to understand how you learn so that you can maximize your potential. Once you do that, your great opportunity will come. Do you believe this?

We learn from failure much more than from success. JOHN H. JOHNSON

1. What did you learn from your last big mistake?

2. Have you learned to bounce back from your mistakes or do they cripple you?

Compose a quote and write it here:_____

_____

_____

Chapter 7

Defeated By Rejection

Definition of rejection: To reject something is to discard it, throw it out as worthless, useless, or substandard. (The term reject is also used in basketball when a player blocks the shot of his opponent.) The young people can really relate to that use of the term.

Connecting With And Learning From Your Rich, Personal, Painful, Productive Past. Rejection can be devastating at any age. A man your age has experienced rejection in many forms. Share with the boys how you have been "kicked to the curb" (rejected). Share the rejection experiences of your youth and adulthood.

CAUTION: As you share this lesson, be sure to always show that we can recover from any form of rejection. Use personal examples of how you have recovered form rejection in various areas. Young people are greatly affected by peer pressure. They will do almost anything to keep from being rejected.

CHARGE: Charge the young men to strive never to take a rejection personally. A rejection by another person is not an assessment of your self-worth. People reject us for many reasons; if we knew the real reasons that they rejected us, we would be amazed and cease to give the opinions of others credibility.

ACTIVITY: Discuss the most painful rejection that you have ever faced. Share a rejection that had to do with a female and one that had to do with an employment or school situation. Encourage the boys to share their most painful rejection. Occasionally reiterate to the boys that what you share in your group should remain confidential.

TIP: An important purpose of a mentoring relationship is for the mentor to assist the mentee in identifying positive qualities. Most of us have habits, behaviors, or blind spots that would go unnoticed and uncorrected if no one ever pointed them out to us. Relationships give us the opportunity to deal with issues that we would otherwise overlook.

Lesson 7

Defeated By Rejection

Not too long ago, I had to take a trip on an airplane. As I approached the plane, I extended my hand to the flight attendant to shake her hand. She stood there with her hands folded in front of her and she refused to shake my hand. She rejected me! I experienced a mild form of rejection. Maybe she thought that I had not washed my hands, so she did not want to shake my hand. Whatever the reason, she rejected me.

At first I became angry at the fact that she did not want to shake my hand. I said to myself: "I can't believe that she thinks she is better than I am!" Then I began to ask myself: "What is wrong with me? Do I have bad breath? Is it because I am a man, is it because I am Black?" When we are rejected we always want to know why. As I sat in my seat on the plane I began to realize how this woman had affected me. I had actually allowed her to make me to feel defeated and angry. Once I realized what had happened, I determined to get myself together and not let her rejection affect me.

Rejection is a powerful force that all of us encounter at one time or another. The most common form of rejection is when a girl rejects a boy who wants to be her boyfriend. I can remember when I was 12 and I wanted Gilta (a cute girl in my neighborhood) to go to the movie with me. She told me no and I felt rejected. She then told me that she would go with me if I took two of her friends also. Like a dummy, I did it. People do many dumb things to keep from being rejected by a date. When a girl kicks a guy to the curb and goes on to someone else the boy is usually devastated. Millions of love songs have been written about being rejected by a lover.

Another form of rejection is the rejection of peers. In school I was always rejected by Freddie, who was the most athletic boy in the school. He never picked me to be on his dodge ball team. I told people that it didn't bother me, but deep down inside I was angry every time it happened. I said to myself: "Forget Freddie!" and I played on the losing team. I also felt rejected by the rich kids who would not talk to me. They would not talk to me because they were rich and by the smart kids who only talked to other smart kids. It was rough enduring the rejection of the other kids in school.

It is important to realize that people who reject others only do so because they don't feel good about themselves. People who don't feel good about themselves need to reject other kids because it helps them feel better about themselves. It is a primitive human behavior to put another person down so that you can feel better. I watch little children do it all of the time. One kid will tell another kid: "I got three pieces of candy, you only got two." The attempt to show that I am better than you is a human behavior that is not good.

I can remember when Freddie rejected Walter and refused to let him play on his team. Later that same day I saw Walter reject another kid the same way Freddie did him. Actually when most people reject you it is because they need to feel better about themselves. You need to always remember that when you are rejected by a person, it is just one person's opinion.

The key to all of this is to remember **not** to let the rejection affect you or defeat you. Too many kids in school feel rejected because **they received a** low grade on a math test or they failed a subject. Other kids feel bad and **rejected because** **they do not play sports** well. Some kids feel rejected because someone told **them they did** not want to be their friend. To feel rejected because of what someone else says about you is to hurt your own self. It is not what the other person says about you but what you feel about yourself.

Well, what about you? Have you been defeated by rejection? Have you rejected other kids and made them feel bad? It is a terrible thing to reject kids and make them feel bad for any reason at all. The proper thing to do is to remember how it feels to be rejected before you reject someone else. If we all considered how bad it felt, we would think before we rejected others.

Questions
(to discuss and think about or to serve as a written assignment)

1. The author starts the chapter by stating that he was rejected by a flight attendant on an airplane. It seems to have really bothered him. Can you remember the last time you were rejected and how it made you feel?

2. Look at the picture of the boy who is being rejected. What does that picture say to you?

3. Do you think that anyone should go through what that boy in the picture went through?

4. If you were asked to define "rejection" without using the word "rejection" how would you define it?

5. How many words can you think of that mean the opposite of rejection? List them.

6. Describe what happened the last time you were rejected._____

7. Find and complete this sentence: "When we are rejected_____"

8. How did the author say that he had allowed the woman to make him feel?_____" What did the author decide to do once he realized what had happened?

9. Find and complete this sentence: "Rejection is a powerful force_____"

10. Have you ever liked a girl that did not like you? Yes__ No__

11. The author says that he was rejected by Freddie who was an athlete. Some people feel rejected in the area of sports, others feel rejected in area of academics. Which area do you feel the most rejection in, sports or academics?

12. What is the dumbest thing that you have ever done to keep from being rejected?_____

13. What thoughts go through your mind when you are rejected?_____

14. How are you rejected the most? _____

15. Find and complete this sentence: It is primitive human behavior to_____

16. Tell the truth and not a lie: Do you ever put a person down so you can feel better?

17. In the next to the last paragraph the author makes an important point for us to remember. What is it?

18. You are not rejecting a young man when you beat him in a game of basketball but you are rejecting him when you tell him he is no good after the game is over. There is a difference in a person's value and his ability to play a game. We should never reject a person because of how well he does something. All human beings are infinite in value no matter how lousy they play ball, sing, or do on a math test. Do you agree with this statement? Yes__ No__ If you agree with this statement should we ever make fun of someone because he does not have the latest shoes or clothes? Yes__ No__

19. The author of this book came home one day and cooked a big meal for his kids. He worked hard in the kitchen for about two hours getting everything ready. When his kids sat down at the table to eat, one of them lowered his head and said: "I want McDonalds." How do you think that made their father feel?_____ Do you ever reject your parent(s) efforts to do things for you and ask them for something better than what they are offering? Yes__ No__ If yes, how do you think that makes them feel?

20. Each year college athletes anxiously sit by the telephone waiting on a call from a pro team. Most of them do not get the call. After years of work they are rejected. How do you think they feel?

21. Find and complete this sentence: "It is not what the other person_____"

22. How do you feel about yourself right now? Good__ Fair__ Bad__

23. When you suffer rejection, who do you talk to about it?

24. Every day we all have an opportunity to reject others. The older you get, the more opportunities you have to reject others. When you become the oldest and you see others who are younger struggling, will you reject them or embrace them?

25. What does the word "rejection" mean? (Look it up)

26. Tell the truth and not a lie: When you are rejected, do you sulk, mope and pout for a long time, or do you get over it quickly? long time__ quickly__

27. Find and complete the following sentence: "You need to always remember that when you are_____"

28. The golden rule says: "Do unto others as you would have them do unto you." How does this apply to rejection?

Wisdom From The Elders

Read the quotes and explain them to the boys. Use the questions to begin the discussion. Be sure to work with the boys to compose your own quote that relates to this chapter.

No one can figure out your worth but you. PEARL BAILEY

1. How much are you worth?
2. Who tells you that you are worth a lot?
3. Do you ever allow other people to make you feel worthless?
4. Do you see yourself as a valuable person regardless of who rejects you?

Fall seven times, stand up eight. JAPANESE PROVERB

1. Tell the truth and not a lie: Are you a quitter?
2. Every man has something that he struggles with. In what area do you quit very quickly?
3. Do you fall seven times and stand up eight or do you fall eight times and stand up seven? What is the difference between the two?
4. This is a Japanese proverb. What is a proverb?
5. How many times do you have to be rejected by other kids before you begin to feel sorry for yourself?

Do not be afraid of defeat. You are never so near to victory as when defeated in a good cause. HENRY WARD BEECHER

1. Are you afraid to fail?
2. In your opinion, what happens to people who are afraid to fail?
3. When you are defeated, does it give you more energy and make you want to fight on or does it make you want to quit?
4. Based on your experience, how can a defeat help you?

To lose is to learn. ANONYMOUS

1. Watching babies learn to walk is a lot of fun. Often they fall flat on their face. They may cry but they always try again. In your opinion, what can adults learn from watching babies learn to walk?
2. What did you learn the last time you lost at sports?
3. What did you learn the last time you flunked a test?
4. Only a fool fails to learn from his mistakes. Do you always try to learn from your mistakes?

What is defeat? Nothing but education, nothing but the first step toward something better.
WENDELL PHILLIPS

1. Tell the truth and not a lie: Is something defeating you right now?
2. If you told the truth you said "yes." We all have areas in our lives where we have not been as successful as we would like to have been. Can you name one area where you have experienced failure and how you plan to overcome it?
3. When you are defeated, do you see it as the first step toward something better or the end?

And a good rejection slip can be more educational than a mediocre workshop. ANONYMOUS

1. In your opinion, how can rejection be educational?

2. What possible lessons can be learned when someone rejects you?

3. Adults attend workshops to learn things they did not learn when they were young. Are you working with your mentor to learn about life now so that when you are grown you will not have to attend a lot of workshops? Yes__ No__

It is said that Walt Disney didn't get excited about any idea unless all the members of the board resisted it. If even a few were in favor, the idea dimmed for him. the challenge wasn't great enough to spark the energy he knew it would require. ANONYMOUS

1. Who was Walt Disney and what did he do?

2. Do you like a challenge?

3. Do you like an academic (school) challenge?

4. In your opinion, was Walt Disney an ordinary man? Yes__ No__ If no, how was he different?

5. Has anyone ever told you that you could not do something and you did it just to prove them wrong? Yes__ No__ Young men often respond to stupid challenges, but for some reason they can be slow to respond to wise challenges. In your opinion, why does that happen?

Believe in yourself and your abilities. There are lots of other folks who'll tell you, "It can't be done." JASMINE GUY

1. In your life, do you have more people telling you that you can do it or more people telling you that you can't do it?

2. When you are rejected, do you believe in yourself or do you believe in what the other person has said about you?

3. Tell the truth and not a lie: Do you believe in yourself and your abilities?

Many people know how to criticize, but few know how to praise. ETHEL WATERS

1. It takes a really mature young man to look at another young man his age and give him a compliment. Do you compliment the students in your class?

2. In your opinion, why does it take a strong person to compliment another person?

Compose a quote and write it here: _____

_____

_____

_____

Peer Pressure knows no age restrictions.
Adults buy things they don't need, with money they don't have, to impress people they don't like.

ANONYMOUS

Chapter 8

Fools and Foolish Behavior

Definition of a fool: a person who has little or no judgment, wisdom or common sense.

Connecting With And Learning From Your Rich, Personal, Painful, Productive Past: Like most grown men, I have encountered many fools in my past. When I think of my school days I can recall a multitude of fools and many foolish pranks. Take a minute to reflect back and remember some of the foolish deeds of the past. Selectively share with the boys, taking care to show the negative consequences of foolish behavior.

CAUTION: Remind the boys that often foolish behavior is made to look exciting or harmless. It is true that many boys temporarily get away with foolish behavior, but just because you don't see the consequences of their actions does not mean that there aren't any. Advise the boys to put foolish behavior behind them because it only causes trouble.

CHARGE: Charge the boys to never call anyone a fool. Although our society uses the word flippantly, it is a very serious accusation to make. No person should call another person a fool. This is especially true for young men.

ACTIVITY: Have the boys seek to identify an area in their lives where they act very foolishly. Ask the boys to seek to improve in that particular area. If they need to, have them keep a journal over a period of time noting success and failure.

ACTIVITY: Ask the boys to pay close attention to television and note the times a person is called a fool. Ask them to note the times people get laughs by acting foolishly.

TIP: There is power in a label. Have you labeled your boys with such labels as: smart, future banker, a great future husband and father, teacher, etc? Labels are powerful and children never forget lofty labels that adults place on them. Don't overdo it, but speak positively to the young men regarding a positive future.

Lesson 8

Fools and Foolish Behavior

The dictionary describes a fool as a person who has little or no judgement, wisdom or common sense. It is an awful, awful thing to be a fool or to be considered a fool by other people. The problem with most fools is that they don't realize that they are fools. They don't listen to those who would help them understand their situation. It is not a good thing to call someone a fool. You should never do this because no one understands why people act the way they do. It is very sad when a young person acts foolishly.

We need to become aware of and challenge our foolish behaviors. Foolish behavior is behavior that is common to fools. One area where most men have acted foolishly is in the area of female relations. I remember my first date with Gilta. I was in junior high school and she was in high school. I was so nervous that I said and did some foolish things. Boys have done many foolish things around girls. It is never too early for a young man to learn how to be wise around women.

People do foolish things because they reject the wisdom of older people. When I was in high school my dad, who was 60 years old, would share wisdom with me. I learned that when I would reject his wisdom, especially as it related to human nature I would suffer for it. The opposite of foolish behavior is wise behavior. Wisdom usually comes from older men. As I look back over my life, I see that I did some wise things and some foolish things. The wise things were done while I was hanging out with wise older men. The foolish things were done while I was hanging out with foolish young men.

In most schools you can find fools and foolish behavior. I repeat that it is not your job to call them fools but it is your job to avoid them. Fools can be very dangerous, especially when you mix them with certain things like guns, cars, firecrackers, drugs, a bad attitude, beer, rejection by a girlfriend and on and on.

As young men, you must be very careful to avoid fools and the foolish things that they do. One bad decision in the presence of a fool can cost you your reputation, your health or even your life. I remember one Friday night when I needed a ride home from a football game and I did something stupid. I got in a car with a fool who had been drinking. That was stupid! When I got in the car, he pressed the gas pedal to the floor and was going 75 miles per hour on a residential street. He could have *killed* me! From that day on, I was *very* careful about whom I rode with.

Fools are dangerous because they do things that other people would only think about doing. It is not uncommon for young people to slip and do something foolish. That does not mean that you are a fool. My friend Merrit was a very intelligent person. One Halloween we were walking down the street and he did something very foolish. He took an egg out of his pocket and threw it at an old lady's house. The egg splattered on the front window and the old lady called the police. They took Merrit to jail and they threatened to take me to jail also. My friend realized that he was foolish and later asked the old lady to forgive him. The good thing is that he did not try to blame it on me. Very often fools get other people in trouble.

It is a full-time job for a young person to guard against foolish behavior. One thing that you can do is to have an accountability system. This is when you have people in your life who will challenge you anytime they notice you acting foolishly. Mentors are good for this role. Remember that we can all slip and occasionally do something foolish. It is good to have wise friends around to tell us when we act that way.

You are really in trouble when foolish behavior is a way of life. If you act foolishly *all* the time, ask yourself these questions:

1. Have I been disciplined enough? Much foolish behavior is caused when parents do not discipline their kids. The child begins to think that there will be no consequences for his behavior, so he fears nothing and acts any way he wants to.

2. Do I realize what happens to fools and those who display foolish behavior? One of the things that an adult can do is look back at the foolish kids they went to school with and see how their lives turned out. In most cases it was bad.

3. Ask yourself the question: Do I need attention so badly that I act foolishly to get it? It is a fact that everybody needs attention. The question is: "How do you get the attention that you need?"

There are many reasons why young people act foolish. The most important thing is for you to control your personal behavior. Out of all the millions of persons on this planet, your behavior is the only person's behavior that you can control. What is it going to be? Will you behave foolishly or will you behave wisely?

Questions

(to discuss and think about or to serve as a written assignment)

1. In your opinion, was reading this chapter important or a waste of time?

2. What type of behavior do you display? Wise___ Foolish____

3. Would your teacher say that you were wise or foolish?_____

4. Find and complete this sentence: "The dictionary describes a fool as_____"

5. What does it mean to have judgment?

6. What is common sense?___ How did the old folks describe common sense? (Horse sense) The author says that it is an awful, awful thing to be what?

7. How many fools do you know?

8. Why does the author say that you should never call a person a fool?

9. Do you occasionally act foolishly? Yes__ No__

10. According to the author, what is one area where many men act foolishly?_____

11. Tell the truth and not a lie: Are you foolish around girls? Yes__ No__

12. Complete this sentence: People do foolish things_____

13. What is the opposite of foolish behavior?_____

14. Where does wisdom usually come from?_____

15. According to the author, it is not your job to call a fool a fool, but it is your job to_____

16. Find and complete this sentence: One bad decision in the presence of a fool_____

17. The author tells a story about a Friday that he made a bad decision with a fool. Can you share a time when you were involved with a fool and found out that it was a bad idea?

18. Of all the people on earth, how many people's behavior can you change?

19. Find and complete this sentence: Very often, fools get other_____

20. Name three men that you get wisdom from?_____

21. What almost happened to the author while he was hanging out with his friend Merritt?

22. Have you ever gotten in trouble because you were hanging out with a fool? Yes__ No__
If yes, what did you learn from that experience?

23. Find and complete this sentence: "It is a full-time job for a young person_____"

24. The author talks about an accountability system. In your own words, explain what that is.

25. Does your mentor ask you from week to week how you are doing? Yes__ No__ If yes, how often are you able to give a good report?____ If no, are you willing to respect his wisdom and concern for you and allow him to ask you each week how you are doing? Yes__ No__

26. At the end of the chapter the author gives three points to consider if you are a person who acts foolishly all the time. Sum up the three points in writing or by discussing them.

27. People learn discipline by being under authority. Young men who have no authority in their lives usually have no discipline. Tell the truth and not a lie: Are you under the authority of a father or other man in your life? Yes__ No__   If no, what are you going to do about it?___
(Suggestions: ask some good men to help guide you through your youthful years-mentors, coaches, uncles, ect.)

28. How do you get the attention that you need?_____

29. Do you have good self-control? Yes__ No__

30. The author says that there are many reasons why young people act foolish. What did he say was the most important thing?

31. Which one are you committed to? Living the life of a wise young man, or suffering the consequences of being a fool? Wise__ Fool__

Wisdom From The Elders

Read the quotes and explain them to the boys. Use the questions to begin the discussion. Be sure to work with the boys to compose your own quote that relates to this chapter.

If fifty million people say a foolish thing, it is still a foolish thing. ANATOLE FRANCE
1. Tell the truth and not a lie: Do you view foolishness differently when a lot of people try to get you to do something foolish?
2. If all the kids in the class are acting stupid, do you join them?
3. When does a foolish thing become a wise thing?

There are some people that if they don't know, you can't tell 'em. LOUIS ARMSTRONG
1. Are you a hard-headed person? Yes__ No__ Where do you think the term "hard headed" comes from?
2. Have you ever met someone who was doing something wrong, but because he was stubborn he continued to do it even after others explained the right way to him?
3. In your opinion, what do you call a person who won't listen to wise advice?
4. Do you know any people like this?
5. Who was Louis Armstrong?

A fool's head never whitens. OLD SAYING
1. The point of this proverb is that fools never get any wiser. Most people think that all old people are wise. This is not true when the old person is a fool. Do you know any older people who are not very wise?
2. Can you think of something worse than living to be old and never getting wiser?
3. In your opinion, what would cause a person to get old and never get wise?
4. What are you doing to insure that you will never be an old fool?
5. Tell the truth and not a lie: Are you wiser this year than you were last year?

A fool's fun is being bad; a wise man's fun is being wise! PROVERBS 10:23
1. How do you have fun?
2. Have you ever seen a young man do something foolish like destroying another person's property or hurting someone and enjoying it?
3. In your opinion, what is the appropriate thing to do when you see some fools having fun?
4. Can you think of any things a wise man does to have fun?
5. Some people say that it is boring, square or dull to do wise things. What is your opinion on this?

It is no fun to be a rebel's father. PROVERBS 17:21
1. Do you think you will ever have a son? Yes__ No__
2. How do you think the parents of foolish kids feel?
3. In your opinion, why do some young men rebel against authority?

4. Jails, institutions and death is what awaits those who develop an addiction to drugs. With this in mind, what type of person would start getting high or using drugs?

A fool always finds a bigger fool to admire him. NICHOLAS BOILEAU
1. Do you ever admire a fool and his foolish behavior?
2. Why do you think it takes a bigger fool to admire a fool?
3. Please notice the words "always finds" in this quote. Why do you think fools are so desperate for someone to admire them?
4. If you know that fools are always on the lookout for someone to admire them, what should you do when you find yourself involved with a fool?

The man of few words and settled mind is wise; therefore, even a fool is thought to be wise when he is silent. It pays for him to keep his mouth shut. PROVERBS 17:28 TLB
1. When you don't have anything to say, do you keep your mouth shut or do you talk anyway?
2. Why do you think people consider you wise when you do not say anything?

The best way to convince a fool that he is wrong is to let him have his own way.
  JOSH BILLINGS
1. Have you ever argued with your parents until they let you have your way? Yes__ No__
2. When you know that your parents are right, do you continue to try to make your point?

Wake up. The hour has come to be more responsible. Change this world by starting with yourself. The world is not going to change until you change. DR. BETTY SHABAZZ
1. Do you agree that it is time to be more responsible?
2. We need more wise young men in the world. Do you plan to be one of them?

When it comes to food for thought, some of us are on a hunger strike. DICK GREGORY
1. Thinking is hard work, for this reason many people do not like to think. Do you enjoy solving a problem by thinking it out?
2. From the time you wake up to the time you go to bed, do you spend more time thinking or playing?

A person completely wrapped up in himself makes a small package. DENZEL WASHINGTON
1. One characteristic of a foolish person is that they only think of themselves. Are you a self centered person?

Compose a quote and write it here:_____

_____

Use Code Words or Phrases

Code words are critical. You should actually develop your own language with the boys based on a quote or favorite portion of a chapter. For example, in chapter three, you find the story about the Harrison boys. This is a favorite of mine because it teaches the benefit of hard work even when you do not understand the logic of it all. When I want to compliment one of my boys for their diligence and hard work, I compare them to the Harrison boys. They take it as a compliment and the Harrison boys have become a code word that I use with the boys and they use with each other. It is our personal secret phrase that we use when we want to stress excellence.

Work to develop code words around the thesis statement and other wisdom that you study. Simply choose a word and use it in your general conversation. One of my favorites is "challenging him with wisdom."
I often say to a young man:
"I am challenging you with wisdom, how are you going to respond?"

DR. HAROLD DAVIS

Chapter 9

Loyalty: What is it? Who Needs It?

Definition of loyalty: The act of sticking with a person or organization that you have indicated a desire to consistently stick with.

Connecting With And Learning From Your Rich, Personal, Painful, Productive Past: We have all been hurt by disloyal people. Friends, lovers, and family have all hurt us in ways that we will never forget. As you share with the boys, keep in mind a particular hurt that you suffered at the hands of someone whom you thought was loyal to you. This will give you power as you share with them because the boys will sense that you are speaking from your heart.

CAUTION: Warn the boys not to expect loyalty from too many people. It has been said that if you make one friend in life you have done very well. Expect loyalty from those who have demonstrated loyalty over a period of time. Loyalty is first demonstrated before it is expected.

CHARGE: Charge the boys to be loyal to the extent that they are expected to be loyal. This should be the case in all areas of life. When you get a job, be loyal to your employer. When you get a girlfriend, be loyal to her. Be loyal to everyone that you represent, your parents, school, teacher and friends. Let them know that there are incredible long term benefits for those who are loyal.

ACTIVITY: Discuss the consequences of disloyalty in various segments of society. What would happen if the police department, fire department, teachers and bankers were disloyal? Discuss the impact that honesty and integrity has in these occupations.

> **TIP:** An important purpose of a mentoring relationship is for the mentor to assist the mentee in identifying his positive qualities. Most of us have habits, behaviors, or blind spots that would go unnoticed and uncorrected if no one ever pointed them out to us. Take the time to remind the young men of the strengths that you see in them. Remember that most young men do not receive compliments, encouragement, and academic challenges from men. Never underestimate the power of your words to encourage.

Lesson 9

Loyalty: What is it? Who Needs It?

When I was fifteen years old I was in a band. Actually, I was the leader of the band. All of the boys in the band were about fifteen years old and we were friends. As the leader of the band, I picked the songs we did, negotiated the contracts for the band to play and paid everybody. I enjoyed being the leader of the band because when everything went well, I got the credit. On the other hand, when things went poorly, I got all of the blame.

My best friend in the band was Jamie. Jamie was the singer and he was my best friend. Friendship is important in a band just like it is in sports. Friends work well together and look out for each other. In other words, friends are loyal to each other. I can remember this one day when I went to practice and a very sad thing happened. As I walked into the room, all of the band members were lined up against the wall looking at me. Jamie, my friend, looked at me and said: "We all quit."

I was stunned, surprised and sad all at the same time. I couldn't believe that my good friend would do this. We had been friends for years. I never expected that this would happen. Well, I left that room with a good understanding of what loyalty was because of how badly I felt. I decided that I was going to be loyal to those who trusted me. I decided that if I needed to leave a situation or break off a friendship, I would do it the right way and not the wrong way.

There is a term that older people use called "burning bridges." They say: "You should never burn bridges." What is meant by this is when people help you in life, they are serving as a bridge that gets you from one place to another. Many young people go over the bridge and then act as if they will never need that bridge again. The fact of the matter is we often need people who have helped us before to help us again. If you treat them badly or act as if you will never need them again, you are burning or destroying the bridge that brought you over and it will be difficult to go back to them for help again. You never know who you will need to help you in the future, so always treat everybody nicely.

Our nation needs a new generation of young men who will be loyal to it. Loyalty is the first cousin to honesty and as never before our nation and communities need honesty. We have businesses that fail because men and women are not loyal to their employers. Marriages are failing because men are not loyal to their wives. Schools are failing because teachers are not loyal to their students and students are not loyal to their teachers. Without loyalty, a nation cannot stand for long because no one can be trusted.

I am challenging you to develop a sense of loyalty in your life. It will be a great asset to your family, boss, community and nation. Loyalty should be extended first to those who helped you when you could not help yourself. It makes me very angry to see a kid sass his mother when she suffered pain to bring him into this world. Boys should be loyal to their mothers because for nine months the mother was loyal to her child while she carried him in her womb.

Loyalty should also be extended to family members and community members who have contributed and are still contributing to your growth and maturity. I am grateful to all of the loyal soldiers who died fighting for our country. Because of their sacrifice, you and I live in a free nation where we can pursue our dreams.

I am loyal to those who have gone before and I show my loyalty by serving the next generation. When I wrote this book to help boys I was being loyal to America and all of the men who have died to keep America a free nation. If you and the boys your age stop being loyal to our American principles of justice and freedom for all, our nation will not last long.

You should seek to be loyal to projects that you begin. Learn how to start something and stick with it until it is completed. The attitude of loyalty to a task will help you be a success in life. Never start a school assignment that you do not finish. Be loyal to your word and complete the tasks that you tell your teacher or parents that you are going to complete. Never begin a task that you do not finish. Be loyal to that task.

I want to encourage you to develop the habit of being loyal to those who love you and sacrificed for you. When young men develop this attitude, it will help our nation stay great and our cities and communities will become better places to live.

Questions
(to discuss and think about or to serve as a written assignment)

1. Before you read this chapter, had you ever thought about how your loyalty is so important to so many people?_____

2. What person has been most loyal to you?

3. Have you ever been hurt by a friend who was disloyal? Yes__ No__

4. Who are you loyal to?_____

5. What is your definition of loyalty?_____

6. Why is loyalty needed in America?_____

7. Have you ever been stunned by someone who was not loyal to you?

8. Find and complete this sentence: "I left that room with a good_____"

9. What did the author decide to do because of what had happened to him?

10. The author says that there is a right way and wrong way to leave a situation. In your opinion, what is the wrong way to leave a situation?

11. What is the right way to leave a situation?_____

12. What does it mean to burn bridges?_____

13. Many times in life you will have to go back to an old friend, an old job, or an old teacher for a reference. If you destroy those relationships you can never go back again. This is what it means to burn bridges. With this in mind, have you burned any bridges lately? Yes__ No__

14. Are there any adults in your life that you have mistreated lately? Yes__ No__

15. Have you ever had someone mistreat you and in your mind you burned the bridge that you previously extended to them? Yes__ No__

16. Find and complete this sentence: "You never know who you will need_____"

17. Is there any person that you have mistreated or "burned bridges with" and you cannot go to them for help? Yes__ No__

18. The author states that our nation needs a new generation of young men who will be loyal to it. Why do you think he said that?

19. Loyalty is the first cousin to_____

20. The author gives several examples of what happens when people are not loyal. Of all the examples that he gave, which one can you relate to the most?

21. Complete this sentence: "Without loyalty a nation cannot_____"

22. What does the author challenge you to develop a sense of?

23. Find and complete the following sentence: "Loyalty should be extended first_____"

24. Why did the author say it made him mad to see a kid sass his mother?

25. Do you sass your mother? Yes__ No__

26. Find and complete the following sentence: "I am loyal to those who have gone_____"

27. Are you loyal to America? Yes__ No__

28. How did the author say that he served the next generation?_____

29. In your own words, state what it means to be loyal.

30. Are you loyal to projects that you begin? Yes__ No__

31. Is there anything that your teacher has asked you to do that you have not done?

32. What type of habit does the author encourage you to develop in the last paragraph?

33. Write the last sentence of the chapter here:_____

_____

_____

Wisdom From The Elders

Read the quotes and explain them to the boys. Use the questions to begin the discussion. Be sure to work with the boys to compose your own quote that relates to this chapter.

Friendship is the only cement that will hold the world together. DUKE ELLINGTON
1. The amazing thing about friendship is that you can be friends with people who are very different than you are. Do you have any friends who are different than you are?
2. Do you have a friend that you feel cemented to?
3. It may be too big a task for you to hold the world together, but you can try to hold your classroom together. Do you work at making friends in your classroom and school?
4. Are you loyal to your friends or do you put them down when a new person comes along?
5. Who was Duke Ellington?

Where ever you are, be there! B.J. TATUM
1. Tell the truth and not a lie: Do you often daydream in class?
2. Are there days when you would rather be some place other than school? Yes__ No__
3. In your opinion, what do you accomplish when you are at school and you think about being some other place?
4. Do you give your all when you are studying, working, playing ball, or do you think about other things at the same time?
5. It has been said that a double minded man is unstable in all his ways. In your opinion, what are the benefits of being able to concentrate on what you are doing right now?

A truthful witness never lies; a false witness always lies. PROVERBS 14:5
1. Do you tell the truth most of the time or all of the time?
2. Can you think of a famous court case where people lied?
3. A witness is a person who tells what he saw. When you are asked to witness all you have to do is to repeat what you saw with no additions or subtractions. In your school are you a truthful witness or a false witness?
4. What would happen if all witnesses were not loyal to the truth and lied?

Without virtue man can have no happiness. BENJAMIN FRANKLIN
1. What does virtue mean? (Look it up)
2. In your opinion, why can there be no happiness without virtue?
3. Did you know that people who are not loyal and honest must struggle to stay happy? Why do you think that this is so?
4. People who are not honest often do well for a while, but if you watch them over a long period of time you will find that they often have big problems in the end. Do you think it is worth it to be happy for a while and suffer in the end?
5. Who was Benjamin Franklin?

Many times we find ourselves turning our backs on our actual friends, that we may go and meet their ideal cousins. HENRY DAVID THOREAU

1. Have you ever stopped being friends with someone because you wanted to make a new friend with someone else?

2. No human being is perfect. The longer you get to know a friend the more bad things you will find out about them. If you find out that they are dishonest or have bad habits that will get you in trouble, you may want to discontinue your friendship. On the other hand, if they just have some minor bad habits that they need to work on, you may want to try to help them overcome them. Which do you think you would choose to do for your friend?

You cannot be friends upon any other terms than upon the terms of equality.
WOODROW WILSON

1. Do you feel that you are better than any of your friends?

2. In your opinion, can a friendship work when one person feels that he is better than the other person?

3. Who was Woodrow Wilson?

You shall judge a man by his foes as well as by his friends JOSEPH CONRAD

1. If you choose to be loyal to family, friends and country, there will always be those who criticize you for it. Are you prepared to handle the criticism that comes from being loyal to those things that are important to you?

2. Do you have any foes?

3. What type of people qualify to be your foes, or what type of people do you not want to be friends with?

Many persons have a wrong idea of what constitutes true happiness. It is not attained through self-gratification but through fidelity to a worthy purpose. HELEN KELLER

1. What does self-gratification mean?

2. Do you live for self-gratification?

4. Nothing is accomplished unless loyal people give time and energy to it. What worthy purpose are you loyal to?

5. Who was Helen Keller?

Compose a quote and write it here: _____

_____

_____

Note to the mentor/teacher: As a result of this lesson, are there any needs that these young men have that can be met by networking with parents, other teachers, social agencies or religious institutions?

Do not be discouraged if you are not getting good grades right now. One little six-year-old took home a note saying he need not come to school since he was "too stupid to learn." That boy was Thomas Edison.

Chapter 10

Getting Even

Definition of getting even: The act of punishing someone for something they did to you.

Connecting With And Learning From Your Rich, Personal, Painful, Productive Past: As men we have all had situations where we wanted to retaliate, but we walked away from them. Call to mind a particular event in which you did this and the long range benefits of your decision. Be honest and let them know that there is still pain associated with the memory but that you know that you did the right thing.

CAUTION: The position that I take in this chapter regarding revenge is not a popular position. Popular culture, songs, movies, and TV shows all say that revenge is sweet. That attitude plays well on the screen, but it is devastating on the streets of America. The attitude of restraint needs to be promoted among the young people of our nation. As you teach the lesson, realize that they may or may not agree with you, but don't let that deter you.

CHARGE: Charge the boys to remember that you don't always see the immediate benefits of not getting even. It usually takes time to see the big picture, and sometimes you never do see the big picture.

ACTIVITY: Discuss how to handle your anger when you want to get even. Consider these possible scenarios when you choose not to get even:
1. The person who wronged you will eventually meet a person who will treat them worse than they treated you.
2. Bad luck will get him.
3. If you try to get even something will go wrong which could result in a tragedy.
4. It is difficult to talk to a foolish person.

ACTIVITY: Ask the young men to pay attention to the next ten television shows that they watch to see how many use revenge as the theme. Often, the revenge is an agent of the government who is trying to catch a criminal which is legitimate, but, too often it is an individual seeking revenge for a personal injury which is not legitimate.

Ask the boys to note how many shows are based on getting revenge and then to further note how many of those who were seeking revenge were seeking revenge as an individual not as an agent of the government.

Lesson 10

Getting Even

I never will forget the day that it happened. I was riding my new bicycle that I had gotten for Christmas. It was my first time having the bicycle out of the house, and boy, was I proud! This was the best bicycle that I had ever owned and it had everything: a mirror, light, horn, streamers, and saddlebags. It was the Cadillac of bicycles, and I was the proudest of owners.

As I was riding my bicycle through the neighborhood, Lamont saw me on my new bicycle. His eyes got as big as two silver dollars. His mouth dropped open and he said: "Wow, this is a bad bike! Can I ride it?" Well, it was not that I did not want him to ride the bicycle but I had just gotten it and I was still riding the bicycle. So, I told Lamont, "Not right now," but I said I would let him ride the bike later that day. Lamont did not like this, and he frowned and walked away in a huff.

I continued to ride until my mom called me inside to eat. Well, I did not want to take my bike in the house yet so I set it on the front porch so that I could sit at the dinner table and watch it. As I was eating my mashed potatoes and meat loaf, I kept one eye on my bicycle. As I looked up from taking a bite of meatloaf, I saw a hand on my bike and I noticed that it was falling over. I jumped up from the table and dashed out of the front door just in time to see two things: Lamont's back going around the side of the house and my bike hitting the ground, breaking my rear view mirror.

I was so mad that I wanted to commit murder! I said to myself: "I'm going to kill Lamont!" I wanted to fight him as soon as I could find him, but he hid from me and time passed. I cooled down but I still wanted to GET EVEN. Summertime came and Lamont thought that I had forgotten about what he had done, but I hadn't. Then my chance came one day in June. Lamont's parents bought him a new skateboard with wide rubber wheels. Lamont was very happy riding his new skateboard, and he was smiling from ear to ear. I waited patiently for my opportunity to strike and three days later Lamont was distracted by a basketball game that some boys were playing. He left his skate board on his front porch at his house. Nobody was home. Nobody was watching. I thought: "Here is my chance."

I took a pair of pliers out of my pocket, took the nut loose on the front right wheel on Lamont's skateboard, took the wheel off and went home. I stopped along the way to throw the wheel over the hill into the weeds where it would never be found again. Finally, I had gotten even! I was not there to see Lamont's face when he found his skateboard, but I am sure that he was very sad, which made me glad.

The next day I saw Lamont walking past my house with his three wheel skateboard in his hand. Just as I thought, he looked very sad. I went out to talk to him so that I could pretend that I was sorry for what happened. As we talked I learned some things that I had not known before. I learned that Lamont's dad was not well and he had taken the money from his last paycheck to buy Lamont that skateboard. I also learned that because of their financial problems that Lamont was going to have to move and live with an Uncle in Detroit. As Lamont continued to tell me all of his problems, tears began to come into his eyes and all of a sudden I began to feel pretty lousy.

I began to think of how good things were with me at my house and how I had nice things but Lamont did not have all the things that I had; he only had a skateboard. After he finished talking, Lamont walked down the street with his head down and I began to feel tremendous guilt. If I had only known all of this before I took the wheel off of his skateboard, I never would have done it. I never told Lamont what I did, and I never replaced the wheel. What I did do was learn a tremendous lesson: *you can never get even!*

The idea of getting even is misleading. There is no way that you can hurt somebody in the same way and to the same degree that they hurt you. You will always hurt them more or less. There is no such thing as even. When you hurt them more than they hurt you, you are just as guilty as they are for starting it in the first place. Because I am a human being, I do not know what other people are going through or what they are thinking, so it is impossible to pay them back. The best thing to do when someone hurts you is to remember that what goes around comes around. If you mistreat someone, someone will mistreat you. It is a law that no human being can break. It is a bad idea to try to get even.

Well, I know what you are thinking. You are saying to yourself: "If I can't get even, what can I do when I am mistreated?" The first thing that you do is to inform the proper people. If you are mistreated in school, tell the teacher. Let someone know what has happened. Secondly, remember that you reap what you sow and it is impossible to escape when you mistreat others. Thirdly, get busy and stay busy improving yourself. The best way to get even with someone is to surpass them in every area. In other words, leave them in your dust as you get ahead in life. The best revenge is success.

Questions
(to discuss and think about or to serve as a written assignment)

1. Do you own a bicycle? Yes__ No__

2. Do you get very mad when someone messes with your stuff? Yes__ No__

3. Have you ever had anything stolen or taken from you? Yes__ No__

4. Do you think about getting even? Yes__ No__

5. What would you have done to Lamont?_____

6. The author said that he was so mad that he wanted to commit murder. Have you ever been so mad that you wanted to commit murder? Yes__ No__

7. What do you do to calm down when you get very mad?

8. What was the last TV show that you watched where someone got even?_____

9. When someone does you wrong, do you plan for a long time how to get them? Yes__ No__

10. The author says that you can't hurt someone exactly like they hurt you. Do you agree with his view on this subject? Yes__ No__ Explain your answer._____

11. Lamont began to cry as he told the author the story. Why do you think he began to cry?

12. The author said that he began to think of how good things were with him at his house and how he had nice things and that Lamont did not have the same nice things that he had. Do you ever think about all the young people in America who are not as fortunate as you are?

13. Once the author realized what he had done, he said that he began to feel tremendous guilt. In your opinion, why do you think he began to feel guilt?_____ Do you think guilt is a good thing or a bad thing?_____ How do you think guilt can help our schools, communities and nation?

14. Do you ever feel guilty for things that you do? Yes__ No__

15. Find and complete the following sentence: There is no way you can hurt somebody in__"

16. In your opinion, why do you think that when you get even you will always hurt people more or less than they hurt you?

17. Lamont was having a lot of personal problems that the author did not know about. Would you have tried to get even if you knew about Lamont's personal problems? Yes__ No__

18. Did you realize that most kids who misbehave have personal problems? Yes__ No__

19. Do you misbehave? Yes__ No__

20. Lamont's dad was sick. Many young men have absent dads, sick dads or dads who have been killed or died. How do you think that affected Lamont?

21. Lamont was being forced to move to Detroit to live with an uncle. He was being moved from one male role model (his father) to another role model (his uncle). How do you think this would affect Lamont?

22. In your opinion, is it important to have a consistent male role model in your life?

23. Some times this role model is a dad, uncle, teacher or friend. Who is the main male role model in your life?

24. Here is the question: Do two wrongs make a right? Yes__ No__

25. The author says that it is impossible to escape when you mistreat others. Why does he say this is so?

26. We have made the point that we should not try to get even, but why do you think so many people feel better when they try to get even?

27. What is the first thing you should do when you feel you are mistreated? (Last paragraph)

28. What is the second thing you should do when you feel you are mistreated? (Last paragraph)

29. What is the third thing you should do when you feel you are mistreated? (Last paragraph)

30. Find and complete this sentence: "The best way to get even_____"

31. Write or discuss the last sentence in the paragraph:_____

_____

Wisdom From The Elders

Read the quotes and explain them to the boys. Use the questions to begin the discussion. Be sure to work with the boys to compose your own quote that relates to this chapter.

The best manner of avenging ourselves is by not resembling him who has injured us.
    JANE PORTER
1. What does avenge mean?
2. Do you know the rest of the words in this quote? Yes__ No__ If no, which words do we need to look up?
3. What can we do to make us look like the person who hurt us?
4. Instead of looking like the person who hurt you, who should you try to look like?
5. When you get even, do you smile and do it or do you frown and get even?

Revenge is biting a dog because the dog bit you. AUSTIN O'MALLEY
1. Have you ever been bitten by a dog?
2. What would you do if a dog bit you? (Kick it, throw a rock at it?)
3. Which is more natural, for a dog to bite a human or for a human to bite a dog?
4. In your opinion, what are the dangers involved in biting a dog?
5. Do you agree that to get even is to be like the one who hurt you?

Vengeance has no foresight. NAPOLEON BONAPARTE
1. What does vengeance mean?
2. What is foresight?
3. Do you have foresight?
4. In your opinion, what are the dangers of having no foresight?
5. Vengeance does not know how much it will hurt the other person. Has anyone ever tried to get even with you and end up hurting you more than you hurt them?
6. Who was Napoleon Bonaparte?

Forgiveness is the highest and most difficult of all moral lessons. JOSEPH JACOBS
1. What does "moral" mean?
2. Building on the definition of the word "moral," what is a moral lesson?
3. In your opinion, why is forgiveness so difficult?
4. Is there anybody that you are struggling to forgive right now?
5. One of the main themes on most tv shows is getting even. In your opinion, is this good or bad?

Forgiveness is man's deepest need and highest achievement. HORACE BUSHNELL
1. Have you ever wanted someone to forgive you and they would not? Yes__ No__ If yes, how did that make you feel?
2. All families often have problems that they must overcome. Often these problems can be solved if one family member will just forgive another family member. Do you need to forgive a family member right now?

Forgiveness is the sweetest revenge. ISAAC FRIEDMANN
1. In your opinion, how can forgiveness be sweet revenge?
2. It takes a really big person to forgive someone. Any small person can hold a grudge. When it comes to forgiveness, are you a big person or a small person?
3. Forgiveness really mixes people up because it does not make any sense to them when you forgive them. Have you ever forgiven someone?
4. The more they hurt you, the sweeter the revenge when you forgive them. Have you ever forgiven someone who really hurt you?

The most effective recourse is the quality of your performance. Your energies should be directed to doing the best possible job you can. CLIFTON WHARTON
1. What does recourse mean?
2. Often people hurt you so that you will stop performing so well. They want you to fail and fall, this is why they hurt you. When this happens, do you get better or get bitter?
3. It takes a lot of energy to flip negativity into positivity. Have you learned to take the anger that you sometimes feel toward people and apply that anger to studying?
4. Do you ever think about the energy it takes to hate someone? When your energies are directed toward hating someone, you are wasting energy. Wise people learn how to direct their energies toward doing the best possible job at all times regardless of how others treat them. Are you mature enough to do that?

Practicing the Golden Rule is not a sacrifice, it's an investment. BYLLE AVERY
1. The Golden Rule says that we should treat other people like we would like to be treated. Do you practice the Golden Rule?
2. In your opinion, how is the golden rule an investment?
3. According to the Golden Rule and based on what the author did to Lamont's skateboard, what do you think might happen to him at some point in the future?

Forgive, forget, and move on. DR. LOUIS SULLIVAN
1. Do you think it is better to forgive and forget or to start a fight which will only make things worse?
2. It takes a very wise young man to look beyond the frustration of the moment and move on with his life. Are you trying to get to that level of wisdom and maturity?

Compose a quote and write it here: _____

_____

Sow an act and you reap a habit.
Sow a habit and you reap a character.
Sow a character and you reap
a destiny.

CHARLES READE

Chapter 11

Grades! (Are They Important?)

Definition of grades: A means of measuring academic achievement.

Connecting With And Learning From Your Rich, Personal, Painful, Productive Past: Look back to those academic days when you shared your report card with the other boys. Remember when everyone asked the question: "What did you get?! What did you get?!" When we refused to let them see our card or did not answer their question, it was obvious to everyone what we got. Call to memory a particular class or teacher that challenged you and share it with the boys.

CAUTION: Point out to the boys that grades do not determine our self-worth. Even if we flunk every class, we are still valuable and important people. Grades do not determine our value as human beings, but they will affect our position in the workplace. If the young men are suffering from shame they will not feel that their grades are bad but that they are bad.

We do know that many young men with genius potential flunk out of school because they struggle with the structure and teaching style. We seek the delicate balance of challenging them to do their best while at the same time not destroying their self-worth.

CHARGE: Charge the boys to work to their full potential. If they do all of the assignments and study hard for the test and make a "C" that is OK. It is *not* OK to miss half of the assignments, study for 20 minutes while watching music videos and flunk the test. Do not accept excuses and push a strong work ethic. When it comes to school it is real simple. . . Work hard now and live good later or have fun now and work minimum wage for the rest of your life.

ACTIVITY: Have the boys ask their teacher to list the things each of them need to do to make better grades. You can discuss her list with the boys at your next meeting. Tell the boys that if they are serious about improving their lives they will do what their teacher says.

TIP: Go back and read a chapter that you have previously read. Read it quickly and then focus on learning one additional quote from that chapter.

TIP: Don't rush through the chapter, questions or wisdom. It is NOT important to finish the book, but it is very important to connect on some point of wisdom each time you meet with your mentees.

Lesson 11

Grades! (Are They Important?)

When I was a kid, there was a time of year that I hated. It was the worst time of the year and it came four times every year. It was report card time. Back when I went to school, we were given our report cards in a brown envelope and told to take them home to our parents. This was very difficult, especially when you knew that there were some bad grades on it. There were times when I would come home late or consider joining the army to avoid showing my parents my report card. I knew they had to see it eventually because they had to sign it.

What is even more amazing is that now that I am a parent, I am very concerned with my children's report cards. Now that I am grown I realize how important grades are. Parents are concerned about their children's grades because parents have entered the work force and know from experience the importance of good grades. Parents have watched some of their friends suffer financially because they could not get good jobs. As a result of seeing what happened to their friends, parents encourage their kids to get good grades.

Our nation is filled with two types of people: skilled people and unskilled people. A skilled person is someone who has learned how to do something or has developed a skill like a doctor, nurse, engineer, teacher, or computer technician. An unskilled person sells popcorn at ball games, sweeps the floor, cuts the grass or sells hamburgers at fast food restaurants. A skilled person generally makes more money than a unskilled worker and has more benefits like hospitalization, insurance and retirement programs.

In order to become a skilled worker, there are things (skills) that you need to learn. These skills are generally learned in school, where there is a grading system. If you can't make a passing grade, you are not passed by that school and you then become classified as a unskilled worker. Please note that all honest work is good work, but usually unskilled workers work harder jobs and longer hours.

Parents want their children to have the skills that it takes to get good jobs. Parents want their children to do well long after they are dead and gone. In the United States of America, you can do well if you develop the right skills. There are many ways to get skills. Before there were so many schools, young people would learn a trade from their dad or another craftsman. I have a friend whose dad was a carpenter and he helped his dad and learned a trade at the same time. He now builds houses for a living. It is always good for boys to help men who are working because you can learn many skills from them.

Good grades should be your goal, but there are some kids who work very hard and still do not make good grades. I can remember how I struggled with my multiplication tables in the third grade and my grades were not good in math. I learned that because you struggle with certain classes does not mean that you can't be successful. More importantly, you should not dislike a class just because you struggle in that class. Just because a class is difficult does not mean it can not be fun. I really enjoyed science class but it took me a few years to learn how to get a good grade out of the class.

One fact that you should keep in mind is that you are going to change a great deal in the next few years. Some subjects that are difficult now will be easier as you get older and wiser. Tell yourself that you are going to do better as time goes by. Do not turn off your hopes in the difficult subjects just because you are having a difficult time. In a few years with some hard work, you could be the smartest kid in the class.

It is important that you learn good study habits to make sure that you are making the best possible grades that you can. There should be a place in your home where you study. Different people study best in different places. For some it is in the kitchen, others study best in their bed room. For others it is on the living room floor. You should know where you study best and spend more time studying than you do watching Television.

Never accept the idea that you can't do any better. Go to your teacher and talk to her about your grades. Learn the grading scale, what it takes to make an excellent or "A" and what is a failing grade. Talk to the kids who make good grades and ask them how do they do it. Educating yourself about grades and the grading process will help you in your school career and will help you develop the skills you need to be successful.

Questions
(to discuss and think about or to serve as a written assignment)

1. There are some people and schools who promote a no grading system. Their idea is that everybody should do the best he can and nobody should be graded. How do you feel about this idea?_____ What are the good benefits and the bad benefits for this idea?

2. Tell the truth and not a lie: Do you enjoy report card time?

3. What are the grades that they give at your school? (Example: A,B,C,D,E,F)

4. Do your parents hassle you about your grades? Yes__ No__ Who else hassles you about your grades?_____

5. Do you understand why the adults who love you want you to make good grades? Yes__ No__

6. Do you do all of your assignments? Yes__ No__

7. Do you study for the test in your most challenging class? Yes__ No__

8. What does the author find so amazing now that he is a parent?

9. Do you think that there will ever come a day when you are grown with kids who bring a report card home to you? Yes__ No__ Maybe__ Don't know__

10. Find and complete this sentence: "Parents are concerned about their children's grades__"

11. Our nation is filled with two types of people. What are they?_____

12. Of the two types of people, which one do you want to be?_____

13. What are some of the jobs that unskilled people do? Name them.

13. According to the author, what are some of the benefits of being a skilled person?

14. According to this author, why do parents want their children to have good skills?

15. Do you ever feel that your parents are unreasonable or too hard on you when it comes to school?

16. How did people get skills before there were so many schools?_____

17. What is your most challenging subject in school?_____ What is your attitude about that class? Do you have a defeated attitude, an I will eventually get it attitude, or this is just another challenge for me attitude?

18. Find and complete this sentence: In the United States of America, you_____

19. The job market in our nation changes on a regular basis. A few years ago, there was no demand for computer programmers. Today that has changed. There was a time when everybody wanted to be a doctor, but now because of the legal challenges, many young people are choosing not to go into the medical field. When you grow up, things will be different than they are today. If you had to make a decision right now, what job would you like to have?

20. Do you talk to kids who get good grades? Yes__ No__ Discussion_____

21. Do you feel people respect you when you make good grades? Yes__ No__ Discussion__

22. Tell the truth and not a lie: Are you sometimes jealous of the people in your class or school who get good grades? Yes__ No__

23. In some schools, the smart students are teased because they do so well in school. Is there a stigma (bad image) associated with making good grades in your school? Yes__ No__

24. In your opinion, why do some young people tease others when they make good grades?

25. Did you know that you can get a free college education worth thousands of dollars with good grades? Yes__ No__ Discussion_____

26. Did you know that you can get out of poverty with good grades? Yes__ No__ Discussion__

27. Find and complete this sentence: It is always good for boys to _____

28. Do you ever watch a repair man who comes to your home or at school to see how he fixes things? Yes__ No__   What can you fix because you watched someone fix it?_____

29. Find and complete this sentence: Never accept the idea_____

30. Do you study more than you watch TV? Yes__ No__

31. Write the last sentence of the chapter here: _____

Wisdom From The Elders

Read the quotes and explain them to the boys. Use the questions to begin the discussion. Be sure to work with the boys to compose your own quote that relates to this chapter.

You're not rewarded for having brains. You're only rewarded for using them.
MORDECAI JOHNSON

1. Tell the truth and not a lie: Do you work as hard as you can (apply yourself) to make good grades?
2. We all want to be rewarded for something. What do you want to be rewarded for? (Example: NBA star, NFL star, Rock/Rap star, etc.)
3. The best way for a young man to use his brain is to make good grades. How do you plan to make better grades this semester?
4. Thinking is hard work. Are you lazy when it comes to thinking?

If you think education is expensive—try ignorance—DEREK BOK

1. Take a guess at how much one semester at a local college costs.
2. How much do you think a teacher makes a year? How much do you think a person who works at a burger joint makes?
3. In your opinion, why is it expensive to be ignorant?
Have you decided how far you want to go in school? College, bachelor's degree, master's degree or a Ph.D. degree?
4. An education requires that you work hard now so that you will have some benefits later. Are you mature enough to put off having fun now so that you can live well later?

I have never let my schooling interfere with my education. MARK TWAIN

1. In your opinion, what is the difference between schooling and education?
2. Grades and education are two different things. There are some people who learn how to get good grades but they don't get an education. Are you learning anything in school that will help you make it in life?
3. Who was Mark Twain?

You don't understand anything until you learn it more than one way. MARVIN MINSKY

1. Can you think of anything that you have learned more than one way?
2. Some boys have more than one man in their lives teaching them things. Can you think of something that two men have taught you in their varying styles?

The best way to fight poverty is with a weapon loaded with ambition. SEPTIMA CLARK

1. Some young men never get serious about life. Is there any way that you see your life as a fight?____ If your answer is yes, what is it?
2. What is the definition of ambition? (A drive to succeed)
3. Are you an ambitious person? Yes__ No__

4. Do you feel that it is automatic that you will do well in life, or is there a chance that you could end up in poverty?

5. In your opinion, how could ambition be a weapon that could be used to fight poverty with?

6. What great weapon is found between your two ears?

The way to be successful is through preparation. It doesn't just happen. You don't wake up one day and discover you're a lawyer any more than you wake up as a pro football player. It takes time. ALAN PAGE

1. Some young men simply do not understand that it takes work to make it. Do you understand this basic principle?

2. What have you done today that will help you reach your goal in life?

3. It has been said that you can walk to California if you take one step at a time.

4. In your opinion, which takes the most work, to become an NBA star or a Dentist?

There are no shade trees on the road to success. LEONTINE KELLY

1. A shade tree is a place where people can sit down and cool out. The point of this wisdom is that if you spend too much time cooling out you are not on the road to success. Do you spend a lot of time in leisure?

2. Good grades come as a result of hard work. How much do you study at home on a average day?

3. Are you on the road to success? Yes__ No__ If you answered yes, can you give me some specific reasons why you feel you are on the road to success?

Remember, luck is opportunity meeting up with preparation, so you must prepare yourself to be lucky. GREGORY HINES

1. Opportunity is something that visits most people at least once and some people a few times.

2. You must be ready to respond when opportunity walks by. When opportunity visits and preparation is not there to meet him, opportunity keeps on walking. What opportunity are you prepared to respond to today?

3. In your opinion, how do good grades bring more opportunities to you?

4. In your opinion, hanging around the wrong people bring what type of opportunities?

Compose a quote and write it here:_____

_____

_____

Do not be discouraged if you are not getting good grades right now. One little six-year-old took home a note saying he need not come to school since he was "too stupid to learn." That boy was Thomas Edison.

Chapter 12

They Made Me MAD!

(How to control your anger)

Definition of being mad: To be in a frenzy, disorderly, out of control.

Connecting With And Learning From Your Rich, Personal, Painful, Productive Past: Acting out in anger is one of the pitfalls of young men. Most adult men can recall situations when they acted in anger and later regretted it. At every stage of my life, childhood, adolescence, young adulthood and middle age, I can recall specific instances when I allowed my anger to get out of control. Recall one of your instances where you regrettably allowed your anger to get out of control and share it with the young men.

CAUTION: The point of this lesson is to show the folly of uncontrolled anger. In your examples please be sure to show the negative consequences of uncontrolled anger. This lesson is taught against the backdrop of a violent society. TV shows demonstrate all types of violence for the young men to imitate. Be prepared to answer their objections to a violence-free life.

CHARGE: Charge the young men to remember that when you are mad you rarely make the best decision. It is not a good time to make decisions when you are angry! Uncontrolled anger and foolishness are first cousins and foolish, immature behavior frequently follows a mad person.

ACTIVITY: Ask the boys what their favorite TV shows are. Ask them specifically what shows that they will watch tonight. Have them take notice of how many times someone gets angry on the show. Have them note what they got angry about and how they responded to their anger. Tell them to take notes so that they can report back to the class next week.

TIP: Go back read a chapter that you have previously read. Read it quickly and then focus on learning one quote from that chapter.

Lesson 12

They Made Me MAD!

(How to control your anger)

I taught elementary school for several years. It was a very exciting time in my life, and I learned many lessons from the kids that were in my classes. I can remember one day, there were two boys sitting next to each other. The boys names were David and Jerry. David was picking on Jerry, calling him names and hitting him. As the teacher, I knew that something was going on but I could not catch them in the act. Well, David kept on picking with Jerry until Jerry snapped. At this point, Jerry jumped over the desk and began to beat David's butt. When I turned around I blamed Jerry for the disturbance, but actually he didn't start it. After I broke up the fight, I sat David and Jerry down to talk and figure out what happened.

As I talked to David and Jerry, I began to understand what had actually happened. Usually Jerry was a very good kid who never caused any problems. This is why I was surprised when I turned to see him kicking David's butt. On this occasion, Jerry had allowed his anger to get to him. Normally Jerry could ignore David when David does stupid stuff, but on this day Jerry allowed David to make him angry. As a result of getting angry, Jerry was in trouble and David almost got away without any blame.

Anger is a very interesting emotion. It can do good or it can do bad. It seems like everybody and most animals will get angry every now and then. I have seen kids get angry, adults, dogs, cats, squirrels and even hamsters get angry. To tell the truth, I used to get angry quite often. Now that I am older, I don't get angry as much as I used to because I understand certain things about anger. Let's talk about what I have learned about anger.

1. Most of the time anger is a choice. Most of the time, we get angry because we choose to. It is a fact that *nobody* can make you angry! I have heard people say: "He or she made me angry!" That is not true. They did not make you angry. You choose to get angry.

The very, very important thing is to decide how you will respond to anger. I remember an incident that happened many years ago when I chose to get angry. Some boys were washing cars on a used car lot. Sitting beside the car lot there was a kind, gentle old man sitting down minding his own business. These mean boys took a bucket of soapy water and dumped it on the old man. When I saw this, I became very, very, very angry and chose to go talk to the car dealership and

111

call the police. What they did to that innocent person made me mad! I responded, not by fighting but by calling the police. It is good to choose to get angry and respond when innocent people are harmed.

2. Much anger is preventable. I have decided that I will not get angry about the things that I cause because of the decisions I make. For example: At work I park my car under a tree. Every spring, the birds mess all over my car and I have to wash it almost every day. That would make me mad. Well, I have learned that if I park my car on the other side of the street, the birds will not mess on the car and I will not have anything to become angry about. Simple solutions are available for many of the things that make us angry.

What about you in your classroom or on the playground? What behavior can you change that will prevent you from becoming angry so often? I know of some boys who ask for problems by not taking preventative action. In most cases if we would do things like: stay in our seats when we're supposed to, turn homework in on time, don't talk when we shouldn't, keep our hands to ourselves, don't say mean things to other people, we would not get in trouble and we would not become angry.

On most occasions we can avoid incidents that would normally cause us to become angry. If you can't avoid the situation, stop and consider what is the proper response when you are about to get angry.

3. Respond, don't react. A reaction to anger is when you are controlled by anger. Some kids throw things, yell and hit other kids. The best thing to do when you are angry is to respond. When you respond, *you* are in control and you have the opportunity to make the right decision.

4. Most anger is not productive. Most of the time when young people get angry, they either sit around and sulk or they become aggressive. I know of students in school who become angry and pout like babies. Other students become angry and throw books, or speak in a mean tone to the teacher.

Only mature, wise people know how to make anger their friend. I am glad to say that at my age, I am pretty successful at making anger my friend. The reason I wrote this book was because I was angry. I was angry because so many boys do not have fathers and no men are spending time with them. There are other good things that I have done while angry, so I have tried to make anger my friend and not allow it to do negative things.

5. When I am angry, I don't think as clearly as I do when I am not angry. I had the opportunity to meet a man who was a 7th degree Karate black belt. This man explained to me that when he was fighting, he knew that he would beat the person if they became angry. He said: "When you get angry, I beat your butt."

The reason that he knew that he would beat you is because it is very difficult to think clearly when angry. Most boxers love to make their opponents angry because they no longer fight smart when they are angry but they begin to brawl.

Questions
(to discuss and think about or to serve as a written assignment)

1. David and Jerry had a problem in class. Have you ever had a problem in class with another young man? Yes__ No__

2. Has anyone ever picked on you until you snapped like Jerry did? Yes__ No__

3. What did the teacher learn about who started it?_____

4. Do you agree or disagree that it is the angry person who almost always gets in trouble?

5. The author states that he used to get angry often when he was younger. Why does he say that he does not get angry as much now?

6. The author states that anger is a choice. Do you agree or disagree with that statement?

7. Based on what you just learned about the fact that nobody can make you angry, what are you going to say the next time you want to say: "He made me Mad!"

8. What did the author say was the very, very important thing?

9. What makes you angry?_____

10. Do you get angry quicker when you see someone else being mistreated or when you are mistreated?

11. When did the author say it is good to choose to get angry?_____

12. Do you ever get angry over things that are not really that important? Yes__ No__

13. In your opinion, how can you make anger your friend?_____

14. Are you wise enough to make anger your friend?

15. What makes you angry at home?_____ What makes you angry at school?_____

16. In your opinion, what is the primary difference between a human and an animal when they are angry?

17. Do you agree with the author who says that much anger is preventable? Yes__ No__

18. The author gives a simple example of how he used to get angry about what the birds did to his car. He devised a simple solution to his problem. What was the solution?

19. Are there any problems in your life that have simple solutions that you could use to solve them? Yes__ No__ For example, if a person is bugging you, would it be possible to move away from him? Yes__ No__

20. Find and complete this sentence: "I know of some boys who ask_____"

21. Tell the truth and not a lie: Do you get angry when things go wrong, even when you could have prevented it by making good decisions?

22. We react to anger when we do the first thing we think when we get angry. Our first thoughts are usually of revenge. We respond to anger when we think it through, considering the consequences of our actions and choosing what would be best for all involved. Which do you generally do, react or respond to your anger?

23. Find and complete this sentence: "When you respond, you are in_____"

24. Do you pout when you are angry? Yes__ No__

25. Which are you more likely to do when you are angry, sulk or be violent?

26. How do you spell "anger"? What happens if you place the letter "d" in front of it?____ Always remember that anger is one letter short of danger.

27. The author states that only mature, wise people know how to make anger their friend. How successful are you at making anger your friend?_____

28. What positive tasks have you accomplished because you were angry?

29. Why did the author say that the 7th degree black belt enjoyed fighting people who were angry?

30. In your opinion, which is best, to fight angry or to fight smart?

31. As a result of reading this chapter, what do you plan to do when you become angry?

Wisdom From The Elders

Read the quotes and explain them to the boys. Use the questions to begin the discussion. Be sure to work with the boys to compose your own quote that relates to this chapter.

He who conquers others is strong; He who conquers himself is mighty LAO-TZU
1. Do you agree that the most challenging enemy that you will face in life will be you?
2. Think of the worst habit that you have, then think of the strongest person in your school. In your opinion, which would be harder to conquer?
3. Are you strong because you can conquer others or are you mighty because you have conquered yourself?

A soft answer turns away wrath. PROVERBS 15:1
1. What is wrath? (Intense anger, rage, fury)
2. Are you one of those people who always yell when they are angry? Yes__ No__ If you are, how do people usually respond to your yelling?
3. Has anyone ever talked to you very softly while you were angry? Yes__ No__ If yes, how did their soft voice affect you?

Let not the sun go down upon your wrath. EPHESIANS 4:6
1. Have you ever gone to bed angry at someone?
2. When you go to bed angry with someone, do you wake up the next morning more angry?
3. The reason it is not good to go to bed angry with someone is that while you are sleeping your brain continues to think about what you are angry about. In your opinion, what is the logical result of thinking about what you are angry about all night?
4. Which would you rather your brain think about while you are sleeping, something that really makes you mad or a beautiful western sunset with it's golden rays slowly fading out of sight?

When angry, count to ten before you speak; if very angry, count to an hundred.
THOMAS JEFFERSON
1. In your opinion, what would be the benefits of waiting before speaking while angry?
2. Do you immediately lash out when you are angry or do you count?
3. Who was Thomas Jefferson?

An angry man is again angry with himself when he returns to reason. PUBLILUS SYRUS
1. What is reason? (Sound judgment, good sense)
2. Do you think that when people are angry, they leave reason or may be unreasonable?
3. What would be the danger in leaving reason?
4. Have you ever said something while you were angry and later regretted what you said?
5. This quote is saying that reasonable people will always be angry twice when they get angry. The first time they will be angry with others, the second time they will be angry with themselves for how they acted while angry with others. Do you agree with this?

Anger is as a stone cast into a wasp's nest. MALABAR PROVERB
1. Have you ever seen what happens when a stone is thrown into a wasp's nest?
2. Have you ever seen a wasp that you could talk to calmly and reason with?
3. Do you feel that you can control how angry you get when you get angry?
4. In your opinion, is it best to throw the rock into the wasp's nest and then try to control them or would it be better not to throw the rock at all?

The longer I live, the more deeply I'm convinced that the difference between the successful person and the failure, between the strong and the weak, is a decision. WILLIE E. GARY
1. Do you agree with this quote that success and failure in life can result from a decision?
2. Many adults have friends who made decisions that were different than theirs. They have lived long enough to see the results of those decisions. Have you ever had an adult to challenge some of the decisions that you have made?
3. Can you decide when you want to be angry and when you don't want to be angry?

You don't make progress by standing on the sidelines, whimpering and complaining. You make progress by implementing ideas. SHIRLEY CHISOLM
1. Fear of failure and the fear of becoming angry cause many young men to stand on the sidelines and never get involved in the game of life. Where are you standing right now?
2. Tell the truth and not a lie: Are you making progress in your life right now?
3. What new ideas have you tried lately?
4. When you get angry, do you sit down and pout or do you get busy to make things better?

This is a tough game. There are times when you've got to play hurt, when you've got to block out the pain. SHAQUILLE O'NEAL
1. Would you like to play in the NBA?
2. Have you thought about how angry some of those guys get?
3. Have you ever seen any NBA players who could not control their anger? Yes__ No__ If yes, what is the worst thing you have seen one of them do while angry?_____ In your opinion, how did a grown man look acting like that?
4. When you play basketball with your friends and they make you mad, do you stop playing the game?
5. Are you able to block out the anger and keep playing or do you have to stop, complain, and demand your rights before you continue?

Compose a quote and write it here: _____

_____

Note to the mentor/teacher: As a result of this lesson, are there any needs that these young men have that can be met by networking with parents, other teachers, social agencies or religious institutions?

Chapter 13

Trash Talkin' (Is it worth it?)

Definition of Trash Talkin': Abusive language toward another person which is designed to diminish the person's self-esteem and elevate the talker to a position of superiority.

Connecting With And Learning From Your Rich, Personal, Painful, Productive Past: When I was a kid, we played what was called the "dozens." This was the act of talking about each other in degrading ways. We mostly talked about the other person's mother, family, sports ability or any physical characteristic that could get a laugh. Actually, as I reflect back on my childhood, the worst fight I was ever in resulted from a successful verbal barrage on a person who was physically bigger than I was. So, playing the dozens or as they say now, crackin' and smashin' could be a dangerous activity.

Reach back into your storehouse of childhood memories and recall instances where someone's mouth got them into trouble. Share your experiences with the boys, and remember they *love* to hear about your childhood, especially your vulnerability to failure as well as success.

CAUTION: Our purpose here is to discourage destroying others with our tongue. It is appropriate to speak up in defense of oneself when needed, but we should never attack people with our tongues for sport.

CHARGE: Charge the young men to discover the power of positive words. Words can be used to build people up and help them be their best. Charge them to remember that any time they choose to tear someone down, they are showing their own weakness and insecurity. People who are secure use words to build people up, not to tear them down.

ACTIVITY: Have the boys make a list of positive words or phrases that they can use to build up others. Some examples: Good job!, You are a nice person, Your hair looks nice. Number these phrases and see how many the group can come up with. After you have exhausted your memories, seek to come up with negative phrases like: butt head, stupid, trash can brain, etc. It will now be interesting to see which list is the longest, the negative list or the positive list. If the negative list is the longest, we need to have a discussion as to why it is the longest. Is it because of TV? If so, which shows? A discussion should follow regarding the benefit of watching shows that increase our negative vocabulary.

Lesson 13

Trash Talkin' (Is it worth it?)

Trash talkin' is something that boys have done for years. For some boys it is considered an indoor sport. When I was a kid, we talked trash to each other all of the time. I remember on one occasion in the 4th grade, I talked trash to a kid in my homeroom named Buster. Buster was the biggest kid in the school. On this particular day he made me mad, so I talked trash to him. I told him that I was going to kick his butt and challenged him to meet me across the street from the school at 3:00. Now, I knew that I was just talking because Buster weighed about 50 pounds more than I did.

I often wondered why I would talk trash to a kid who was big enough to squash me. It was not a smart thing to do. At the end of the day when the bell rang, I got in the front of the line and I was out of the door and home before Buster caught me. Actually, I was a trash-talkin' chicken. I could not back up what I said. In some cases, boys can back up what they say, but in this case I couldn't back it up. Let's consider some reasons why boys talk trash:

1. Pride. Men and boys have a lot of pride. Pride is an overrated opinion of yourself. Because men are very prideful they have the urge to protect themselves when someone says something bad about them. Our pride is usually aroused when someone talks about us personally, talks about our mom, calls us dumb or something like that. Most of the time, when our pride is attacked we would like to fight. If we can't fight right then we sometimes talk trash.

2. It makes us feel better. Talking trash gives us a sense of satisfaction. We feel like we have hit them with words. When kids and adults can't hit with their hands, they hit with words. Sometimes we really feel better when we hit with words and sometimes hitting with words hurts people more than hitting with hands.

3. It really hurts some kids. There are kids who don't feel good about themselves. They may not have a good home life or there may be some physical condition that they struggle with. I remember a kid in the 4th grade who could not control his bladder. He would have accidents in school and wet himself. It was not his fault; it was a medical problem. One day a mean kid talked trash to him after he had an accident and it hurt him so much that he did not come back to school for three days. Words are powerful. Words can really hurt when they are aimed at our weak spots. Everybody has weak spots, even grown men have weak spots.

4. Famous people do it. Sometimes if you watch closely, you can see basketball players talkin'

119

trash to each other. In the movies, the stars do it all of the time. It is easy to back up what you say in the movies, but it is much harder to back what you say up on the basketball court or in real life. We need to remember that in the movies, nobody really gets hurt. In real life, trash talkin' can be very painful to the victims.

It is important to remember that your tongue is one of the smallest organs in the body, but it has a power far greater than many of the other organs. The tongue can start a fire in the minds of men. Many wars have begun because of a loose tongue. Marriages have been destroyed because of loose lips. It is not good to talk all of the time. People will consider you a smart person if you just keep your mouth shut.

When you talk a lot of trash, the people around you soon know all that is in your mind and they do not consider you a very smart person. When you keep quiet, people will wonder what you are thinking and when you talk they will listen. Leave the trash talking to people who are going to live trashy lives. Decide to live with a mouth that benefits those around you.

Questions
(to discuss and think about or to serve as a written assignment)

1. Are you a trash talker? Yes__ No__

2. Do the people that you hang out with talk trash? Yes__ No__

3. Do you consider trash talkin' a sport to be mastered? Yes__ No__

4. Does trash talkin' help you win the basketball game? Yes__No__

5. What athlete is known for talkin' a lot of trash?

6. Find and complete this sentence: Pride is a_____

7. Do you agree or disagree with the statement that men and boys have a lot of pride?

8. Having a healthy pride is good. This is when you have an attitude of appreciation for who you are and what you can do. An unhealthy pride is when you think you are more than you are.

9. Can you tell when someone's pride is hurt? Yes__ No__   Have you ever done something stupid like tripping and falling in front of the class? Yes__ No__ When that happened was your pride hurt? Yes__ No__   If you answered yes, what did you do?_____

10. What do we want to do when our pride is attacked? _____

11. What subject makes you mad when people talk about you?_____

12. We have all heard the saying: "Sticks and stones will break our bones but words can never hurt us." That is a nice saying but it is not true. Words can hurt us very much when said at the right time by the right person. Do you like to hit people with words? Yes__ No__ Are you good at out talking people or are you slow in that area?

13. Have you been hurt by a trash talkin young person? Yes__ No__

14. Name three trash talkin' athletes or movie stars._____

15. Is trash talkin' necessary when you play sports? Yes__ No__ Is it a regular part of the game? Yes__ No__

16. Some people grow up in homes where everybody talks trash to each other. In your opinion, how do you think that affects them?

17. Tone of voice is very, very important when communicating with others. Do you think trash talkin' would be effective if people did it in a very low and polite voice?

18. The author stated that trash talkin' makes some people feel better. Do you agree with this and if so, why do you think it makes some people feel better?

19. The author gives the example of a young man who was hurt when another young man talked trash to him and teased him about a medical problem. There are other true stories about teenagers who committed suicide when they were embarrassed by someone who talked trash to them. In your opinion, what can you do about this?_____

20. Is it worth tearing another person down to boost your self-esteem? Yes__ No__ Depends on who it is__

21. Find and complete this sentence: "Words can really hurt when_____"

22. The opposite of trash talkin' is complimenting or edifying someone. Take a moment right now to compliment someone sitting close to you. Write or state a sentence that will make someone feel good._____

23. Do you imitate what people say on the movies? Yes__ No__

24. Do you understand the difference between movies and real life? Yes__ No__

25. According to the author, when people trash talk in the movies, who gets hurt?

26. What did the author say that the tongue can do?_____ What can loose lips do?_____

27. Find and complete this sentence: "People will consider you a_____"

28. The author gives four reasons people talk trash. Can you add another reason why people trash talk?_____

29. Write the last sentence of the chapter here:_____

Wisdom From The Elders

Read the quotes and explain them to the boys. Use the questions to begin the discussion. Be sure to work with the boys to compose your own quote that relates to this chapter.

The tongue is more to be feared than the sword. JAPANESE PROVERB

1. Do you believe that you can hurt someone more with your words than you can with your fist?
2. The tongue can destroy relationships between people who love each other. Are you able to hold your tongue, be quiet when you want to fuss at a family member?
3. Whose tongue are you afraid of?

I'm the son of a minister and I just can't tell dirty jokes. Even if I could, I wouldn't. You can be funny without cursing and doing sex jokes. SINBAD

1. The mouth is connected to the mind. The mouth does what the mind tells it to do. What does it say about your mind when garbage always comes out of your mouth?
2. Do you sometimes say things that are not nice just to get attention?
3. Many people tell dirty jokes because that is what they listen to all of the time. There was a time when there were no dirty jokes on television. That is not true today. Do you sometimes watch shows that you shouldn't watch on television where adults tell dirty jokes?
4. There is a lot of comedy on television now days. Many of the comedians tell dirty jokes to get a laugh. In your opinion, is it necessary for jokes to be dirty in order to be funny?
5. Many young people curse because they hear it at home. If you would talk to them what would you tell them to help them stop cursing?

If you were to make little fishes talk, they would talk like whales. OLIVER GOLDSMITH

1. Why do you think so many little dudes talk so much trash?
2. Many people compensate for their weaknesses with their mouths. Have you ever known anyone who did this?

Some things are better left not said. BERNARD SHAW

1. A nice person does not repeat mean things about people. When you hear some dirt (bad news) about someone, do you let it die by not repeating it or do you tell everybody who will listen?
2. Many people do not know that everything that they hear should not be repeated. They are not wise enough to know the difference between helpful words and hurtful words. When you hear words, are you wise enough to know which words are helpful and which are hurtful?
3. Not only are some things better left not said, some things should be forgotten. Are you good at forgetting those things that need to be forgotten?
4. Ministers, Doctors, Lawyers and other professionals must be able to keep personal information about the people that they serve. None of them would have their jobs very long if they told other people's personal business. Do you think you could do that?

Honey, it's so easy to talk a good game. What we need are folks who will do something!
MAXINE WATERS
1. It has been said that talk is cheap. Explain what that means.
2. Are you a producer or a talker?
3. Do you know anyone who talks a lot but does very little?

Courage is being brave when you know something isn't going to happen to you.
WILLIAM H. GRAY
1. Do you only talk trash when you know that the other person won't fight you?
2. Tell the truth and not a lie: Have you ever talked trash to a person who was bigger than you are?
3. Courage is the ability to say you are going to do something that may be difficult or challenging and then follow through and do it. Do you have the courage to be a man of your word and do what you say you are going to do?

Thousands of people can speak at least two languages—English and profanity. JOE CLARK
1. When you really need to make your point, do you use profanity?
2. Do many students in your school use profanity?
3. In your opinion, how does television influence the use of profanity by young people?
4. People with small vocabularies use profanity. When was the last time you learned a new word?

The older he grew, the less he said, and the more he spoke. BENJAMIN E. MAYS
1. Do you run your mouth all of the time or do you wait until you have something to say before you speak?
2. As you get older, are you saying more or saying less?
3. The reason you are able to say less as you grow wiser is because you understand more about life and people can see wisdom on your face and by your actions. Do you ever display wisdom by your facial expressions and your body?
4. With wisdom comes the ability to keep your mouth shut. It is actually possible to have a powerful influence without opening your mouth. Can you name an older person you know whose presence has an impact (speaks) without him saying a word?

Learn to speak kind words. Nobody resents them. CARL ROWAN
1. Were the last words you said to your teacher kind words or harsh words?

Leadership begins with sound, verbal communication skills. TERRIE WILLIAMS
2. Are you able to communicate your thoughts calmly and clearly using a healthy vocabulary?

Compose a quote and write it here:_____

_____

EVERY BOY NEEDS
A MAN IN HIS FACE
CHALLENGING HIM WITH
WISDOM REGARDING CRITICAL
ISSUES AND DECISIONS IN HIS
LIFE.

Chapter 14

Every Boy Needs A Man In His Face

Definition of In His Face: To challenge foolish statements, reasoning or action with objective truth based on wisdom and experience.

Connecting With And Learning From Your Rich, Personal, Painful, Productive Past: Men from my generation were raised by a stricter code of discipline than the current generation of young boys. It was common for boys in my era to be corrected by a variety of men. Most men who were considered a part of your life would freely get in your face when the need arose. In your mind, assemble a list of men who were in your face. Recall specific instances when their simple statements challenged your thinking and may even have changed your life. Assemble your list of heroes who were in your face and give tribute to these men in front of the boys. Freely praise and thank them for their effort toward your success.

CAUTION: It is an unfortunate fact that today we have many narcissistic, self-centered men who never lower their gaze to look down at a boy and nurture him. To make it worse, many young men have only experienced this type of man. As a result of this experience, the concept of a man in your face (in the context of love) may be foreign to the boys.

Be sure to explain that men who care about you will get in your face. When men do not care about you, they do not take the time to talk to you. So, a man in your face challenging you with wisdom is an asset. Make this point as many times as is necessary for the young men to grasp the concept.

CHARGE: Set the example of a man in your face by sharing your memories of a man in your face. When you share, involve your whole body to make the memories come alive. Smile as you talk about it and even look up as if you are lost in a wonderful memory. This will impact the boys greatly as they see how deeply you were impacted by loving men.

ACTIVITY: Have the boys make a list of men who have impacted them the most. Have the boys tell one thing that the men on their list have taught them. Explain to the boys that the way we honor those who have invested in us is to be the best that we can be.

TIP: By now, the young men should know the thesis statement and explanation very well. Continue to explore the thesis statement to obtain new levels of understanding regarding it's meaning.

Lesson 14

Every Boy Needs A Man In His Face

Boys are born to test the limits. Every boy will try to see how far he can go before he gets in trouble. This is a normal characteristic that boys display as they get older. I acted like this when I was a boy. The only problem that I had was that I had a father who would look at me, point his finger and tell me what was going to happen if I did the wrong thing.

I remember on one occasion that I almost smarted off to my mother. My father got in my face and said: "Son, if you smart off to your mother, I will knock your teeth out!" I knew that he was serious so I never smarted off to my mother. My father was the first man to spend some time in my face.

Another man who spent some time in my face was my first boss, Mr. Pratt. Mr. Pratt owned a music store and taught me how to work, be on time and treat customers well. I was required to be at work by 4:00p.m. each day. Mr. Pratt would meet me at the door and shake my hand. I knew that I could not be late because Mr. Pratt would be in my face if I was late.

When I went to college I was just about grown. In spite of how old I was, I still needed a man in my face. Mr. Gillispie was the man in my face while I was in college. He taught me many things and challenged me to be my best.

The fact of the matter is that all men need an older, mature man in their face to help them do all that they should do and to be all that they can be. When you have a man in your face, several things will happen:

1. Wisdom is available to challenge you. Now that I am grown I often think of all of the stupid things that I almost did when I was younger. It was the older men that I talked to who prevented me from doing the stupid things. They challenged me with good wisdom and convinced me that what I was getting ready to do was stupid. When an older man is in your face, he is there to bring you wisdom and he is there because he cares.

2. Strength is available to control you. Every boy has what I call "wild horses" in him. Wild horses make you think that you are stronger than you are. The wild horses in you encourage you to take risks. I never will forget one day when I was in college, I decided to try to body-slam my dad who was sixty years old, but still in shape. I grabbed him from the side and was trying to lift him up when all of a sudden the world began to spin. Dad had somehow managed to pick me

127

up, spin me around and throw me down. Even though he was older, he was still able to control me.

Young boys need to realize that there are men who are stronger than they are. They are able to control you if they need to. This is good and not bad because most boys go through periods in their lives where they need help managing their wild horses.

3. Wisdom and strength are available to cover your back. In this life there are many things that you cannot control, things that are behind your back and you cannot see them. There are other things that you are not wise enough to see that an older man is aware of. A man in your face can warn you of the things that are behind your back and can alert you to the dangers that you can't see.

When we make mistakes in life, we need wisdom and strength to help us to recover and get our feet back on the ground. A man in your face will provide that for you. The idea of having a man in your face will work to make you a better man when you get older. I often think of the men who were in my face while I was forming my personality. Young men are in the process of forming their personalities and lives. A man in your face will guide the process and help you reach your full potential in the years to come. The only thing that society has to make men out of is boys. A man in a boy's face is a great gift to the boy and the community. I challenge you to get some men in your face so that you can be the best that you can be.

Questions
(to discuss and think about or to serve as a written assignment)

1. Are you the type of young man who constantly tests the limits or see how much you can get away with? Yes__ No__

2. Tell the truth and not a lie: Are you labeled as a discipline problem? Yes__ No__

3. The author states that he tested the limits when he was young. He said that he had one problem. What was that problem?

4. The author said that he almost smarted off at his mother. Do you ever smart off at your mother? Yes__ No__ If yes, what man gets in your face about that?

5. Many young men have problems with the idea of a man getting in their faces. They fail to understand what we are talking about. We are not talking about abuse or someone going off on you for the fun of it. What we are talking about is a man who will challenge you when you are wrong with wisdom. The reason he does this is because he wants to see you do well in life, so he challenges your faulty thinking when you say or do stupid things. Now that you understand what we are talking about, do you have any men in your face? Yes__ No__

6. The author names several men who were in his face during his formative years. Now that he is grown he looks back and smiles when he thinks of those men who challenged him when he did or said stupid things. Do you think one day you will be thankful for the men who are in your face today? Yes__ No__

7. What man challenges you with wisdom?_____

8. Do you have a male teacher, principal or counselor? Yes__No__ If yes, have you given them your school permission to get in your face? Yes__ No__

9. The author says that when he went to college he was almost grown. In spite of his age he said that he still needed a man in his face. How old do you think you will be before you no longer need a man in your face challenging you with wisdom?_____

10. Find and complete this sentence: When an older man is in your face, _____

11. Look at the picture in your book. What do you think the man in the picture is telling the boys? In your opinion, how is the tall boy responding? How is the boy holding his shirt responding? How is the boy with his arms folded responding?

12. Tell the truth and not a lie: Do you feel that you need a man in your face? Yes__ No__

13. Before you read this chapter, had you ever thought about how having a man in your face was a good thing? Yes__ No__

14. It is unfortunate but true that some men never grow up. Men like this often take their frustration out on young men by yelling at them and in severe situations hitting them. This is called abuse and it is not healthy. Be careful not to confuse a man that wants to help you and challenges you with wisdom with a man who is abusive. In your opinion, what should you do when you do not know how to distinguish between the two?

15. Do you listen when a man who cares about you gets in your face? Yes__ No__

16. Under point number 1. "Wisdom is available to challenge you" what does the author say prevented him from doing more stupid things when he was younger?

17. Find and complete this sentence: "When an older man is in your face_____"

18. What are wild horses and what do they do?_____

19. Do you have wild horses in you? Yes__ No__   Do you control them or do they control you?

20. Under point number two, the author states that his sixty year old dad picked him up and threw him down. You can understand it when a man is physically stronger, but can you understand it when a man is mentally stronger (smarter) than you are? Yes__ No__

21. Tell the truth and not a lie: Do you have any problem listening to a man that you know is smarter than you are? Yes__ No__

22. The author states that most boys go through a period when they need help controlling the wild horses in their lives. Do you think that you will be able to listen to the men in your life when the wild horses inside of you begin to rear up? Yes__ No__

23. Have you memorized the TALKS Thesis Statement yet? Yes__ No__   If yes, recite it. If no, write it down, or copy it out of the book and begin to work on it.

24. As a result of this lesson, I want you to thank the men in your school for being in your face. Name the men that you need to thank._____

25. Write the last sentence of the chapter here:_____

Wisdom From The Elders

Read the quotes and explain them to the boys. Use the questions to begin the discussion. Be sure to work with the boys to compose your own quote that relates to this chapter.

A good example is the best sermon. THOMAS FULLER
1. Do you have a man in your face who sets a good example for you?
2. A sermon is a speech that is designed to change the way you think and act. Would you rather have someone preach to you about how to act or would you rather have someone demonstrate it?
3. It is unfortunate that many young men do not have a father at home to be a good example for them. In your opinion, what should a young man do if he is in this situation?

Don't ask for anyone's advice unless you are prepared to use it. SAMMY DAVIS
1. Wise men only give advice to young men who listen. Once the wise man realizes that the young man is not listening, he stops giving him advice. Have you ever had a wise man stop giving you advice because you were not listening?
2. Are you going to use the advice that you are getting from your mentor?

A person isn't educated unless he has learned how little he already knows.
THOMAS A. FLEMING
1. The author of this book has many friends who have Ph.D degrees. There was a time when he thought that a person who had a Ph.D degree knew everything. He has since learned that a Ph.D degree is a good place to start learning. It is not the end. Most people with Ph.D. degrees will tell you that they are just beginning to learn. Do you feel that you know everything?
2. Do you feel that you can learn a lot from a man in your face or do you feel that you already know what you need to know?
3. In your opinion, what is the danger in thinking that you know everything?
4. Tell the truth and not a lie: Have you ever felt that you knew everything?

Children could keep on the straight and narrow path if they could get information from someone who's been over the route. MARIAN WRIGHT EDLEMAN
1. The straight and narrow path has been used to describe a direction or road that leads to success. That route is easiest to follow when someone you know and love has gone down that path before you. Do you have a man in your family who is successful that you can model?
2. Are you going to use the information that you are getting from your mentor to help you stay on the straight and narrow?
3. Who is Marian Wright Edleman? (Look it up)

It embarrasses me to think of all those years I was buying silk suits and alligator shoes that were hurting my feet; cars that I just parked, and the dust would just build up on them.
GEORGE FOREMAN

1. George Foreman is a former heavy weight boxing champion. He earned a lot of money when he was very young and according to this quote he wasted a lot of it. What would you do if you had one million dollars right now?

2. Do you feel that George Foreman would have wasted his money like that if he had an older man challenging him to save it and spend it more wisely?

3. A fool and his money are soon parted. This wisdom has proven to be true again and again. Can you think of a famous person (athlete, rap artist) that has wasted a lot of money?

A person is never what he ought to be until he is doing what he ought to be doing.
BUSTER SOARIES

1. Often adults can look at young people and see qualities, strengths and talents in them that they cannot see. Adults are good at this because they have watched hundreds of people grow up and they have learned from experience how life works. Are you listening to the adults who are trying to help you do what you ought to be doing?

2. It is tragic when people grow to be old and never find their spot in life. This happens as a result of bad decisions. Are you currently making good decisions or bad decisions in your life?

3. Do you appreciate a man in your face trying to get you to do what you ought to do?

The wounds of a friend are better than the kisses of an enemy. PROVERBS 27:6

1. Some young men feel that everyone is picking on them. Their mind is programmed to respond to everyone that corrects them the same way. They say: "Why are you picking on me?" I call this a victim mind set. In their minds they are never wrong and always the victim when corrected. Do you know anyone like this?

2. Think about this. When a friend who really cares about you corrects you with hard words, he is trying to help you. Do you think this is true or false?

3. Wounds (pain) from friends are good because they are trying to help you. But when an enemy kisses you, you can be sure that he is trying to get close enough to stab you in the back. A kiss here represents many things like: giving you something, saying nice things about you, pretending to be your friend and things like that. Have you ever had someone slide up to you and try to be your friend just because they wanted something?

Compose a quote and write it here: _____

_____

_____

Teachers, who educate children, deserve more honor than parents, who merely gave them birth; for the latter provided mere life, while the former ensure a good life.

ARISTOTLE

Chapter 15

My Teacher, My Friend

Definition of a teacher and friend: a person who teaches you in the classroom each day who also has your best interests in mind.

Connecting With And Learning From Your Rich, Personal, Painful, Productive Past: When I think of the list of teachers that I have experienced, I must say that some of them were not my friends. As I look back, there were those who had my best interests at heart but because of my youth, I did not understand it at the time. Recall several teachers and share with the boys characteristics of those who were your friends and characteristics of those who were not your friends.

CAUTION: Because of our immaturity, it is easy to accuse a teacher of hating you when all he/she is trying to do is to get you to perform at your best level. Actually, teachers who make you stay in before school, during recess or after school to do your work do not hate you. They are actually trying to help you keep up with the class. The teacher that you need to beware of is the teacher who lets you get behind and flunks you or passes you to get rid of you. His/her actions are saying that he/she does not care enough to challenge you to do better.

CHARGE: Charge the boys to strive to be every teacher's friend. Challenge them to make the first step by being polite, kind and understanding. Everybody gets a bad teacher at some time during their educational career. This should never turn you against all teachers or make you think that all teachers don't like you. If any boy feels that the teacher does not like him, it is probably because he has become unlikable. Charge the boys to look at themselves if they think the teacher does not like them.

ACTIVITY: Help the boys make an assessment of their young educational career. Have them list or discuss the teachers, aids, principals, that they have had so far. Then have them note the ones that they liked and the ones they disliked. Try to determine what was the motivation for their feelings. If they feel that the teachers disliked them, help them realize that there is a reason. Help them search for that reason. Was it their attitude? Was the teacher mean to everyone or just you? Are you a rebellious child who needs an excuse?

Lesson 15

My Teacher, My Friend

My favorite teacher in middle school was Mrs. Thompson. I can remember her today just as if I was still in her 7th grade science class. I have often tried to figure out why I liked Mrs. Thompson so much. I believe that one reason I liked her was that I knew that she wanted what was best for me. I knew that when she fussed at me, it was because she wanted me to do my best.

To tell the truth, there were many days when I did not do my best, and she would fuss at me. I think it is important to know the difference between when a teacher gets on you because she wants you to do better and when she gets on you because she is having a bad day. Mrs. Thompson would get on me because she cared for me and she would not accept second best.

A good teacher is like a gold mine that you need to dig in to get all of the riches out of your relationship with her. Teachers have the ability to look at kids and see abilities and strengths that may one day make them great. When a teacher tells you that you can do better, she generally does it for two reasons:

1. She feels that you really can do better. When my teacher made me do a project over it was because she wanted me to do my best. When I was young I thought that she wanted me to do it over because she was mean. When teachers don't like you, they let you do badly and don't care about it. When teachers like you very much, they insist that you do your best and they may bug you until you do the work correctly.

2. She wants to encourage you to do better. Young people don't realize the benefits of doing your best. Many kids just want to do enough to get by. When you do this, you are cheating yourself. A good teacher will try to help you see that you can do better and encourage you to do better. If your teacher is that kind of teacher, then she is a good teacher.

One of the problems with being a kid is that you do not understand the future. Teachers understand the future because they are older than you are. When a teacher looks at you and says that you are not doing your best, she is usually thinking about your future. She knows that time is moving on and that if you don't do your best you will be behind and have a hard time catching up.

It really hurts elementary school teachers when they hear that students that they had are now in high school and are not doing well or dropping out. As a matter of fact, teachers often feel a sense of personal failure when their students don't do well. Teachers also know that no matter how hard they work, success in the classroom is ultimately up to the student. A teacher is not your mother or father but a person who comes along to help your parents give you an education.

Let me give you some suggestions on how to really benefit from the time you spend with your teacher:

1. Always cooperate fully with your teacher. It is a fact that you are the student and he/she is the teacher. There will be times when you do not understand what he/she is doing or why she is doing it. If you understood it all, you would be the teacher.

2. Be honest with your teacher and tell him/her when and where you are struggling with particular subjects. The worst thing that you can do is to pretend that everything is all right when it isn't. If you don't ask for help when you need it, you are not helping your teacher to help you. Learn to look your teacher in the eye and say: "I need some help with this subject." Not only will it help you in that particular subject, but it will also help you as you relate to adults.

3. Use the best manners that you know. Saying things like: "Yes, Miss Johnson, and No, Miss Johnson," will most definitely help your relationship. It is a funny thing, but adults will generally go out of their way to help a kid who has good manners.

4. Remember that your teacher is a person too. She may have kids and problems of her own. If she makes an occasional mistake, don't be surprised, but allow her to be human just like you are. There are days when teachers are low on energy and need to take it slow. Be helpful on days like this and don't make her day worse.

What can you do today to help your teacher have a better day? I want to challenge you to be the student in your class who keeps a good attitude toward your teacher. Regardless of what the other kids do, you should be the one who shows your teacher appreciation by keeping a good attitude.

Questions
(to discuss and think about or to serve as a written assignment)

1. Do you like your teacher? Yes__ No__

2. Do you feel that he/she is your friend and looks out for your best interests? Yes__ No__

3. Do you say nice things to her and treat her with kindness? Yes__ No__

4. What was the last nice deed that you did for her?_____

5. If you don't like your teacher, is it his/her fault or your fault?_____

6. The author says that he liked Mrs. Thompson. Why did he say he liked her?

7. What did Mrs. Thompson do to make the author know that she liked him?

8. Find and complete this sentence: "I think it is important to know the difference between__"

9. Can you tell the difference between when a teacher fusses at you because she cares about you or when she fusses at you because she is having a bad day? Yes__ No__

10. In your opinion, is it OK for teachers to occasionally have bad day? Yes__ No__

11. Do you ever have a bad day? Yes__ No__

12. Find and complete this sentence: "A good teacher is like a gold mine that you need to___"

13. Do you ask your teacher questions? Yes__ No__

14. Are you kind to your teacher? Yes__ No__ Have you ever given her a gift? Yes__ No__

15. Do you understand that teachers who care about you insist that you do your work and it is a bad sign when your teacher never gets on your case? Yes__ No__

16. Does your teacher get on your case when you do not do your best? Yes__ No__

17. Do you answer your teacher with: "yes ma'am, no ma'am" and "yes sir and no sir?" ____

18. Have you ever thanked your teacher for caring about you? Yes__ No__

19. What comes to your mind first when your teacher makes you do a project over?

20. Find and complete this sentence: "When teachers like you very much, they_____"

21. Tell the truth and not a lie: Do you do just enough to get by? Yes__ No__

22. According to the author, who are you cheating when you do just enough to get by?

23. Do you ever think about the fact that when you fail to do your best it may cause your teacher to feel like he/she is not doing their best? Yes__ No__

24. Do you always cooperate fully with your teacher? Yes__ No__

25. Are there days when you feel like you could do a better job than your teacher? Yes__ No__

26. Find and complete this sentence: "The worst thing you can do is_____"

27. Do you help your teacher help you? Yes__ No__

28. What did the author tell you to look the teacher in the eye and say?

29. Find and complete this sentence: "It is a funny thing, but adults_____"

30. Tell the truth and not a lie: Do you have good manners? Yes__ No__

31. I have actually heard of young men in school who use profanity in class with their teachers. You wouldn't do that, would you? Yes__ No__

32. The author makes the point that teachers are human. Have you ever thought about your teacher in that way or do you view him/her like a machine that does not have feelings and works all the time?

33. How do you act when your teacher makes a mistake? Do you laugh, get angry or be understanding?

34. Name three things that you can do today to help your teacher have a better day._____

33. Write the last two sentences of the chapter here: _____
_____

Wisdom From The Elders

Read the quotes and explain them to the boys. Use the questions to begin the discussion. Be sure to work with the boys to compose your own quote that relates to this chapter.

A teacher affects eternity; he/she can never tell where his influence stops. HENRY ADAMS
1. What is the best thing a teacher has ever done for you?
2. What is eternity?
3. In your opinion, how does a teacher affect eternity?
4. What is influence?
5. The author of this book has grown men approach him at the mall and other places and thank him for teaching them when they were young. Would you speak to your teacher if you saw him/her in public?

Each friend represents a world in us, a world possibly not born until they arrive, and it is only by this meeting that a new world is born. ANAIS NIN
1. Just imagine one of your friends walking in the door and sitting next to you. Their presence would make you think of all the things you have done together. If another friend walked in and sat down, there would be a new set of memories and experiences that would come to mind. What world of experiences come to mind when you see your teacher?
2. Do you have any fond memories of something that your teacher taught you this year?
3. What has your teacher taught you this year that you did not know before you met him/her?
4. Have you ever thought about how much there is to learn about the world that can be learned from teachers?

Teachers, who educate children, deserve more honor than parents, who merely gave them birth; for the latter provided mere life, while the former ensure a good life. ARISTOTLE
1. Do you agree with Aristotle when he says that teachers deserve more honor than parents?
2. In other countries, teachers are highly respected and paid very well. Who do you think should be paid the most, an NBA star or your teacher?
3. Teachers teach you what you need to know to go to college. What do you feel that your parent(s) teach you?
4. Who was Aristotle?

You shall judge a man by his foes as well as by his friends. JOSEPH CONRAD
1. If your teacher is your enemy, that is not a good sign. If your teacher is your friend, that is a good sign. Is your teacher your friend?
2. I understand that every teacher that you have had may not have been your best friend, but they can be highly respected and obeyed. Have you obeyed most of the teachers you have had so far in your educational career?

Chance makes our parents, but choice makes our friends. JACQUES DELILLE

1. Nobody can decide who their parents are but they can decide what their attitude is going to be about everything else. Have you decided to make your teacher your friend?
2. Have you decided to have a good attitude about the subjects your teacher teaches?
3. The decision to work hard in spite of your circumstance must come from you. Everybody can find something wrong in his life that he can complain about, but only the strong can determine to be positive and move on regardless of his circumstances. Are you a determined person or a defeated person?

A teacher is the child's third parent. HYMAN MAXWELL BERSTON

1. Teachers can become very close to us. Do you feel like your teacher is your third parent?
2. Do you ever talk to your parents about the things your teacher shares with you?

The friend is the man/woman who knows all about you, and still likes you. ELBERT HUBBARD

1. Your teacher knows a lot about you. He/she knows about your good days and your bad days. Do you feel that your teacher likes you?

Perhaps the most valuable result of all education is the ability to make yourself do the thing you have to do, when it ought to be done, whether you like it or not. WALTER BAGEHOT

1. Is your teacher helping you get your life organized and disciplined?
2. Do you have the ability to do the thing you have to do, when it ought to be done, whether you like it or not?
3. Education opens your mind up to all the possibilities in the world. When I was a kid, we would read the National Geographic Magazine and see all of the new worlds that were out there. The new vision of the worlds would motivate us to work hard to accomplish our goals. Has what you learned in school given you a vision of a world full of potential? Yes__ No__
4. Does this vision of a new and expanded world motivate you to work harder? Yes__ No__

A hand up is better than a hand out. SYBIL MOBLEY

1. Do you feel that your teacher should give you grades or do you feel that she should help you earn them?
2. Do you ever ask other kids to do your work for you or help you with your work?
3. Are you prepared to work hard to reach your goals or are you expecting handouts along the way?

Compose a quote and write it here:_____

_____

_____

Chapter 16

TV And Reality

Definition of television and reality: a medium of entertainment that frequently uses fantasy to the extreme. Reality is that world in which we live where fantasy is rarely productive and can be detrimental to mental, social, and physical development.

Connecting With And Learning From Your Rich, Personal, Painful, Productive Past.
As a child, I struggled with daydreaming. I can remember when the Apollo astronauts were going into space I would physically sit in school, but would be mentally in space. Children today have so many forms of entertainment to focus on that they must learn to distinguish between fantasy and reality. Connect with your past and recall your hero that kept your mind occupied and off of things like homework, chores, and other productive things.

CAUTION: We are not trying to paint imagination as a bad thing but we are trying to keep it in proper context. The comforts of life that we enjoy today were once thoughts in someone's mind that they worked to bring to reality. So, we do not want boys to stop dreaming, but we want them to dream creatively and not in an attempt to escape reality.

CHARGE: Charge the boys to use their dreams for the benefit of society. Challenge them to test the value of their dreams by the criteria of how useful they will be to society. Dreams that only make you feel good and cannot be realized for the benefit of society eventually end up wasting your time. Learn to get some benefit from your dreams.

ACTIVITY: Discuss with the boys reality versus their favorite TV shows. Pick a popular movie that you have all seen and discuss what was real in the movie and what had to be fantasy. Most TV shows require that you leave your brains in the bathroom while you watch the show. List the shows that are not realistic.

Lesson 16

TV And Reality

I am so old that I can remember when television was still new. At that time, only a few people in the neighborhood had televisions. I remember when the day came when we finally got one at our house. Back then, everything on television was good and there was no need for ratings or for your parents to tell you not to watch certain programs. Today, young people need to be careful what they watch because there are some programs that are only for adults and are about things that may be too stressful for young people. Things like violence, sex, and other shows that teach young people things that they should not learn until they are 17 years old or older.

There are some young people who have a problem telling the difference between fantasy and reality. For example, one of my favorite shows when I was a kid was The Three Stooges. They would do all sorts of things like falling down stairs, hitting each other on the head with hammers and stuff like that. The interesting thing is that they never got hurt. Well, my friend Dugan tried to do one of the tricks that we watched the Three Stooges do, and he ended up in the hospital with three stitches in his forehead. His mom was mad! She said that we could not watch television for a whole month.

Television is not all bad, but you must learn to watch it with your brain really alert to tell the difference between what is real and what is not real. I love to watch TV and see if I can see what is real and what is not real. I can remember watching one episode of *Gun Smoke* when Matt Dillon, who was the Sheriff in Dodge City, got into a fight with a bad guy. They rolled around in the dirt, punching, kicking and choking each other for about two minutes. The amazing thing was that when Matt Dillon got up, his shirt was clean. So, I realized that Matt Dillon was not rolling around in the dirt but that it was a stunt man. I still enjoy watching movies today to find mistakes like this.

Today, I believe that we need to look for flawed messages when we watch TV and movies. There are many messages given through TV shows that you really need to think about. For example, I watched a show about a man who was running from the law. This man very successfully escaped from the law several times. Each time he escaped, he made the police look very foolish. Now, this is fantasy because I know some policemen who are ten times smarter than the policemen in the TV show and they would have caught him the first time they tried.

We must be careful to look at things realistically rather than believing everything that we see on TV. Today we have a lot of copycats who imitate anything that they see on TV. Guns on TV don't

143

hurt anybody because they use blanks. In real life, guns kill you dead and should be avoided at all costs. On TV they punch you in the stomach five times, kick you in the head eight times, and stomp on you four times, and you still get up and fight some more. In real life, one kick to the head can kill you.

One of the joys of being young is that you are impressionable. In other words, you believe much of what you hear and see. The problem with being young and impressionable is that you don't have the discernment to know what is real and what is fantasy. Discernment is the ability to tell something real from something not real. The older you get, the more discernment that you have. This is why it is so important to ask an adult about the TV shows that you watch. Adults know that you don't have as much discernment as you will have in a few years. This why they don't want you to watch certain shows.

When I was a kid, I was afraid of the monster shows. And yet, I would stay up late Saturday night and watch *The Monster Who Ate Up New York*. The problem was that after watching the show, I could not go to sleep. I did not have the ability to discern between TV and reality. I felt that the monster that ate up New York would soon eat up my house, so I stayed up all night.

It is important that we guard our minds and protect them from things that would affect us in a bad way. Violence, sexual activity, profanity, and other bad things should not be seen by young people because the images will stick in your mind and affect you negatively. Television is a wonderful invention that can be used for good or for bad. If you choose to watch all shows with discernment, turning off the bad shows, you will use television for good. When you do this, you will control the television and it will not control you.

Questions
(to discuss and think about or to serve as a written assignment)

1. Can you imagine not having a television set? Yes__ No__

2. What is your favorite TV show?_____

3. Why is it your favorite TV show?_____

4. Is it fantasy or is it reality?_____

5. Do you imitate some of the actors on your favorite shows? Yes__ No__

6. Do you guard your mind from bad TV shows? Yes__ No__

7. In your opinion, is there too much violence on TV?

8. Find and complete this sentence. "Today, young people need to be careful_____"

9. Do you get mad when adults tell you not to watch certain shows? Yes__ No__

10. Find and complete this sentence: "There are some young people who have a problem telling the_____"

11. Why is it that actors never get hurt doing dangerous things on television?

12. Would you like to be a stunt man? Yes__ No__

13. What was the mistake that Dugan made?_____

14. The author stated that he watched Matt Dillon when he was young. Who is your favorite televison personality?

15. The author states that he still enjoys watching movies. Why does he say he likes watching them?

16. When you watch TV, do you watch it in a mindless manner accepting everything that you see, or do you watch to look for the flawed messages in it?

17. In your opinion, does TV reflect reality? Yes__ No__

18. The author talks about how stupid police look on TV. Who else do some TV shows make look stupid?

19. Tell the truth and not a lie: How much of what you see on TV do you believe? All__ Most__ None__

20. Find and complete this sentence. Today we have a lot of copycats_____
_____

21. Have you ever tried something you saw done on TV? Yes__ No__

22. Do you copy the vocabulary that is used on TV? Yes__ No__

23. What did the author say about the effects of being kicked in the head?

24. Many TV shows have to do with getting even with someone. In your opinion, what does that teach the young people who watch it?

25. The author states that when you are young you do not have the discernment to tell what is real from what is fantasy. What does the word discernment mean?

26. Do you get angry when you are told by adults that you cannot watch certain TV programs?

27. Find and complete this sentence: The problem with being young and impressionable is that you_____

28. Are you very impressionable? Yes__ No__

29. The author says that he was frightened by a show where the monster ate up New York. What show has frightened you?_____

30. When a show frightens you the first time you watch it, do you go back and watch it again?

31. Write the last two sentences in the chapter here: _____
_____
_____

Wisdom From The Elders

Read the quotes and explain them to the boys. Use the questions to begin the discussion. Be sure to work with the boys to compose your own quote that relates to this chapter.

Human kind cannot bear very much reality. T.S. ELIOT

1. Which do you enjoy most, fantasy or reality?
2. In your opinion, why do amusement parks, video arcades and other amusement businesses do so well?
3. Would you rather play video games or deal with the problems that you need to solve in your life?

All television is educational television. The question is: what is it teaching? NICHOLAS JOHNSON

1. Do you understand the role that commercials play in television?
2. Have you ever noticed that often times the commercials are better than the TV show. Why do you think this is the case?
3. Do you turn the channel when something comes on that is for adults only?
4. Have you learned any bad words from television?

Everything is a dangerous drug except reality, which is unendurable. CYRIL CONNOLLY

1. Do you feel that reality is too hard to bear?
2. Reality is school work, chores at home and getting up early in the morning. Fantasy is playing video games, taking imaginary trips by watching a movie where everybody is beautiful, happy and wise. If you could choose, which life would you rather live?
3. Many people in our society become addicted to fantasy. They feel that they must be entertained at all times. When there is a dull moment with no media, TV, DVD's, CD's or Radio, they become very disturbed and rush to turn something on. Have you ever met anyone like this?

Facts are facts and will not disappear on account of your likes. JAWAHARLAL NHRU

1. The realities of life, like school, work, eating and sleeping will not go away just because you don't want to do them. What do you feel happens to kids who ignore the facts of life?
2. For centuries men have tried to discover a way to avoid reality. This is why drugs are so appealing because for a few minutes (the high) you forget about your problems. But when you come down you are often depressed because you are forced to face reality. Do you know any people who try to escape reality through drugs?

Living in Hollywood can give you a false sense of reality. I try to stay in touch with my inner feelings—that's what's really going on. WILL SMITH

1. Hollywood is designed to make you forget about reality. When you watch TV, do you lose touch with reality?
2. How do you think living in Hollywood can give you a false sense of reality?
3. How do you think the people that we call "stars" are any different than we are?

4. Have you ever met a Hollywood star? Yes__ No__
5. Do the Hollywood stars have problems with their kids, marriages, health and other things just like the rest of us? Yes__ No__
6. Who is will Smith?

Thoughts have power; thoughts are energy. And you can make your world or break it by your own thinking. SUSAN TAYLOR
1. Do you watch TV that promotes strong, healthy, productive thoughts, or do you watch TV that dulls your brain?
2. TV is not bad as long as you use it and do not allow it to use you. In your opinion, how can you use the TV and not let it use you?

No life will ever be great until it is dedicated and disciplined. PETER C. B. BYNOE
1. Do you feel you can reach your goals and be disciplined by watching 4 hours of TV each day?
2. In what way can watching TV hurt your attempts at being disciplined?
3. Have you ever thought about how much TV great people watched when they were young?
4. Have you dedicated your life to anything yet? Yes__ No__

Television is an invention that permits you to be entertained in your living room by people you wouldn't have in your home. DAVID FROST
1. Would your parents let you invite the people you watch on TV into your home?
2. Name a TV personality that you would like to invite into your home?
3. Which shows would you NOT watch if the people on TV could step out of the TV into your house?

Of all the dramatic media, radio is the most visual. JOHN REEVES
1. Which takes more imagination to enjoy, radio or television?
2. Which do you enjoy most, what you see in your mind when you use your imagination or what you see on TV?
3. Many years ago before the TV was invented, whole families would sit around the television and listen to radio drama. There would be voices, sounds and music to make the story real. Is your imagination powerful enough to listen to radio drama and enjoy it? Yes__ No__
4. Each person in the family saw something different because each person had his own imagination. Do you think TV helps people use their imagination or does it hurt them?

Compose a quote and write it here:_____

_____

Family life is too intimate to be preserved by the spirit of justice. It can be sustained by a spirit of love which goes beyond justice.

NEINHOLD NIEBUHR

Chapter 17

Family Equals Joy And Pain

Definition of family: Brothers, sisters and parents constitute your family.

Definition of Joy and pain: Emotions found on both extremes of the emotional scale. Joy can be described as great happiness; pleasure. Pain can be described as an uncomfortable feeling deep in your stomach.

Connecting With And Learning From Your Rich, Personal, Painful, Productive Past. Making it through childhood with a younger or older sibling is a task that impacts us at our very foundations. There are wonderful memories and there are painful memories associated with each sibling that we have. As you spend this time with the boys, go to the archives in your memory and call forth good and bad memories from your childhood to share with your boys. Remember that transparency is one of your most effective tools in reaching the young men.

If you are an only child then it will be necessary for you to use a near relative or close friend for your examples. You can also talk about your relationship with your parents.

CAUTION: Be sensitive to those kids who are victims of broken homes. We are focusing on the fact that problems and differences that we have as children can be understood and healed as we get older. Our goal is to put in place early in their lives the attitude of eventual victory in their relationships with their siblings. Be sure to draw from your own experience examples where you have overcome in this area and share with the boys.

CHARGE: Charge the boys never to accept problems between siblings as permanent. Tell them that time helps change attitudes and that there will always be an opportunity to mend broken relationships. Charge them to be the imitators in the process, be the ones who make the first phone calls, and have patience with their siblings.

ACTIVITY: Ask: are there any relationships that need to be healed in your family? Encourage the boys to develop a friendly attitude toward their siblings. Tell the boys that they are strong enough to initiate the healing process. It takes a real man to go to someone and say: "We need to talk." Remind them that they are future men and future leaders, and that the ability to reconcile is crucial to their success. It is best to start with those who are closest to you.

Lesson 17

Family Equals Joy And Pain

I am the son of a man who had ten children. These people are called my family. There are days when I am very glad that I have them as my family, and there are other days when I wish that they were not born. Take my younger brother David (names have been changed to protect the guilty) for example. He is a great guy. If you met him, you would want him to be your friend. The only problem is that he has a drug problem that he can't control. So, on one hand, I love to be around him and I love him, but on the other hand, he hurts my heart because of what he does. Family equals joy and pain.

I know many young people who have family members whom they love very much. Unfortunately, some of their bad habits or actions also cause pain. When you are young you often feel helpless to change some of the pain that you are feeling about your family. What I find interesting is that even when you grow up, there will still be pain and disappointment that you will have to learn to live with. It takes years to learn how to live with a family that brings joy one day and pain the next day. I have learned some things about families that I want to share with you.

1. We love family members even if we don't love what they do. A human being is the most valuable thing on this planet. It is very important that we learn at an early age to love people even if we hate what they do. I love my brother David but I hate what he does. What he does brings me pain, but he brings me joy. Remember that family members deserve and need your love even when they do not behave as they should.

2. You can't change the way anybody acts. No human being can change the behavior of another human being. Children often plead, pray, and beg for their parents and other loved ones to behave a certain way. Many times young people will feel very guilty about the behavior of other family members. Some kids even feel that it is their fault when their parents divorce. This is not true! No human being is responsible for the behavior of another, and you can not change the way another person acts.

3. Learn to separate yourself from their bad behavior. I can remember that one day I gave David a ride in my car. What I did not know was that David had a rock of cocaine in his pocket. We were not stopped by the police or anything, but if we had been stopped, I would have gone to jail because of my brother. What I learned to do was to be careful how and when I would hang out with David. People who have unacceptable behaviors can get you in trouble if you are

151

not careful. It is possible to start doing what they do if you don't pay attention. Bad company corrupts good habits. Don't be afraid to tell them "I am not going to do that with you or hang with you while you do that."

4. Always leave the door of hope open because they might change. I have a friend who was an alcoholic for many years. One day he decided that he was not going to take another drink. Believe it or not, it has been nine years and he has not had another drink. Friends and family members must always believe that change is possible. You may even want to encourage them by telling them that you believe that they can change and maybe one day it will happen.

Because families are central to our lives, we need to learn how to deal with the ups and downs they bring to our lives. Every family has its ups and downs, and when you get married and have children there will be ups and downs, good days and bad days. The only thing that we can do is to continue to love our families. We must remember that we cannot make them act a certain way. We also must determine that we will not copy their negative behavior.

Questions
(to discuss and think about or to serve as a written assignment)

1. The greatest organization in the world is the family. Unfortunately, when people live together there will be problems. There will be misunderstandings and mistakes that cause some family members pain. Have any of your family members ever hurt you? Yes___ No___

2. In every family there are those members who help bring the peace, those who break the peace, and those who are encouragers. Do you try to encourage family members who have problems? Yes___ No___

3. What do you plan to do in your life to keep from making the same mistakes that some of your family members have made? _____

4. The author mentions a younger brother who was on drugs. Drugs are a major source of pain for many families. Are you committed to being drug free and sparing your family the pain that would be associated with you developing a drug habit? Yes___ No___

5. If there is pain in your family, do you feel helpless to change it? Yes___ No___

6. In your opinion, will there ever be a family that is perfect and never causes anyone any pain? Yes___ No___

7. Find and complete the following sentence: "It takes years to learn how to live with a_____"

8. What does the author say about what his brother David does and what he is?

9. Are you mature enough to love a person and hate what he does? Yes___ No___

10. Find and complete this sentence: No human being can_____

11. Do you ever feel guilty about the behavior of other family members? Yes___ No___

12. What did the author say about trying to change the behavior of other family members?

13. Find and complete this sentence: "No human being is responsible for the_____"

14. What do you do to separate yourself from the negative behavior of family members?___

15. Do you know of anyone who went to jail because they were with someone who did something wrong?

16. Do you believe that you will start acting like the people that you hang out with? Yes__ No__

17. Find and complete this sentence: Don't be afraid to tell them, "I am _____"

18. Do you believe that people can change their bad habits? Yes__ No__

19. What do you think your attitude should be when people refuse to change their bad habits?

20. Are you wise enough to love a family member but not hang around them when they have habits that will get you into trouble?

21. The only person that cannot change is a dead person. As long as people are living there is a chance that they will get their lives together. Is there anyone in your family that you are hoping will change? Yes__ No__

22. What do you think you could do to encourage someone to change?

23. Do you feel that people are encouraged to change when you join them and do what they do?

24. What happens to your credibility (ability to be trusted) when you join people who are doing undesirable things?

25. There has been a lot of talk about dysfunctional families in the last few years. Dysfunctional means that something is not working the way it should. Actually, all families are dysfunctional because no family is perfect in every way. Because of this fact, you should be encouraged regarding your family. If your family is dysfunctional in one way, celebrate the ways that your family is not dysfunctional. For example, if your dad is not there, celebrate the fact that your mom is there and loves you. . . Do you celebrate the good things about your family?

26. Have you decided that you will be the family member who brings joy to your family whenever you can?

27. Read the last three sentences of the chapter out loud.

Wisdom From The Elders

Read the quotes and explain them to the boys. Use the questions to begin the discussion. Be sure to work with the boys to compose your own quote that relates to this chapter.

I don't know who my grandfather was; I am much more concerned to know what his grandson will be. ABRAHAM LINCOLN

1. Do you plan to be a stronger, smarter, greater man than your father was?
2. Who is the best role model for you, your father or your grandfather?
3. How many generations back can you go when you consider your fathers? Father__ Grandfather__ Great grandfather__ Great great grandfather__
4. Have you ever thought about what type of man your son will turn out to be?
5. Have you ever thought about what your father will say when you tell him that he is going to be a grandfather?
6. Who was Abraham Lincoln?

To the family—that dear octopus from whose tentacles we never quite escape, nor in our inmost hearts, ever quite wish to. DODIE SMITH

1. We are all molded in the image of our families. What things would you like to do differently when you have a family?
2. In this wisdom the family is referred to as an octopus with tentacles that we never quite escape. What do you think is meant by that statement?
3. It is normal when you are a child to want to run away from home. When I was young I told my Father that I was going to run away from home. He told me that I did not have to run but that I could walk and take my time. His response took the fun out of the idea and I did not run away from home. As you mature, you do not want to run away from home but run to home. Which do you want to do right now, run to or away from home?

The proper time to influence the character of a child is about 100 years before he is born. DEAN WILLIAM R. INGE

1. In your opinion, how can you influence a child 100 years before he is born?
2. How have your grandparents influenced you?
3. What kind of reputation does your family have?
4. At the top of the page we read a quote by Abraham Lincoln. Abraham Lincoln's descendants are still around. How do you think they are impacted by the fact that their Great, Great Grandfather was Abraham Lincoln?
5. What are you doing now to influence your child or children who have not been born yet?

Find the good and praise it. ALEX HALEY

1. Every family has good in it and every family has bad in it. What is the best thing you can say about your family?
2. Do you praise other family members in front of them so they can hear it?

From the day you're born until the day you ride in a hearse, there's nothing so bad that it couldn't be worse. SMOKEY ROBINSON

1. Whatever your worst disappointment is with your family, do you feel that it will get better some day?

2. If you are having family problems today and they are making you sad, focus on the fact that it could be worse. Is that easy or difficult for you to do?

My mother told me I was capable of doing anything. "Be ambitious," she said. "Jump at de sun." ZORA NEALE HURSTON

1. Does your mom or dad tell you that you can accomplish anything?

2. How much of what your mother tells you do you believe?

3. When people encourage you does that give you the power to try more challenging things?

4. What was Zora Neale Hurston's mom trying to tell her when she told her to "Jump at de sun?"

I'm not a self-made man. I cannot forget those who have sacrificed for me to get where I am today. JESSIE HILL

1. Do you thank your parent(s) for how they sacrifice for you?

2. Are you a grateful, thankful person or do you expect people to help you?

3. Do you feel that you are bad all by yourself or do you realize that somebody changed your diaper, fed you, took you to the doctor and kept you from falling down the steps?

4. How many people can you name who sacrificed for you?

5. You may name immediate family who sacrificed for you but what other individuals, often complete strangers can you name who sacrificed for you?

The most lonely place in the world is the human heart when love is absent. SADIE ALEXANDER

1. Have you ever felt all alone?

2. How many people in your family really love you?   (If you do not get enough love from your family, where do you get it from?)

Everything in the household runs smoothly when love oils the machinery. WILLIAM H. GRIER

1. Love is the most powerful force in the world. Do you help make your home a loving place?

2. Everybody loves the holidays because love is in the air. In your opinion what can you do to keep love in the air all year long?

Compose a quote and write it here:_____

_____

_____

Chapter 18

Girls (Sugar, Spice And Everything Nice)

Definition of a girl: a female child

Connecting With And Learning From Your Rich, Personal, Painful, Productive Past. The purpose of this chapter is to help boys understand and capitalize on the differences between boys and girls. Personally, girls have been a mystery to me from the beginning. Sigmund Freud said: "The great question which I have not been able to answer, despite my 30 years of research into the feminine soul, is: what does a woman want?" Many husbands have often quoted these words: "Women, you can't live with them and you can't live without them."

As you read this chapter with the boys, reflect back on the mystery of your mother, sister, first girlfriend and current relationship. Share from your rich reservoir of experience with women who are friends, family, colleagues in the work force or strangers. Share with the boys the richness that can be gained from interacting wisely with the females that they encounter.

CAUTION: Because girls are different than boys are does not mean that they are inferior in any way. Because males may be able to run faster, jump higher and lift more weights than females, this does not make men better than women.

CHARGE: Charge the boys to accept the fact that they will be learning about women for the rest of their lives. Charge the boys to always treat girls like they would want other boys to treat their sisters. Charge the boys to remember that when they grow up they may have daughters of their own.

ACTIVITY: Have the boys list the important females in their lives: mother, sisters, friends and even someone they may like. Discuss with them how they treat them. Do they treat them with kindness? Do they try to understand their differences? Ask the boys how patient they are with the girls when they play sports.

Lesson 18

Girls (Sugar, Spice And Everything Nice)

Girls are special. Wait a minute, wait a minute! Let me explain what I mean. If you were to talk to a grown man, most of them would tell you that some of the most exciting times that they have had in life is the time they have spent with girls. Now, when you are in the fourth grade, you don't know very much about girls and you are not supposed to. As boys get older, they begin to take an interest in girls and really start studying them.

It takes most boys a long time to understand girls. Most husbands work hard to understand why their wives do what they do. I really think this is great because it keeps us interested in them. Girls would be boring if we completely understood them all the time.

One of these days you will be interested in girls and when you grow up you may get married and live with a woman every day. There are some important facts that every boy should know about girls. These facts will help him as he relates to all females, including his mother, teacher, and future girlfriend.

1. Treat them with kindness and respect. Girls love to be treated kindly. As a matter of fact, most human beings like to be treated that way, but I think that girls really appreciate being treated that way.

2. Give them sincere compliments. We all like to be complimented. Be sure to always compliment girls on who they are and not only on how they look. Please notice that I said: "sincere compliments." Don't overdo it.

3. Treat them like you would want a man to treat your mother. There is a principle that you cannot escape which says whatever you dish out to others will eventually come back to you. If you have seen women being abused in any way, you must determine that you will not do that. You have the privilege of starting a new way of doing things when you get a girlfriend. Always think about your mother when you deal with girls.

4. Never, as long as your heart is beating, hit a woman! Any man who would hit a woman is a low-down dirty dog. I can hear someone asking the question: "What if she hits me first?" Well, if she hits you first you have several options: 1. Walk away. 2. Tell an adult. 3. If possible, reason with her and tell her that you do not like to be hit upon.

159

In most cases you can avoid hitting her back if you use your head.

5. Learn to become a servant to women and you will find that all of your needs will be met.
When you get older and enter into a relationship, what you are actually agreeing to do is to serve the other person. Marriage is a commitment to serve the person that you are married to. All relationships with women prior to marriage are warm-ups for the real thing. So, in other words, if you want a good relationship, you must learn to develop the mindset of a servant.

Now, let me hurry up and say that this applies to the woman too. In a relationship she will be your servant also. So each person is serving the other person's needs.

Questions
(to discuss and think about or to serve as a written assignment)

1. Do you have any sisters? Yes__ No__

2. Do you feel that girls are special? Yes__ No__

3. Do you feel that you understand girls? Yes__ No__

4. What did the author say that a grown man would tell you about girls? (First paragraph)

5. Find and complete this sentence: As boys get older, they begin_____

6. Do you study girls? Yes__ No__ Sometimes__

7. Actually, once you become a man, girls will be the main object that you will study for the rest of your life. Does this make any sense to you now? Yes__ No__

8. A man is surrounded by females most of his life. He starts off with a mother whom he loves very much. Often he will have sisters who teach him what girls are like. Then as he matures he has girlfriends and eventually a wife. The greatest joy a man can have is to marry a beautiful young woman, love her and raise a family. The key in all of this is to avoid the mistakes that so many men make with women. As you get older, what do you plan to do to avoid making the same mistakes many men make with women?

9. Do you believe that you will get married one day? Yes__ No__ If yes, what type of wedding would you like? If no, what do you plan to do for the rest of your life?

10. Have you been taught at home to be nice to girls? Yes__ No__ If the answer is no, where did you learn how to be nice to girls?

11. Everybody likes to be spoken to nicely. What was the last nice thing that you said to a girl?

12. Give three nice things you could say to a girl:_____
(Your hair looks nice, you did well on that assignment, I think you are smart)

13. What is fact number three?_____

14. Find and complete this sentence: "There is a principle that you cannot escape which says_____"

15. A very safe way to deal with girls is to treat them like they are your sisters. Older women you should treat like they are your mother. This will keep you out of trouble. Does this sound reasonable to you?

16. It is very unfortunate that many men are violent with the women in their lives. Do you think you would ever hit a woman? Yes__ No__

17. Girls have bodies that are softer than guys. Even when they make you mad you cannot hit them. Have you ever wanted to hit a girl? Yes__ No__ Did you hit her? Yes__ No__ If you did not hit her, what did you do?

18. The author remembers on one occasion when he and his sister got into an argument in their kitchen. He tried to grab her on the shoulders and shake her but instead of reaching her shoulders he accidently hit her nose. Her nose began to bleed and she ran off crying. Although it was an accident, he really felt bad about it for a long time. You must be careful when you get angry around girls. Tell yourself now while you are young that you will never even consider hitting a girl. Say this three times: "I will never consider hitting a girl."

19. Television often makes girls seem as strong as men are. You may see a woman on TV fighting a man and overpowering him. In real life that rarely happens. Make sure that you get your information about girls from real life and not the fantasy world of television. Where do you think you get your information about girls from?

20. There are some girls that will hit boys and hit them hard. The author gives you three options to choose from. Read them again.

21. Under point number 5, the author states that if you learn to serve women you will find that all of your needs will be met. Marriage is nothing more than serving the person that you are married to. When two people in a marriage serve each other they will usually have a great marriage. Make yourself the promise that you will not get married until you are ready to serve.

Wisdom From The Elders

Read the quotes and explain them to the boys. Use the questions to begin the discussion.
Be sure to work with the boys to compose your own quote that relates to this chapter.

A woman is the only thing I am afraid of that I know will not hurt me. ABRAHAM LINCOLN
1. Are you afraid of girls? Yes__ No__
2. Do you think Abraham Lincoln was joking when he said this?
3. Females are mysterious to most guys. Do you see girls as mysterious?

Treat the older women as mothers, and the girls as your sisters, thinking only pure thoughts about them. TIMOTHY
1. In your opinion, what would be the result of treating females as Timothy suggested?
2. Do you treat the girls in your class like you would want other boys to treat your sister if you have one?
3. Do you treat the older women (teachers) in your school like you treat your mother?
4. What types of thoughts do you think about the girls in your class?

A woman is like a tea bag—only in hot water do you realize how strong she is.
    NANCY REAGAN
1. Who is the strongest woman you know?
2. What makes her strong?
3. You really don't know much about how strong women are until you marry one, live with her and watch her have a baby. Women have strengths that will fascinate you for the rest of your life. Are you looking forward to become a man and experience the joys of marriage and fatherhood?
4. Although women are strong, do you think that they should raise babies by themselves?

A woman's strength is the irresistible might of weakness. RALPH WALDO EMERSON
1. This wisdom is making the point that men love a damsel in distress. Men enjoy helping women and girls when they need help. What was the last kind thing that you did for a girl?
2. In your opinion, in what ways are women weak?
3. Have you ever seen a girl acting weak when she wasn't really weak?
4. Who was Ralph Waldo Emerson? (Look it up)

Women who set a low value on themselves make life hard for all women. NELLIE McCLUNG
1. If you find one girl who acts silly and is hard to get along with, will you believe that all girls are silly and hard to get along with?
2. Every girl that you interact with helps you understand more about girls. Why do you think it would be wise to avoid a girl once you discover that she is not very wise?
3. Why do you think some girls or women set a low value on themselves?

A homely girl hates mirrors. PROVERB

1. What does "homely" mean?

2. Some girls feel that they are not pretty. Have you ever told a girl that she was ugly? If you did, how do you think this made her feel?

3. Some girls as well as boys do not like the way they look. Our society puts pressure on young people to look like the stars from Hollywood. Do you think this is a good thing or bad thing?

4. You should NEVER call a girl fat! Many teenage girls see themselves as fat no matter how skinny they get. They develop a condition called anorexia nervosa where they develop an aversion to food and become obsessed with weight loss. You could actually help a young girl develop this condition if you tease her about being fat. Have you ever called a girl fat?

5. Homely girls (unattractive girls) need encouragement and acceptance from the group. Are you willing to be a person who reaches out to girls and guys who may not be attractive and need friends?

A girl is Innocence playing in the mud, Beauty standing on its head, and Motherhood dragging a doll by the foot. ALLAN BECK

1. Do you ever stop to think that the girls in your class will be very beautiful young women in just a few years?

2. Have you ever considered the fact that just a few years ago, your mother was a little girl?

Don't be upset if your dreams don't come true. It could be the best thing that ever happened to you. SHARI BELAFONTE

1. Do you have any dreams that have not come true? Yes__ No__

2. Have any of you had a crush on a girl yet? Yes__ No__

3. If you have and she didn't like you, do you feel it was good or bad?

4. This wisdom is saying that everyone has some dreams that are not good for them. The best thing that can happen is for them not to come true. You may one day dream of being with some girl that you like and that dream may shattered by disappointment. If this happens, don't be sad, but realize that it was probably the best thing in the long run.

Compose a quote and write it here:_____

_____

_____

Note to the mentor/teacher: As a result of this lesson, are there any needs that these young men have that can be met by networking with parents, other teachers, social agencies or religious institutions?

Chapter 19

I Got Busted, And I Didn't Do It!

Definition of getting busted: Caught in the act of doing something wrong.

Connecting With And Learning From Your Rich, Personal, Painful, Productive Past. Unfortunately, we have all been accused of doing something that we did not do. Being falsely accused is a very painful experience. As a child, I suffered at the hands of teachers whom I felt were blind because they misconstrued what happened. As an educator, I now know of situations where I have inaccurately diagnosed a situation and punished the wrong child. It is unfortunate but these things do happen.

Call from your memory a situation where you were falsely accused. Share your response with the boys and the outcome. Use a situation where you kept your mouth shut and were validated in the end. Use another situation where you never got the justice you deserved.

CAUTION: Don't allow this lesson to degenerate into a pity party for the falsely accused of our nation. Keep the lesson focused on the fact that our justice system is run by human beings who often make mistakes. Make the point that teachers cannot see everything and will occasionally make mistakes. Everybody is falsely accused from time to time and what is important is your response to it.

CHARGE: Charge the boys to keep in mind that the people who bust you are human and will make mistakes. The only recourse for a young man is to keep his nose so clean that he would be the last one to be accused. Charge the boys to be on the positive side of every situation and not the negative. This includes screening the people that you hang with and those whom you allow to influence you.

ACTIVITY: Show the boys how difficult it can be to discern who did it by playing this game. Have one boy turn and face the wall while an item that belongs to him or one designated to be used is held by one of the three remaining persons. The boy is allowed to ask each person one question to determine who has the missing item. This little demonstration will show the difficulty teachers have in determining who is guilty and who is innocent.

Lesson 19

I Got Busted, And I Didn't Do It!

I will never forget that Tuesday morning after recess when all the boys were allowed to go to the bathroom. We had been outside playing, and the teacher told us to come in. We were told to go to the bathroom before we went back to our classroom. While in the bathroom, a very interesting thing happened. My friend Richard and a few other guys started making a lot of noise, screaming, banging on the paper towel dispenser and other things. Now, everybody was making some noise. but only a few guys were making most of the noise.

When we came out of the bathroom, Miss McFever was very angry. She started fussing at everybody when Richard, my supposed friend, turned around, looked at me and said: "He was banging on the paper towel dispenser." Now, I was in shock because that was a "bold face *lie*!" I didn't think that the teacher would believe him, but she did. Now, you won't believe what happened next. The teacher took me, only me, to the side and sent the rest of the class to the room. She then took one of those little paddles you bounce the ball on and gave me five swats on my butt. That hurt really bad. Now, I want to tell you the truth. I wanted to KILL Richard! I wanted to KILL Richard! I wanted to rip his brains out with my bare hands!

We all know that it is illegal to kill people even though they are the cause of you getting a paddling. Now, I want you to put yourself in my shoes:
1. Your butt is throbbing!
2. You hate Richard and want to kill him!
3. You are not guilty but nobody believes you!

These are days when you wish you had stayed in bed. These are days when you really need to think as you try to figure out what to do. It is very hard to think when you have been lied about and you are forced to suffer unjustly, but if you want to succeed in life, you need to learn how to do it.

It takes great wisdom to keep your mouth shut when you are busted for no reason. Sometimes it is better to let things cool down and then go to the teacher and ask her if you could speak to her for a minute. If you give situations time they will often work themselves out. I know of a situation where a girl lied, lied, lied all of the time and got people in trouble. The only problem was she looked like a little angel and the teacher always believed her. One day when she wasn't paying attention, the teacher was standing behind her and the teacher heard her using profanity and lying. From that day on, whenever she told the teacher something, the teacher would really check out what she was saying.

Whenever you get caught up in a negative situation where there is a lot of confusion, cool out. Let the dust settle and then try to talk it out. If it happens that you are busted and you didn't do it, no big deal. The person who got you in trouble will have their turn. What goes around, comes around.

I often thought about getting even with stupid Richard. What if I had thrown my history book at him while sitting behind him in class, or, sliced the tires on his bicycle, or got even in some very creative way? In reality, the guy who hits back always gets caught. In basketball, the referee will often miss a foul, but he always sees it when the guy hits back.

Wise men learn how to overlook minor offenses. In other words, wise men don't seek to get even for every little wrong that they suffer because if you do, it will only get you into further trouble. What about you? If you were me and Richard got you busted, what would you do?

Questions
(to discuss and think about or to serve as a written assignment)

1. What does it mean to be busted?_____

2. Have you ever been busted for something that you did not do? Yes__ No__

3. In your opinion, do all the people who need to be busted get busted? In other words, do a lot of people in your school get away with stuff? Yes__ No__

4. Have you ever gotten away with something several times and then you got busted?

5. In the picture at the beginning of this chapter, what do you think the kid is saying to the teacher?

6. The author was accused of making noise when he got busted. What were you accused of?

7. Have you ever got busted because somebody lied on you? Yes__ No__

8. A lie really hurts especially when it is totally opposite of the truth. To make things worse, those who saw what happened said nothing to help me but stood there silently while I was taken away to be punished. Have you ever had anything like this happen to you?

9. Have you ever been the one who lied on others and got them in trouble? Yes__No__

10. A lie is even more devastating when the liar points his finger at you while he is telling the lie on you. Have you ever pointed your finger at someone and lied on them?

11. The author said that the teacher singled him out for punishment although everybody was involved in making the noise. Has this ever happened to you? Yes__ No__ If yes, what did you learn from the experience?

12. How did the author say that he felt about Richard?_____

13. What goes through your mind when you are being punished and the guilty person is looking at you with giggles in his eyes?

14. Have you ever had an old fashioned paddling like the author had? Yes__ No__

15. Find and complete this sentence: "It is very hard to think when you have been lied about and you are forced to suffer unjustly, but_____"

16. How clearly can you think when you get busted?

17. A calm mind is a great asset during confusing times. What do you think you could do to help yourself calm down when you get busted?

18. When you get busted for something you did not do, do you start yelling, protesting, and basically going off with the teacher? Yes__ No__

19. What should be your tone of voice when you get busted?_____

20. Do you think that the Teacher, Dean or Principal are frightened when you are upset?

21. Wise men overlook minor offenses. A minor offense is something that is not that important, not a life or death situation. It is something that only inconvenienced you a little. Describe some of the minor offenses that you have overlooked._____

22. Find and complete this sentence: "It takes great wisdom to keep_____"

23. Are you wise and mature enough to calmly ask the teacher if you could speak with her for a minute when you have been falsely accused?

24. What happened to the girl who lied, lied, lied?_____

25. Find and complete this sentence: Whenever you get caught up in a negative situation where_____"

26. What does the author mean when he says let the dust settle?

27. Do you now the meaning of the saying: "What goes around comes around?" Yes__ No__

28. Find and complete this sentence: In basketball, the referee will_____

29. Do you believe that when people do wrong that it will eventually catch up with them? Yes__ No__

30. What would you have done to Richard?_____

31. I read a story in the newspaper about a man who had been in prison for nine years before it was discovered that he was innocent. The amazing thing was that he said that he was not mad at anyone. If he can do that, don't you think that you can get over someone telling a lie on you? Yes__ No__

Wisdom From The Elders

Read the quotes and explain them to the boys. Use the questions to begin the discussion.
Be sure to work with the boys to compose your own quote that relates to this chapter.

It is a smaller thing to suffer punishment than to have deserved it. OVID
1. This wisdom is saying that it is better to be paddled for something that you did not do rather than being paddled for something that you did do. Do you agree with this?
2. When you are innocent, you have a sense of peace inside even though you are accused of being guilty. When you are accused of something, are you usually innocent or guilty?
3. Which is more important to you, peace on the inside or for people to understand you?

The innocent is the person who explains nothing. ALBERT CAMUS
1. There will be times when you will be innocent and nobody will believe you. Are you prepared to keep quiet and get on with life or will you insist on making the point that you are innocent?
2. Why do you think that the innocent person does not need to explain anything?
3. Have you ever seen a guilty person start explaining what happened before anyone asks him what happened? Yes__ No__   Why do you think he does that?

Whosoever blushes is already guilty; true innocence is ashamed of nothing.
    HENRY DAVID THOREAU
1. The author of this book has never been good at telling lies. His parents could always look at him and tell when he was guilty. Are you good at telling lies?
2. Tell the truth and not a lie: Can you tell a lie and not blush?
3. Do you agree that it feels wonderful when something happens at home or school and you are the one who did not do it?
4. Who was Henry David Thoreau?

In law a man is guilty when he violates the rights of another. In ethics he is guilty if he only thinks of doing so. IMMANUEL KANT
1. If you are with two other boys and they hit someone and you laughed and enjoyed watching them do it, you are morally just as guilty as they are even though you did not lay a hand on the kid. Many times, teachers accuse you because you were part of what happened even though you did not actually hit anyone. Remember that you can be guilty when you are there and enjoy the damage done even though you did not personally hit the kid. Have you ever enjoyed seeing someone hurt although you did not do it yourself?

Even doubtful accusations leave a stain behind them. THOMAS FULLER
1. An accusation is when you are accused of something. A doubtful accusation is one that is difficult to believe. The point of this wisdom is that even farfetched lies damage people. This is why it is very important that you never lie on a person because you stain (damage) his reputation. Do you lie on people? all the time__ some of the time__ never__
2. When you are falsely accused there will be questions left unanswered in some people's minds.

When this happens are you willing to continue to work hard to promote your good reputation?

Character is what you have left when you've lost everything else. PATRICIA HARRIS
1. Are you a person of character?
2. When you have been accused and you didn't do it, do you remind yourself that you are a good person, a honest person in spite of what has happened?
3. A lie on you does not change who you are. What do you say to yourself about who you are when you are lied on?
4. What would you rather have, character or three million dollars?

There is more power in the open hand than in the clenched fist. MARTIN LUTHER KING JR.
1. The open hand is a symbol of reason while the clenched fist is a sign of warfare. Which sign do you show most often?
2. Do you feel that it is better to puff up in anger because you were falsely accused or try to stay calm and reason with your teacher?
3. When it comes to talking and reasoning with others, are you a powerful person?

One of the highest forms of human maturity is taking full responsibility for what happens to you. B. J. TATUM
1. When you get busted and it was not your fault, it becomes your responsibility to be wise and get your self out of that situation. Are you mature enough to understand that?
2. Are you the type of person who takes responsibility for what happens to you or do you blame others for what happens?
3. Are you willing to work hard to take the unfair things that happen to you in life and work to make good come out of it?
4. Many people in America are taking the position of a victim. When you are a victim of something you can't be held responsible because it is not your fault. Do you want to be a victim so you can feel sorry for yourself or are you going to work hard to overcome whatever negative thing that has happened to you?

Compose a quote and write it here:_____

_____

Note to the mentor/teacher: As a result of this lesson, are there any needs that these young men have that can be met by networking with parents, other teachers, social agencies or religious institutions?

Chapter 20

Stupid Stuff

Definition of stupid stuff: Stupid is showing a lack of sense. Stupid stuff would be behavior that shows a lack of sense. Actions that are very immature and will get you in trouble.

Connecting With and Learning From Your Rich, Personal, Painful, Productive Past. While writing this chapter, I was reminded of the time in junior high school when I responded to a dare and taped an X-rated sign on a pretty girl's back. I never got in trouble because she did not find out who did it. I later realized that her three brothers would have killed me had they found out that I did it. Think of something stupid that you have done that can be shared with the boys. As usual, make sure that it is age-appropriate.

CAUTION: Do not make light of your past acts of ignorance. Just because you and I have survived acts of stupidity does not mean that the next kid that tries it will be so lucky.

CHARGE: Charge the boys to exhibit sensible behavior. Chance is nothing to play with. Each year children are injured and killed because they feel that they will not get caught in their foolishness. Discuss and discourage the imitation of acts of stupidity that can be seen nightly on TV.

ACTIVITY: Discuss pain and age as two cures for foolishness. Think of children who are in the hospital, who are hungry, who are forced to live on the street. These children do not have time for stupid stuff. When we have pain in our lives, we stop acting foolishly and doing stupid stuff. Age also helps you stop acting foolishly and doing stupid things. Age usually brings experience, which shows the emptiness of foolish behavior.

Lesson 20

Stupid Stuff

One of the problems of being a boy is that boys sometimes do stupid stuff. Girls often tell us that we do stupid stuff and we blow them off and try to ignore them, but the fact of the matter is, boys do stupid stuff. As a grown man, I often look back to when I was a child and I remember the stupid stuff that I used to do. I can remember that I would operate on all of my sisters dolls and take the little motors out of them. Not only was this stupid, but it was mean. My sister would pick her dolls up and try to get them to move, but she did not know that I had taken the motors out of them.

I can remember riding my bicycle off the top of the hill at full speed, getting up to about 40 miles per hour without a helmet on. That's just plain stupid! Some of my friends did some really stupid stuff. I can remember them trying to talk me into doing some stupid stuff with them. Sometimes I did and sometimes I didn't. One time, they put a long board up to the side of the school and they climbed up the board and got on the roof. They challenged me to climb up too. They were all older than I was and much bigger. I remember struggling to climb up the board like the big boys. When I finally got on the top of the ladder, the big boys jumped off and took the board down. I had to stay up on the roof until my father came and got me. Now, that was stupid!

I have often tried to think of the reasons why people do stupid things. I have come up with some reasons:

1. To get attention. It is a fact that everybody needs attention. The problem is that some people don't know how to get it without acting stupid. They act stupid hoping that others will look at them. When people look at them, they feel better about themselves because they are getting the attention that they desire.

2. Because they don't know any better. Some people don't have what I call "Good Home Trainin'." Good home trainin' is where your parents teach you basic social skills like not to dig in your nose in public, to open the door for elderly people, to say "Yes sir" and "Yes ma'am, "Yes, Mr. Johnson" or "No Mr. Johnson." We have many young people today who have not been taught basic social skills, and they don't know any better than to act up in public to get attention.

3. They don't understand the consequences. I have a friend who was very stupid when he was younger. He told me that he and some of his boys did some wrong things and got caught. When they stood before the judge, they were arrogant (thought they were baad). They told the judge to go ahead and give them time, they could do whatever he dished out. Well, the judge gave

175

them all one year in the penitentiary. They turned and walked out of the courtroom like they were baad. What is interesting is that once they got in prison, my friend said that he and all of his buddies cried every day and every night. They realized that they did not understand what prison was like and that they were stupid when they acted like they acted.

4. They hang around with stupid friends. It is a fact that all people eventually act like those they hang out with. The reason why so many young people do drugs is because they hang out in a drug- infested environment. It is a fact of human behavior that you act like the people you hang out with. In the next chapter we'll talk more about this.

I am so excited that as a man I do not do as many stupid things as I did when I was a boy, but men occasionally do stupid things. As I get older and wiser, I am learning how to leave the stupid things to stupid people, and I am trying to live a wise life and do wise things. What about you?

Questions
(to discuss and think about or to serve as a written assignment)

1. What is that boy in the picture at the beginning of this chapter about to do?

2. Have you ever done anything stupid?

3. Have you done anything stupid today? Yes__ No__ If yes, what did you do?_____

4. Is the boy on the picture doing something stupid? Yes__ No__ What do you think will happen to him?

5. In what area do you struggle with doing stupid things: school__ home__ at the mall__ in the neighborhood__ with friends__ all alone__ other_____

6. What is the stupidest thing you have ever seen a friend do?_____

7. Stupid people do stupid things all the time. Wise people occasionally slip and do something stupid. Are you stupid or are you wise?_____

8. Find and complete this sentence: "One of the problems of being a boy_____"

9. Name the wisest man you know:_____

10. What are you doing to try to be like him?_____

11. Find a grown man and ask him what is the stupidest thing that he has ever done._____

12. Do you do stupid stuff to get attention? Yes__ No__

13. The author said that his friends would often try to talk him into doing stupid stuff. Do your friends ever try to talk you into doing stupid stuff? Yes__ No__ Do you do it most of the time or do you reject them most of the time?

14. The author tells the story about allowing some older boys to talk him into doing something stupid. Do you think that it is easy for older boys to talk you into doing something stupid?

15. In your opinion, is it a good idea to show off for older boys?

16. Doing something stupid is bad enough but doing something stupid and getting caught is doubly bad. How do you feel when you get caught doing something stupid?

17. The author gives several reasons people do stupid things. One of those reasons is because people need attention. Tell the truth and not a lie: Do you do stupid things because you need attention?

18. It is a terrible thing to need attention and not be able to get any. It is a fact that many young men do not get attention from older men. What man gives you some attention?

19. Can you name some practical things to do when you feel the need for more attention?

20. Find and complete this sentence: "Good home trainin' is where your_____"

21. Have you ever met any young people who do not have good home trainin'?

22. Home trainin' not only comes from home, but it comes from all of the adult care takers you have had in your life. Home trainin' is something that will help you for the rest of your life as you interact with people at school and on the job. Another word for home trainin' is manners. Do you have good home trainin'?

23. Many young people do not understand the consequences for doing stupid stuff. I wonder what happened to the boy in the picture in the front of the book. I bet he got into some serious trouble. The author tells a story about some of his friends who went to court and smarted off in front of the Judge (STUPID!) What did he say that they learned from that experience?

24. Find and complete this sentence: "They realized that they did not understand_____"

25. Under point number four the author talks about what happens when you hang around stupid people. What is the main point he makes here?

26. Drugs are poison. People must be out of their mind to start doing drugs. When a young man allows a friend to talk him into doing drugs, he has no idea how the drugs will affect HIS body. Just because drugs make one person feel good does not mean that they will do the same thing for the next person. In your opinion, what type of friend would talk another friend into doing drugs?

27. What are you doing now to start eliminating stupid things from your life?

28. What is the one major stupid thing that you need to stop doing?

29. Do you say: "Yes sir and yes ma'am?" Yes__ No__

30. Are you committed to living a wise life and doing wise things? Yes__ No__

Wisdom From The Elders

Read the quotes and explain them to the boys. Use the questions to begin the discussion. Be sure to work with the boys to compose your own quote that relates to this chapter.

It's like this: When I was a child I spoke and thought and reasoned as a child does. But when I became a man my thoughts grew far beyond those of my childhood, and now I have put away the childish things. I CORINTHIANS 13:11

1. Childhood is a wonderful time of learning and discovery. Are you enjoying your childhood?
2. What does it mean to reason? (the ability to think, form judgments)
3. Do you think that you can reason as well as a man in his thirties?
4. The thoughts of men are far beyond the thoughts of boys. Are you excited about becoming a man and reasoning as a man does?
5. It is proper for a grown man to stop acting like a child. Have you ever seen a grown man who still acted like a child?
In your opinion, why do some men not grow up?
6. What role do you think a father plays in helping his son put away childish things and grow up?
7. Do you do the same stupid things that you did two years ago?

A fool always finds a bigger fool to admire him. NICOLAS BOILEAU

1. Have you ever noticed that fools are never happy alone but always seek out someone to admire them?
2. Are you willing to be a bigger fool by laughing at a fool's antics?
3. When someone in class acts in a foolish manner and you laugh at him, what does that make you?
4. A fool can be a very dangerous person. In your opinion, why is this so?

Common sense is very uncommon. HORACE GREELEY

1. Common sense, horse sense, the sense it takes to come in out of the rain, is not something that everybody has. Do you feel that you have common sense? . . What does your teacher think?
2. There are people who have obtained Ph.D. degrees but they lack common sense. Which would you rather have a Ph.D. or common sense?_____ How about a Ph.D. degree AND common sense?

Lost time is never found again. THELONIOUS MONK

1. Your youth is precious and it is important to accomplish certain things while you are young. There are grown men who are just doing some of the things they should have done in Jr. High School. Do you feel that you are on track with your life or have you lost some precious time?
2. Have you ever been goofing off in school and failed to get your work done?

It is better to look where you are going than to see where you have been.
FLORENCE GRIFFITH-JOYNER

1. Do you think about where you are going or do you spend most of your time thinking about your past?
2. In your opinion, will your future require more wisdom than you needed in your past?
3. We are all supposed to learn from the mistakes of the past. When we learn from our past we benefit from it and our future will be better. What mistake have you made this year that you NEVER want to make again?
4. Who is Florence Griffith-Joyner?

The difference between genius and stupidity is that genius has its limits. ANONYMOUS

1. This wisdom is saying that stupidity has no limits. It can go on and on and on and on. There is a saying: "Stupid is as stupid does." What do you think that means?
2. In your opinion, do stupid people get tired of acting stupid?

Stupidity is an elemental force for which no earthquake is a match. KARL KRAUS

1. Stupid people can cause a lot of trouble because of the things they say and do. Have you ever seen a stupid person start a fight, break something, tell lies that hurt people and things like that?
2. It has been said earlier that you should stay away from fools and stupid people. Are you quick to move away from a person once you figure out that he is stupid?

Never underestimate the power of stupid people in large groups. ANONYMOUS

1. Riots, wars, and fights in the bathroom can be started by stupid people in large groups. What should you do when you find yourself in a large group of stupid people?
2. History is filled with stories about riots that were started when one stupid person in the group threw a rock at another person. Stupid people are more dangerous in a group than they are one on one. Do you ever sit quietly and study the behavior of a stupid person?

Stupidity is the night of the mind, but a night without moon or star. CONFUCIUS

1. Stupid people refuse to listen to those who would lead them to wisdom. One clear sign that a person is stupid is when that person refuses to listen to anyone who is older and wiser that seeks to guide them. Do you listen to the wisdom of wiser men?
2. Who was Confucius?

Compose a quote and write it here:_____

_____

Note to the mentor/teacher: As a result of this lesson, are there any needs that these young men have that can be met by networking with parents, other teachers, social agencies or religious institutions?

180

Peer Pressure knows no age restrictions. Adults buy things they don't need, with money they don't have, to impress people they don't like.

ANONYMOUS

Chapter 21

Who Do You Act Like?

Definition of acting like someone: Consciously or unconsciously imitating the behavior of another person.

Connecting With and Learning From Your Rich, Personal, Painful, Productive Past. As I reflect back on my young and impressionable years, it frightens me to think of the people that I idolized and imitated. The super heroes of my day had the same numbing effect on my brain as today's heroes have on today's children. One aspect of this chapter is to look at how we purposefully imitate others. The other thing that we want to look at is how we unconsciously imitate others, such as parents, friends or TV personalities.

CAUTION: Let's not paint the picture that to imitate others is a bad thing. Let's attempt to show that we should be selective in how we allow others to influence us.

CHARGE: Charge the young men to take inventory of their behaviors, scrutinizing them to determine their origin. When they determine that a behavior is bad, it then becomes necessary to eliminate that behavior from our conscious mind. It often helps to eliminate bad behaviors once we discover where they come from.

Each generation should do better than their parents did. In order to accomplish this goal, it is necessary to eliminate our parents' negative behaviors from our lives. Challenge the boys to decide to act better than anyone that they know by eliminating the negative influences in their lives and determining that they will not be victims to negative behavior.

ACTIVITY: Have the boys make a list or discuss three to five behaviors that need to be eliminated from their lives. Ask the boys if they have any idea who they modeled that behavior after. Once they identify the behavior and identify where they picked up that behavior, it will be time for them to make a decision to rid that behavior from their lives. Awareness is the first step to overcoming negative behavior.

Lesson 21

Who Do You Act Like?

I am amazed that many children act just like their parents act. When you live with people, you unconsciously begin to talk like them and pick up many of their behaviors. These behaviors may be negative or they may be positive. As I get older, I find that I have many of my dad's good and bad habits. I really did not realize that I acted so much like him, but my wife and my mother are always noticing many of his characteristics in my behavior.

We are all prisoners of our environment. We pick up words, movements, and mannerisms from those around us. Stop and think for a moment about the words that the kids in your class use. How many words have you learned from them this year? What is the latest slang word that has hit your class or school? We all are influenced by our environment, whether negative or positive, and we all act like somebody.

The million dollar question is: "Who do you act like?" Do you really know the person who most influences you? Do you know why you act like that person? Have you thought about whether you should act like this person? As a parent, I am very careful about the TV shows and movies that I allow my children to watch. I have learned that my kids start to act like whoever they see on TV. Not too long ago, I purchased a video for my kids to watch, and they learned all of the words on the video. They watched it over and over and over again. Soon they had almost memorized the whole video.

We must remember that we all learn about life by watching others. This can be a really good habit if we are watching the right people. Let me ask you a question: When it comes to study habits, who is the best person in your class to watch? When it comes to good manners and politeness, who is the best person in your class to watch? When you go outside to play ball, who has the best talent out there?

My advice to you is to find people who are good at doing the right thing and then watch them and imitate them. There is nothing wrong with giving them a compliment and letting them know that you admire them in that area. No person has it together in every area, but we all have something that we do well and others can learn from us. Who do you act like? Well, for me, I act like different people in different things.

When it comes to being a good father, I act like my dad. When it comes to cooking, I act like my mother. When it comes to teaching, I act like Mr. Jenkins, my favorite junior high school teacher.

183

It is good to know who you copied all of your good habits from.

When my daughter was in kindergarten, we learned that we could not allow her to hear any bad language because she would repeat it. One day she stayed with a friend who was watching an adult-rated movie. This friend did not think that my daughter would pay any attention to the movie, but she came home saying some of the bad things that were in the movie. It was easy for us to tell where she learned the words because she had not been anyplace else.

Discovering why you act the way you act is a great accomplishment. Once you discover why you act the way you act, you can change the things you want to change. I want to challenge you to take the time to think about your family and some of the behaviors that you see in your home. Every home has some good behaviors and some bad behaviors. We should always try to imitate the good behaviors of our parents and not imitate their bad behaviors.

My mother was a wonderful mother for us kids. She had many good behaviors that I tried to imitate. She also had one bad habit that I did not want to imitate, and that was cigarettes. Back then, it was cool to smoke and everybody did it but it just didn't seem right to me. I am glad that I did not act like my mother in that area. Well, your life will be modeled after someone that you are around. It is up to you to choose who you want to act like. You can control your behavior by making a decision not to imitate the way certain people act. When you make these decisions every day, you are taking control of your life. Good luck as you decide who you want to act like.

Questions
(to discuss and think about or to serve as a written assignment)

1. In your opinion, is it important to examine your behavior? Yes__ No__

2. Some people never consider how they look or act in public. Have you ever seen anyone like that? Yes__ No__

3. Who do you act like?_____

4. In your opinion, what person has had the greatest impact on your behavior?

5. What person do you not want to act like?

6. Name one good behavior that you have learned from your mom._____

7. Name one good behavior that you have learned from your dad or a male figure in your life.

8. Name one good behavior that you have learned from your teacher._____

9. Name one good behavior that you want to learn from your mentor._____

10. The author says that we are all prisoners of our environment. What he means is that we learn from those around us. In your opinion, how should we protect ourselves from people around us who do not know how to behave?

11. Do you imitate any movie stars? Yes__ No__ If yes, then who?_____

12. The personal lifestyles of many athletes and rap stars are not worth imitating. When you see them doing their thing are you mature enough to appreciate what they do without imitating their personal life style?

13. When you play ball, whose style do you model?_____

14. Find and complete this sentence: We are all prisoners_____

15. Who do people say you remind them of?_____

16. It is a documented fact that the TV shows that you watch have a powerful influence on you. What are your favorite TV shows?

17. Have you memorized any of lines from your favorite videos?

18. To prove the point that TV impacts you, I want you to stop and think for a moment about the TV show or video that was your favorite when you were a little child. Can you remember any of the words to the songs they sang?

19. How many hours a day do you watch TV and play video games?

20. What type of video game machine do you have?_____ Is it the latest version?

21. The author says that we all learn about life by watching others. He goes on to say that this can be good if we are watching the right people. How can watching others be bad?

22. Find and complete this sentence: "My advice to you is to find people who are good____"

23. What bad behavior do you need to get rid of?_____

24. Where did you get that bad behavior from?_____

25. Who is the person in your class with the best manners?_____

26. Do you hang out with the person with good manners? Yes__ No__ If you don't, do you think that you could benefit from hanging out with them? Yes__ No__

27. Find and complete this sentence: Discovering why you act_____

28. Today we have a lot of medical knowledge about smoking. We know that it is terribly damaging to your health. Even with all the information that we have about the dangers of smoking, many young people are deciding to smoke. Can you explain why they do this?

29. Find and complete this sentence: We should always try to imitate the good_____

30. The author said that his mother had one bad habit when he was a kid. What was it?__

31. At the very end of the chapter the author states what needs to be done to take control of your life. What did he say needed to be done?

Wisdom From The Elders

Read the quotes and explain them to the boys. Use the questions to begin the discussion. Be sure to work with the boys to compose your own quote that relates to this chapter.

If I try to be like him, who will be like me? YIDDISH PROVERB

1. It is most important to be yourself. As you age and mature this will happen, but during the formative years all human beings imitate others. So, while you are young it is OK to try to be like someone as long as that person that you imitate is a good role model. Do you ever feel uncomfortable when you try to imitate others?
2. In your opinion, who do you cheat when you choose to act like someone other than yourself?
3. Why do you think that some people work hard to be like others?

We love in others what we lack in ourselves, and would be everything but what we are. R. H. STODDARD

1. Are you trying to be anything other than what you are?
2. Is there anybody in your school that you feel is really cool? Yes__ No__
3. Have you analyzed why you think they are cool? Yes__ No__
4. Tell the truth and not a lie: Do you love in others what you feel you do not have in yourself?
5. If you could have one quality of another person in your school, what would it be?
6. When you wake up in the morning are you thankful that you are who you are?

When people are free to do as they please, they usually imitate each other. ERIC HOFFER

1. Do you have on any clothes or shoes that have a famous person's name on them?
2. What basketball star's shoes do you wear?
3. Do you ever get bored with yourself? Yes__ No__ If yes, what do you think you could do to make yourself more exciting?
4. Tell the truth and not a lie. Who do you model your life after, a famous person, a family member, someone in your school?
5. Do you like the freedom we have in our country to act any way we want to act or would you rather live in a country where people are told how to act?

Nothing is so soothing to our self-esteem as to find our bad traits in our forebears. It seems to absolve us. VAN WYCK BROOKS

1. This wisdom is saying that when we learn that our fathers had bad habits it makes us feel better because we realize that they were not perfect either. Do you think we should base how good we should be on our fathers or on what is right?
2. When you discover that you are practicing a bad habit learned from your family, what do you do?
3. When you see someone do something wrong, does that make it right for you to do it?

The question is not always where we stand but in which direction we are headed.
MARY FRANCES BERRY

1. Has today been a day of good direction for you? In other words, have you made good decisions and done all of your school work today?
2. You can reach any destination if you keep moving in the direction of your goals. On the other hand, what destination do you think you will reach if you keep making bad decisions?
3. The right direction for young people your age is toward an education. You are too young to make any decisions other than that decision. Do you think that you are old enough to decide that you do not like school and not work hard?
4. Do you hang out with the right people and are you going in the right direction?
5. Are there any people in your school who can influence you to go the wrong direction?
6. When was the last time someone talked you into doing something that you knew was wrong?

To do exactly the opposite is also a form of imitation. GEORG C. LICHTENBERG

1. Do you agree that we often imitate people and are not aware of it?
2. Many young men have decided to wear their pants drooping down. Do you think they realize that when they do that they are imitating people in prison?
3. Is it reasonable to think that we could imitate some things by doing the opposite of them?

A man becomes like those whose society he loves. HINDU PROVERB

1. Society here means your friends and associates. The Hindu people taught that you will become like those people you love. We know this to be true in America also. Do you think that people all over the world become like those they hang out with?
2. Do you have a group of friends who have secret words that nobody knows about?
3. Our behavior is very personal and private. We only change it when we want to. Do you act the same way around your friends as you do when you are around your mother?

Compose a quote and write it here: _____

_____

_____

Note to the mentor/teacher: As a result of this lesson, are there any needs that these young men have that can be met by networking with parents, other teachers, social agencies or religious institutions?

Let no pleasure tempt thee,
no profit allure thee,
no ambition corrupt thee,
no example sway thee,
no persuasion move thee to
do anything which thou knowest
to be evil; so thou shalt live jollily,
for a good conscience is a
continual Christmas.

BENJAMIN FRANKLIN

Chapter 22

Moral Restraints

(What are they, and who needs them?)

Definition of moral restraints: The ability to understand the difference between right and wrong and then doing right.

Connecting With and Learning From Your Rich, Personal, Painful, Productive Past. I give an example in the chapter of not using moral restraints, and I also discuss the pain that resulted for me and others. Recall from you past an event where your failure to use moral restraints resulted in pain for you and others.

CAUTION: Tell the kids that no one is perfect, but we should get better as we get older. Don't allow anyone to go on a guilt trip because of their failures, but encourage them to seek to improve as they mature.

CHARGE: Charge the boys to do what is right. When we follow right teachings, the pain we suffer in life is diminished. It is impossible to avoid pain in our lives, but we can lessen that pain by having moral restraints working in our lives.

ACTIVITY: Discuss the pain that people have suffered because they did not have any moral restraints. Discuss the extreme behaviors that are possible when there are no moral restraints in place, behaviors such as murder, drugs, assault, robbery, lying, stealing, rape, etc.

Lesson 22

Moral Restraints

(What are they, and who needs them?)

Not too long ago I heard of a terrible, terrible situation where two boys, both in elementary school contributed to the death of another boy their age. Actually, what they did was they killed him and they did it like it was a game. I asked myself how these young boys could do such a dastardly deed and make a joke out of it. The truth is that there are some things that are morally wrong and others things that are morally right. Unfortunately, there are those in our society who either don't know the difference or don't care.

Some people in our society do not have what is called moral restraints. In other words, there is no little voice in their head telling them what is right or wrong. They do whatever they want to do, regardless of how it will affect themselves or other people. Another way to say this is that some people do not have a conscience. Our conscience is our moral warning system that goes off when we do something wrong. When you do wrong, your conscience will make you feel guilty even if you never get caught by an adult.

I can still remember the day that I did something really bad. I played a trick Terry Wayne. There was a hornet's nest in a path behind our house. I told Terry Wayne to race me to the other side of the field, knowing that he would have to run through the hornet's nest. I knew that what I was doing was wrong, but I did not use restraint. In other words, I did it anyway. Well, we raced and Terry Wayne was stung very badly by three bees. I can remember looking in his back door watching his mother pull the stingers out of his head. At first it was funny, but later I really felt bad about what I had done. My conscience was bothering me.

I am glad that I had a conscience when I was a kid. My conscience kept me out of a lot of trouble. On many occasions I would listen to that little voice that would say: "Don't do that" when I was about to do something wrong. I have learned that if you listen to that little voice before you do wrong, it will be a little voice that warns you. If you don't listen before you do wrong, that little voice will become a big voice that will bug you after you do wrong.

Moral restraints are needed to keep our society healthy. If everybody decided that they were going to do what they wanted to and ignore moral restraints, our society would collapse. The bad things that you see happening to other countries on television would soon occur in our cities

191

here in the United States of America.

If there were no moral restraints in our society, people would raid the malls and take what they wanted. They would kill you or me for any reason at all. Robbery, rape, beatings and burnings would be happening all around us. Life as we know it would soon end.

We cannot allow this to happen to our country. The only way to stop it is for people to impose moral restraints on themselves. For example, I do not allow myself to steal. I don't mess around with other men's wives. I vote for laws that will help men and women with their moral restraints. I vote against laws that would encourage people to do wrong.

History tells us that the greatest nations that ever existed were not destroyed by invading armies that came from far away. Instead, they were destroyed by their own citizens when almost everybody in the country refused to have moral restraints and did what they wanted to do even when it was wrong. The ancient empire of Rome is the best example of a nation that destroyed itself. Take time to look it up in the encyclopedia and see for yourself.

Having a good system of moral restraints will help you in all of your endeavors. You develop your moral restraints from your early training when you are told to respect other people and treat them like you would like to be treated. Decide now to be a moral leader in your school, community and country. America needs more young men like you to keep it the great nation that it is. If you don't do it, it won't be done.

Questions
(to discuss and think about or to serve as a written assignment)

1. What is a restraint?_____

2. What are morals? (principles, standards with respect to right or wrong conduct)

3. Do you have a system of moral restraints in place in your life? Yes__ No__

4. Could you hit another person and not feel guilty? Yes__ No__

5. Do you understand what your conscience is? Yes__ No__

6. A conscience is a knowledge or sense of right and wrong with an urge to do right. Our conscience is what speaks to us when we do wrong and encourages us to do right. Does your conscience ever speak to you? Yes__ No__

7. Do you often argue with your conscience? Yes__ No__

8. The author started this chapter with a story about a terrible crime that had been committed by two young boys. Have you ever heard of anything like this on the news or in your city?

9. Do you believe that there are people in our society who do not know the difference between right and wrong? Yes__ No__

10. Moral restraints have been described as a little voice in our head telling us what is right and wrong. Have you ever been about to do something wrong and you heard that little voice in your head? Yes__ No__

11. How does it make you feel knowing that some people do not have that voice in their heads correcting them when they are about to do something wrong?_____ It is because of those people that your parents want you in after dark and must know where you are at all times.

12. A good conscience is good for society because it helps people make good decisions. Find and complete this sentence: "When you do wrong, your conscience_____"

13. The author tells the story about how he played a dirty trick on Terry Wayne. The trick resulted in Terry Wayne suffering a lot of bee stings. The author said that it was funny at first but what did he say happened later?

14. Find and complete this sentence: "Our conscience is our moral_____"

15. Has your conscience ever bothered you? Yes__ No__

16. What did the author say his conscience did to help keep him out of trouble?

17. Find and complete this sentence: "I have learned that if you_____"

18. What is the difference in the voice of conscience before you do something wrong and the voice of conscience after you do something wrong?

19. The author states that moral restraints are needed to keep our society healthy. In your opinion, how do moral restraints help keep our society healthy?_____"

20. What did the author say would happen if everybody decided that they were going to do what they wanted to and ignored their moral restraints?

21. What great nation did the author say was destroyed because there were no moral restraints?

22. According to the author, who is supposed to impose moral restraints on you?

23. The author gives a list of things that he does not allow himself to do. Can you name some of the things that you do not allow yourself to do?

24. Using this chapter as a reference, why do you think the two boys killed the other boy?

25. Do you watch TV shows where the people have no moral restraints? Yes__ No__

26. Name some of the shows where the people have no moral restraints._____

27. What does history tell us about how have the greatest nations been destroyed?

28. Find and complete this sentence: "You develop your moral restraints from_____"

29. What does America need? (last paragraph)

30. Are you going to decide to become a moral leader? Yes__ No__

Wisdom From The Elders

Read the quotes and explain them to the boys. Use the questions to begin the discussion. Be sure to work with the boys to compose your own quote that relates to this chapter.

What you ought to do, you should do; and what you should do, you ought to do.
> **OPRAH WINFREY**

1. Do you know the things that you should do?
2. What do you do when you know that you should do something but you really do not want to do it right now?
3. Are you mature enough to do the things you should do?
4. Tell the truth and not a lie: Have you done all of your school work?
5. Do you agree with your parents when they tell you things you should do?

Of all the qualities necessary for success, none comes before character. ERNESTA PROCOPE

1. Character has been described as moral strength and discipline. Do you have the reputation of a person of character?
2. If you do not currently have a reputation as a person of character, are you working on being known as an honest, trustworthy person?
3. Abraham Lincoln's nick name was Honest Abe. He was called that because he was honest and could be trusted. If you were given a nick name based on your character, what would that name be?

The collapse of character begins with compromise. FREDERICK DOUGLASS

1. A compromise is when you do something that you know is wrong. Every time you do this your character is damaged. For example, if you lie to your teacher you compromise your character. If you take something that does not belong to you, you compromise your character. Have you compromised your character in any way today?
2. What little thing have you recently done wrong that could lead to you doing bigger wrong things?
3. When character collapses nobody will believe you. People see you as a total cheat and liar. Do you know anybody whose character has collapsed?
4. If the collapse of character begins with compromise (giving in to wrong) what should our attitude be about doing little things that are wrong?
5. Who was Frederick Douglass? (look it up)

Not to have control over the senses is like sailing in a rudderless ship, bound to break to pieces on coming in contact with the very first rock. MAHATMA GANDHI

1. Can you imagine how dangerous a car would be if it was traveling at 40 miles per hour and the steering wheel did not work. This is the way many people run their lives. They travel very fast through life but they are not able to guide or control their passions and desires. What do you think is going to happen to them?

195

2. Can you think of any adults who have ruined their lives because they could not control themselves?

3. What do you plan to do to avoid making the same mistakes that many young people and adults have made?

Moral restraint is feeling temptation and resisting it. SIGMUND FREUD

1. Temptation is not bad or wrong. Everybody is tempted in some way. It is only when we do the bad things that we are tempted to do that we have done wrong. Do you sometimes feel bad when you are tempted?

2. When you are tempted does it help to that you have not done anything wrong?

3. The author of this book was often tempted to steal when he was young. He would go to the store and there were many items that he wanted to take but the important point is that he did not take them. Do you ever feel guilty about being tempted? Yes__ No__   If yes, the next time this happens tell yourself: "I haven't done anything wrong."

4. The author's father told him not to steal because it was wrong. This is where he found the motivation not to steal. Where do you find the motivation to resist doing those things that you shouldn't do?

5. Who was Sigmund Freud?

Moral restraint is drawing the line somewhere. GILBERT KEITH CHESTERTON

1. Are there certain things that you will not do? Do you draw an imaginary line that you refuse to cross as it relates to certain issues? Some kids will lie, but they draw the line at stealing. Other kids will hit you, but they draw the line at kicking you. Where do you draw your lines?

Moral courage is a more rare commodity than bravery in battle or great intelligence.
ROBERT F. KENNEDY

1. According to Robert Kennedy, it is a greater task to have moral courage than to do all of the things that people call great. Do you agree with him on this point?

2. Do you have the courage to say "NO" when you are asked to do something wrong?

You've got to be brave and you've got to be bold. Brave enough to take your chance on your own discrimination--what's right and what's wrong, what's good and what's bad.
ROBERT FROST

1. Do you feel that you have a good sense of what is right and wrong? Are you brave enough to stand up for what is right when you need to?)

Compose a quote and write it here:_____

_____

_____

The only discipline that lasts is self-discipline.

BUM PHILLIPS

Chapter 23

How to Change Your Bad Habits

Definition of bad habits: Behaviors that you exhibit on a continual basis that are not in your best interest and need to be eliminated from your life.

Connecting With and Learning From Your Rich, Personal, Painful, Productive Past. Reflect on those bad habits that you have eliminated from your life and share with the boys how you overcame them. Be realistic and let them know that you still have some habits that need to be eliminated. It is for this reason that you can identify with them as they work on their habits. Take time to share how you overcame some of the habits that they are still struggling with. For example, getting out of bed, doing your school work, respecting authority, respecting girls, etc.

CAUTION: Do not accept the attitude of "I can't do it" from any of the boys. It is easier to accept the victim mind set than it is to decide to overcome bad habits. Tell the boys that you reject the victim mentality. Tell them that you do not tolerate it first in yourself nor in those that you are close to.

CHARGE: Charge the boys to tackle one bad habit at a time. Tell them that in order to change a bad habit, you must practice the desired behavior at least 21 days before it becomes natural. Don't allow discouragement to stop you before you develop the behavior that you want to have. As the mentor, you should work to take any negative stigma away from this subject. Strive to create an environment where it is OK to discuss your successes and failures. The task of breaking bad habits is a life long activity. As hard as we try, we seem to pick up new bad habits that we must get rid of. So, encourage the boys to use what they learn in this chapter as they mature into manhood.

ACTIVITY: Help the boys identify one bad habit that they want to break. Once identified, discuss the proper behavior to replace the bad behavior. Check with the boys each week to see if they are staying on course.

Lesson 23

How to Change Your Bad Habits

When I think of my elementary school days, I think of a period in my life when it seemed like I was trying to do what everybody told me what to do. My mother always had a list of things for me to do. So did my dad. If you add to that my teachers, aunties, and older brothers and sisters, I know that you will see what I mean. It seemed like everybody was my boss. So, the way I dealt with that situation was this: I rebelled. In other words when my mother told me to pick up my clothes, I would try to see how long I could let them stay on the floor. I developed an attitude of trying to do things my way, regardless of how illogical it was.

When young people do this, they will eventually develop some bad habits. Needless to say, here I am, a grown man and I am still trying to get rid of some of the bad habits that I developed when I was in the fifth grade. One habit I am working on is to make sure that all of my clothes are hung up as soon as I take them off. When my mother told me to do this, I felt that she was nagging, but now that I am married, my wife says the same things that my mother did.

What I have come to realize is that if you have a bad habit, you will never be able to outlive or outrun it. The only hope is to overcome it. So, here I am, a grown man, still working hard to make sure that my clothes are hung up at the end of the day. I guess there are some things that we naturally rebel against. I have a friend who just won't stop smoking. He started when he was younger and he knows that it is bad, but he just won't stop. I have another friend who has a bad habit of reading while he drives. Even though he has had one accident, he still won't work to break that bad habit.

Well, enough about me and my friends. What about you and your friends? We need to remember that bad habits do several negative things:

1. They affect others. If you smoke, drink, do hard drugs, lie, steal or cheat, your bad habit hurts other people. I know a man who steals to support his drug habit and he told me that he didn't hurt anyone. The fact of the matter is that even though you may not hurt people directly, you can hurt people indirectly. For example, if you smoke it hurts you directly but it hurts others indirectly when you get sick and others must take care of you.

2. They slow us down. Just take my bad habit (that I used to have) of not hanging my clothes up. This habit cost me time and money because when you don't hang up your clothes you will have a disorganized room and it will take you longer to get going in the morning. Also, your clothes get dirty and wrinkled faster.

3. They cause us to get lower grades. Can you remember the old excuse: "The dog ate my homework?" This is the excuse of a person who was not organized, which is a bad habit. Your bad habits will contribute to low grades. For example, if you don't have a place in your home where you do your homework, you are disorganized. You should find a spot that your family will agree to be your homework spot. It may be the kitchen table, the living room floor or your bedroom, but you need a spot where you can get in the habit of working.

People who get ahead in life are those who are never happy with second best. If you have bad habits that you can change, that is second best. Let me tell you what to do if you want to change a bad habit.

1. Talk to yourself and tell yourself that you can change. Convincing yourself is a very important place to start. If you don't believe that you can change, you never will change. When there is no one to encourage you, talk to yourself. I have learned to talk to myself when I am discouraged or weak. I tell myself that I can do it.

2. Find a friend who will encourage you. If you have another person in your life who wants to see you do better and will encourage you, that will help. I have a friend who is very neat. There are times when he makes me sick, but most of the time he encourages me to do better with my neatness and I encourage him to stop reading while he drives.

3. With a very stubborn attitude, start practicing the behavior that you desire. For me, it was picking up my clothes no matter how lousy it made me feel, no matter how big a rush I was in or if my brother had stolen all of my hangers.

4. Continue practicing the new behavior until it becomes natural. Believe it or not, any behavior that you repeat often enough will eventually become natural. You can do anything over and over and over and it will become a habit. The first thing that I think of is the first time I saw someone smoke their first cigarette. After the first puff, they cough and choke a few times. After a few days, they can suck smoke into their lungs and never cough. The reason this happens is because the human body adjusts to the intrusion of the smoke into the lungs and will even begin to demand cigarettes on a regular basis.

This is the same thing that happens when we begin to change our habits. Believe it or not, if you were to come to my bedroom you would not find any clothes on the floor. They would all be hanging up. Did this happen overnight? No way! It took some time while I practiced appropriate behavior.

I have a background in music and I can say from experience that when a person begins to play an instrument that it will be awkward and difficult to play a scale but after a little practice it can be done with ease. This is how you can overcome your bad habits and help others overcome theirs.

5. If you are not working on your bad habits, you are not growing. Some people never grow in life because they never challenge their bad habits. If you are challenging your bad habits, then you will someday soon be a mature adult who has it together. Good luck as you tackle those bad habits that are in your life. Remember, be sure to celebrate every time you overcome one.

Questions
(to discuss and think about or to serve as a written assignment)

1. Do you have any bad habits? Yes__ No__

2. Are you working on them? Yes__ No__

3. The author said that when he was young, everybody tried to tell him what to do. How did he say he dealt with it?

4. Find and complete this sentence: "I developed an attitude of trying to do things my_____"

5. Do you have any illogical behaviors that you keep on doing in spite of the fact that they are illogical and non-productive?

6. Find and complete this sentence: "Needless to say, here I am, a grown man_____"

7. What bad habit did the author say that he was still trying to get rid of?

8. How did the author say that he developed this bad habit?

9. The author says that his mother and his wife do the same thing. What is it?

10. According to the author, can you out run or out live a bad habit? Yes__ No__

11. How does the author say we need to deal with our bad habits?

12. What is the major bad habit that you are dealing with right now?

13. Have you ever looked at someone's bad habits and thought how stupid they are?

14. When was the last time someone told you how stupid your bad habit is?

15. Do you have a partner to help you and encourage you as you work on your bad habits?

16. The author states that bad habits affect others, slow us down and cause us to get lower grades. Which bad habit of yours affects others the most?

17. Which bad habit causes you to get lower grades?_____ Tell the truth and not a lie: Do you have one bad habit or several that affect your grades?

18. Where do you do your homework?_____

19. What does the author say about a place to do your homework?

20. Find and complete this sentence: "If you have bad habits that_____"

21. Are you happy being second best? Yes__ No__

22. Do you ever talk to yourself and encourage yourself when you are trying to change a bad habit? Yes__ No__

23. In your opinion, is talking to yourself a good habit to develop to help you reach your goal?

24. An accountability partner is a person who checks on you as you work on changing your bad habits. Do you have an accountability partner?

25. You must be aggressive when you attack a bad habit. If you are weak or passive you will probably not get the job done. With what attitude are you attacking your bad habits?

26. Find and complete this sentence: "Believe it or not, any behavior that_____"

27. The author uses the habit of smoking cigarets to make a point. What point does he make?

28. What does the human body do the first few times a person smokes?_____ What will the human body eventually do if a person keeps smoking?

29. A smoking habit is one of the most difficult habits to break. Since everybody knows this, why do you think people continue to start smoking?

30. State or write three bad habits you want to change_____

31. The author talks about people who get ahead in life. He goes on and gives five steps that will help you change a bad habit. Read the list again or write them down._____

Wisdom From The Elders

Read the quotes and explain them to the boys. Use the questions to begin the discussion. Be sure to work with the boys to compose your own quote that relates to this chapter.

A habit is something you can do without thinking—which is why most of us have so many of them. FRANKLN CLARK

1. Have you ever thought about the fact that habits are done without thinking?
2. Do you think that people would have as many bad habits as they do now if they had to think real hard before doing them?
3. In your opinion, which is more difficult to keep, a good habit or a bad habit?

Habit is the test of truth: It must be right, I've done it from my youth. GEORGE CRABBE

1. Actually, this quote is not true. It is not true that because you have done something since you were a kid that it is right. Many habits that we developed early in life need to be changed. What is your oldest bad habit?
2. Since you are aware of that habit, what are you doing to change it?

Habits are chains too small to be felt till they are too strong to be broken. SAMUEL JOHNSON

1. The beginning of a bad habit is often overlooked. It is not until the habit is part of your life that you sit up and notice how ingrained it is. Do you remember when you started your bad habits?
2. Do you know any people who are hooked on smoking? Do you think they realized how addictive the behavior was when they started?
3. Some habits are too powerful for a person to break by himself. Professional help may be needed. Can you think of any habits that are in this category?

Excellence is to do a common thing in an uncommon way. BOOKER T. WASHINGTON

1. What is it that you are really good at?
2. In what areas of your life do you strive for excellence?
3. Life is never boring when you strive for excellence in all that you do. In what area of your life are you bored?

It's no disgrace to start over or to begin anew. BEBE MOORE CAMPBELL

1. When you try to break a bad habit and fail, do you feel too bad to try again?
2. Great people have no problem starting over as they strive to reach their goals. Are you a great person?
3. Failure crushes many people. These people never move beyond a certain level in the areas that they fail in. Many young men have failed in school and stopped striving for excellence. Is there any area in school that you have stopped trying?

I've always believed no matter how many shots I miss, I'm going to make the next one.
ISIAH THOMAS

1. Do you feel that you can change your bad habit the next time you try?

2. Do you live life with the mind set that victory is just around the corner or that another failure is just around the corner?

3. Do you know who Isiah Thomas is? He came up through inner city poverty in Detroit to become a NBA star. His persistence and talent made a place for him on a championship team. Are you persistent or do you give up easy?

It's not a question of can you succeed; a better question is will you succeed.
GEORGE JOHNSON

1. It is a fact that you can succeed in life if you work hard and make some good decisions. People with much less talent than you have are doing quite well. Have you decided that you will succeed in life?

2. It only takes one bad habit to make you a failure. Are you willing to work hard to get rid of all of your bad habits so you can succeed in life?

3. Do you believe the adults who tell you that you can make it in life?

The person who is self-centered is off-centered. SIMON ESTES

1. Small people focus on themselves and do not consider the needs of others. Large people take care of themselves and consider the needs of others also. Are you a small person or a large person?

2. Most bad habits make us feel good in some way or another. What bad habit do you have that makes you feel good and at the same time hurts you or other people?

Responsibility develops some individuals and ruins others. ROBERT WOODSON

1. What responsibilities do you have around the house?

2. Does responsibility develop you or make you shrink under their pressure

3. Do you have bad habits that make you undependable?

The secret to getting things done is to act! BENJAMIN O. DAVID

1. Which are you known for, talking or acting?

2. Are you challenging your bad habits or talking about changing your bad habits?

Compose a quote and write it here:_____

_____

Note to the mentor/teacher: As a result of this lesson, are there any needs that these young men have that can be met by networking with parents, other teachers, social agencies or religious institutions?

Chapter 24

Peach People (Understanding Different Races)

Definition of Peach People: Those who are of a different culture than you are or who have different physical features.

Connecting With and Learning From Your Rich, Personal, Painful, Productive Past. I was raised in the 60's, during the thick of the Civil Rights movement. One thing that I learned early in life was that there were some good white people and some bad ones. I also learned that there were some good black people and some bad ones. Because of my understanding of this fact, I determined to be friends and associate with those who I could identify with regardless of their physical features. Draw from your rich past as it relates to different races. Be honest with the kids and share your struggles and how you have overcome or how you are still overcoming.

CAUTION: The younger generation does not carry the same scars as the older generation. Also, you are dealing with children, who are normally very loving and forgiving. Be cautious not to taint them with your personal prejudices.

CHARGE: Charge the boys to seek the good in all people. Remind them that there are good people and bad people in all races. Charge them to be the ones who represent their race well. The best thing anyone can do to represent their race is to be fair and equitable to all people.

ACTIVITY: Have the boys make up character names for individuals whom they know. The name should describe the personality of the person and have no relation to the external physical characteristics. Have them seek to be as complimentary as possible. It is not necessary to share the names publicly. The goal here is to have the boys consider character above the color of the skin. This is a fun exercise that can also be used to sensitize them to the personalities of young ladies as opposed to focusing on the physical.

Lesson 24

Peach People (Understanding Different Races)

I really enjoy being around little kids because they are a lot of fun. One of the joys of being a parent is that kids bring a feeling of innocence to your world. Little children believe in kindness, gentleness, sharing and good stuff like that. Unless an older person teaches them to, they do not hate anybody.

When my first child was little, she went to a preschool where for the first time, she met kids who were different than she was. Some of these kids had skin of a different color and different hair. My daughter found this very interesting but not threatening. I will never forget the day that I picked her up from pre-school and she told me about her day. She said: "Daddy, I made a new friend today." I said: "You did? What is your new friend's name?" She said: "My friend's name is Jennifer, she is one of the Peach People." I said: "Peach People?" She said: "Yes, Peach People."

I was puzzled, trying to understand what this 5-year-old meant by "Peach people." I had never heard of Peach People. Well, she went on to explain that Peach People had straight hair and skin that looked like a peach. I finally understood what she was talking about. She was talking about "white" or Caucasian people.

What I found interesting was that this 5-year-old did not know that they were called "white people" so she made up her own name and called them Peach People. This innocent child did not understand anything about different races. All she knew was that she had a new friend whose skin reminded her of a peach, so she called her a Peach Person. I think it is great when a child innocently makes up a name for people of different races. It is terrible when kids learn bad names about other races from mean adults.

We live in the United States of America; a great nation that has been built by many different races. Regardless of what race you may be, we all need to learn to be like the 5-year-old who sees all people as possible friends regardless of the color of their skin.

As an adult, I have learned to pick my friends because of how nice they are and not by the color of their skin. All races have nice people and all races have mean people. I want to have nice people as my friends, regardless of what race they are. There is a lot we can learn as we spend time with people who are different than we are. I am not saying that everybody has to be your friend but I am saying that you should not prejudge a person because of how they look.

We must also be careful about the words we use when no one is looking. What language do you use in your home to describe different races of people? Do you use words that others would approve of? What we say about people behind their back is a good indicator of how we really feel about them. This is why it is very important to be careful about the words we use to describe others.

People who choose not to interact with people who are different than they are miss opportunities for growth that will help them get ahead in life. As a black man, I have several white guys that I am good friends with. We have helped each other grow and we are all stronger, better men as a result. When considering a friend of a different race ask yourself these questions:

1. Do we think alike? Thinking alike is an important requirement for any relationship.
2. Do we have similar goals? All relationships go through changes. If you have similar goals you will change together for good.
3. Are we both strong enough to be friends in spite of what others may say? There are people who will have negative things to say about you choosing to be a friend with someone of a different race. Can you handle that criticism?

America needs a new generation of men who will take an innocent approach toward dealing with different races. Let us strive to be like the five year old who was not pre-programmed about different races but dealt with them based on how they acted.

Questions
(to discuss and think about or to serve as a written assignment)

1. Has this chapter helped you understand different races better? Yes__ No__

2. The author talks about how little children believe in kindness, gentleness and sharing. Do you still believe in those things? Yes__ No__

3. Do you have friends who are of a different race than you are? Yes__ No__

4. When you talk about your friends, do you describe them by their color first or do you describe them by their personality first?_____

5. What does the picture in the front of the chapter say to you?_____

6. Do any of the kids in your school look like the kids on the picture?

7. Read the last sentence in the first paragraph._____ Do you agree with the author when he says that young kids do not hate unless they are taught to? Yes__ No__

8. America needs for the different races to get along. Do you want to be like old mean people who say mean things or do you want to be like the 5-year-old who gives everybody a fair chance?
_____

9. Sometimes adults are mean because somebody of a different race has treated them badly at some point in their life. If someone of a different race treats you badly, are you going to blame everybody of that race for what one person did to you? Yes__ No__

10. Name three friends that you have of a different race. _____

11. What do you feel we can do to help people of different races get along better?_____

12. Why was the author puzzled when his daughter called white people, peach people?___

13. Had you ever heard of white people being called peach people before? Yes__ No__ In your opinion, why is it that when she referred to white people as peach people, nobody got mad?

14. Find and complete this sentence: "All she knew was that she_____"

15. Children with pure hearts are always making up names for things. The author says that he thinks it is great when a child does what? (find it)

16. America is different from many nations because America is made up of many different nations and races. This is why we have to work so hard on race relations. How does the author say we should see all people regardless of the color of their skin?_____

17. Find and complete this sentence: As an adult, I have learned to pick_____

18. What does the author say that all races have?_____

19. Find and complete this sentence: There is a lot to learn as_____

20. Does the author say that everybody has to be your friend? Yes__ No__

21. What words do you use to describe people of different races?_____

22. What does the author say about that the words we use behind a person's back?

23. When you hear a person talking about someone, do you wonder if they talk about you like that when you are not around?

24. Find and complete this sentence: People who choose not to interact with people who are different_____"

25. The author states that he has benefitted from having friends of a different race. How did he say he benefitted?_____

26. The author gives three questions you should ask when considering a friend of a different race. Which of the three questions do you agree with the most?

27. In your opinion, can you be friends very long with a person that you do not agree with?

28. It is very difficult to travel with a person who has a different destination than you do. When you are friends with a person whose life goal is different than yours, there will be strains in the relationship. For example, what type of problems do you think you would have if you are determined to go to college and your friend wants to play video games all of the time?

29. Write the last two sentences in this chapter here:_____

30. As a result of what you have learned in this lesson, what specific things do you need to do?

Wisdom From The Elders

Read the quotes and explain them to the boys. Use the questions to begin the discussion. Be sure to work with the boys to compose your own quote that relates to this chapter.

Understanding leads to acceptance, acceptance leads to influence and influence leads to change. B. J. TATUM

1. There are four steps in this process: Understand, accept, influence and change. Think about this. If you understand a person, you can accept them. If you accept them, they will let you influence them. Once you influence them, they will begin to change. The first step begins when you make the effort to understand them. Is there anyone in your class that you have not taken the time to understand?
2. According to this wisdom, if you do not take the time to understand them, what will not happen?
3. In your opinion, how can understanding a person help change the way you feel about them and the way they feel about you?
4. Do you seek to learn about other cultures so that you can understand them?

Prejudice is the child of ignorance. WILLIAM HAZLITT

1. To be prejudiced is to prejudge someone before you meet him. Have you ever prejudged someone before you met him?
2. In your opinion, how stupid is it to judge someone before you meet him?
3. There are two types of ignorance: 1. Ignorance of simply not knowing. 2. Ignorance of not wanting to know. Are there any areas where you are number 2 ignorant?

We hate some persons because we do not know them; and will not know them because we hate them. CHARLES CALEB COLTON

1. It is always necessary for someone to make the first move when there is a disagreement. Are you willing to be the one who takes the first step in getting along with other people?
2. Do you have a good friend who is of another race?

I don't care where you come from, I want to know where you're going. ANDREW YOUNG

1. In America, many adults who were involved in the civil rights movement have put the past behind them and are moving forward in life. Are you more concerned about past racial issues or future racial issues?

One way to make the world better is by improving yourself. WILLIE WILLIAMS

1. When you choose to be kind to other people, your environment immediately becomes a better place. Are you willing to be a person who brings kindness to your classroom and school?

We must define ourselves by the best that is in us, not the worst that has been done to us.
    EDWARD LEWIS
1. When you think of another race of people, do you think of their good qualities or do you think of something bad about them?

People with clenched fists cannot shake hands. RALPH BUNCHE
1. There will always be people who do not want to get along. There will always be people who feel that they are better than everybody else. How will you deal with these people when you meet them? (show them kindness and move on)
2. Do you meet people of different cultures with an open mind?

Why hate when you could spend your time doing other things? MIRIAM MAKEBA
1. Have you ever thought about how much energy it takes to hate someone?
2. Can you remember the last time you were angry with someone and thought about them all day and night, then you went to bed with them on your mind? What did all of that accomplish for you?
3. It is just as easy to look for the good in someone as it is to look for the bad. Which do you look for when you meet someone who is different from you?

Kindness is the language that the deaf can hear and the dumb can understand.
    DESMOND TUTU
1. There are many languages other than words. Have you ever thought of kindness as a language before?
2. Do you extend kindness when you meet someone from a different race?
3. Who do you think of when we discuss kind people?
4. Do you want to be known as a kind person or a tough person?
5. Who is Desmond Tutu?

To love the world is no big chore. It's that miserable guy next door who's the problem.
    GARDNER TAYLOR
1. How do you feel about the kids who sit next to you in class?
2. In your opinion, why is it so difficult to love the people who live next to us?
3. What is it about the people who know us so well that challenges us?

Compose a quote and write it here:_____

_____

Chapter 25

I Will Stay In My Seat
(A Lesson On Concentration)

Definition of concentration: The ability to collect one's thoughts toward one purpose.

Connecting With And Learning From Your Rich, Personal, Painful, Productive Past. There are many things that can distract a person from concentrating. One of the signs of maturity is the ability to focus your thoughts and accomplish what you are working on. In my school years, I was distracted by almost anything: girls, sounds, smells, cars and my imagination. What is your experience as it relates to your ability to concentrate? Reflect and be prepared to share with the boys a situation they will benefit from.

CAUTION: Make it clear to the boys that your ability to concentrate is better now than it was when you were their age. Share with them that if they begin to work on that skill, it will improve greatly as the years pass.

CHARGE: Charge the boys to develop their concentration skills to the point where they are just like the boy in the bubble. They should learn how to block out sounds and events around them so that they can focus on their goal.

ACTIVITY: Try this experiment to test the boys ability to concentrate. Give each boy one of these sentences and challenge him to remember it no matter what happens:
1. The spotted dog fell down the red steps.
2. The blue bird swallowed the red worm.
3. The brown cat ate the grey mouse.

Next, ask one boy to say his ABCS's, another to count to 28 by 2, and the third boy to say the pledge of allegiance. They are to do this at the same time. (Be careful not to let them get too loud.) After they complete saying what you assign them, ask each boy to state the sentence that you previously gave him. To take it a step further, see if any of the boys could say all of the sentences.

Lesson 25

I Will Stay In My Seat

(A Lesson On Concentration)

I remember very clearly the day it happened. It was a bright summer day in Ms. Spat's fourth grade classroom. I became restless and could not sit still. One of the worst things I can think of is when I want to go outside, or at least get out of my seat and the teacher gives us work to do. Finally I couldn't take it any longer, so I got out of my seat to go to the back of the room. I thought that I would sharpen my pencil because that was as good an excuse as any to get out of my seat. As I went to the back of the room, Mack Hendrix, a kid who sat toward the back of the class, stuck his foot out. When his foot went out, I tripped over it and fell. I made a lot of noise and everybody in the class stopped what they were doing and looked at me. Miss Spat's face turned red and she took me to the office.

While I was in the office, I was supposed to explain to Mr. Thompson (the principal) why I was out of my seat. The real problem was that I did not know why I was out of my seat, other than because I was sick of sitting there. I have always wanted to figure out why I had to get up and sharpen my pencil. Why couldn't I have stayed in my seat? Now that I am grown, I think that I know the answer to some of those questions.

I think that a lack of concentration is one of the problems that I had when I was young. I always had difficulty thinking about what I was supposed to be thinking about. For example, we had math class at 11:00. It was very difficult for me to think about anything at 11:00 because that was just before lunch and the cooks were already cooking the lunch and it smelled sooooooo good.

At 2:00 when we studied science, we were talking about the Apollo spaceship. As soon as we started talking about the spaceship, my imagination would get busy and I would pretend that I was the pilot of the ship and we were gliding through the Milky Way. So, one problem that I had as a kid was that I had difficulty concentrating. If you have this problem, I have some suggestions for you that may help you concentrate.

1. Pretend that you are in a bubble and that the other kids around you are outside of that bubble. This way, you cannot hear them or talk to them. Use this bubble only when you need to get work done. After the work is done, you can deflate the bubble until you need it again.

2. When unwanted thoughts pop into you mind, command them to go away. If they do not go away, determine that you will not listen to them. This is what I learned to do when something frightened me. I would ignore the frightening thoughts and tell my brain to think about my ten-speed bike, my train set, or Gerlene, the prettiest girl in our class. With a little practice, you can tell you mind what to think.

3. Learn to imagine what will happen when you are finished with your project. When the teacher gives you an assignment, always imagine what her response will be when you complete the paper and hand it to her with the right answers to the questions.

4. Think about how you will be able to relax and play after you are finished with the project. The ability to concentrate is a skill that you must develop if you are to be successful in life. Teachers and other adults can help you learn how to concentrate. Feel free to ask them to help you.

Remember this point. You can always concentrate on the things that interest you. The difficulty comes when we are required to concentrate on things that may not interest us. The smart young man works very hard at developing an interest in things like math, science and other subjects that he is required to study. Telling yourself that you like these subjects will make concentrating on them easier and will result in better grades.

Questions
(to discuss and think about or to serve as a written assignment)

1. Have you ever had difficulty staying in your seat in school when the sun is shining out side?

2. On a normal day, how long can you stay in your seat?_____

3. Find and complete this sentence: "One of the worst things I can think of_____"

4. Most people sharpen their pencils when they want to get out of their seats. What excuse do you use when you want to get out of your seat?

5. Do you have a problem with daydreaming in school? Yes__ No__ If yes, what do you daydream about?

6. Can you concentrate on a math problem until you solve it? Yes__ No__

7. Look at the picture in the front of the book. What does that picture say to you?

8. Based on how the young man in the picture has blocked the rest of the class out it appears that he has learned how to concentrate. Do you have the ability to block out everybody and concentrate like the boy in the picture? Yes__ No__

9. Are there any additional lessons that you learned from the picture?

10. What do you do when you get bored in school?_____

11. Which TV shows bore you?_____

12. Is your mind strong enough that you can block out the noises in the classroom? Yes__ No__

13. Some people can concentrate on fun things like making a foul shot while the crowd is yelling. Can you concentrate when you play sports? Yes__ No__

14. Can you concentrate on tasks that may not be fun? Yes__ No__

15. Who do you know that really concentrates well?_____

16. The ability to concentrate helps you get your school work finished quickly. Is all of your school work done today? Yes__ No__

17. The author states that when he was young, he could not understand why he could not stay in his seat. Now that he is grown, he says that he thinks he has figured it out. The purpose of this book and the mentoring program is to help you figure out why you do what you do before you become a grown man. What is it that you do that you do not understand why you do it?

18. Find and complete this sentence: "I think that a lack of_____"

19. What did the author say happened at the same time that his math class happened that caused him to have problems concentrating?

20. The author gives several suggestions to help us concentrate. The first suggestion has to do with a bubble. Have you ever tried to do this before? Yes__ No__ Do you think it will help you? Yes__ No__ Look at the picture again and tell me if you think it is helping the boy on the picture.

21. According to the author, you need to learn how to inflate the bubble when you need to concentrate and deflate the bubble once you get your work done. Do you think your imagination is strong enough to do this? Yes__ No__

22. The author says that with a little practice you can command unwanted thoughts to go away. He suggests some things that he would think of instead of the unwanted thoughts. When you do this it is called thought swapping. In other words, you swap unwanted thoughts for the thoughts that you want. Have you ever tried this before? Yes__ No__ Can you name a thought that comes to your mind that you need to swap with a better thought? Yes__ No__

23. Do you ever get excited about finishing a project as you start it? Have you ever started with a blank sheet of paper and pretended that the page was already filled with what you had written? The art of seeing the end before you begin is a great aid in stimulating your mind to focus on the task at hand. What project or assignment are you working on that you need to see as already finished?

24. Find and complete this sentence: "The ability to concentrate is_____"

25. There is a good feeling that comes when you finish a task. All tasks are finished faster when you concentrate. As we come to the end of the questions, are you beginning to understand the importance of learning how to concentrate? Yes__ No__

26. Find and complete this sentence: The smart young man works very hard_____

Wisdom From The Elders

Read the quotes and explain them to the boys. Use the questions to begin the discussion. Be sure to work with the boys to compose your own quote that relates to this chapter.

It doesn't matter what you're trying to accomplish. It's all a matter of discipline. . . I was determined to discover what life held for me beyond the inner-city streets. WILMA RUDOLPH

1. Wilma Rudolph is one of the fastest women in the world. When she was young, she decided that she would develop her craft (track). She concentrated, focused, worked hard and became one of the greatest female track stars of all time. What is the craft that you need to concentrate, focus and work on now while you are young?

2. In your opinion, is there any way to become a track star without working hard? Yes__ No__ Do you know any people your age who want to be great but are not ready to work hard to accomplish that goal?

3. Do you believe that with hard work and discipline, you can accomplish any goal?

There's nothing mysterious about success. It's the ability to stay mentally locked in. MONTEL WILLIAMS

1. Do you look at successful people and see them as different, more talented than you are?

2. According to Montel Williams, what is the key to success?

3. Do you have the ability to lock in and concentrate on a subject until you accomplish your goal? Yes__ No__ If the answer is no, when do you plan to start developing that skill?

Each of us must earn our own existence. And how does anyone earn anything? Through perseverance, hard work, and desire. THURGOOD MARSHALL

1. Perseverance means to keep working and not give up. What subject are you persevering in right now?

2. Does it ever cross your mind that you will be required to earn your own existence and that in just a few years, nobody will feed you and support you?

3. Who was Thurgood Marshall?_____ What significant things did he do?_____

Nothing is easy to the unwilling. NIKKI GIOVANNI

1. Is your attitude toward work positive or negative?_____

2. Many young men in today's society want to sit in front of the video game all day and never work. Does this describe you? Yes__ No__

3. Are you willing to work hard at concentrating in class or is it difficult because you are unwilling to do it?

4. Nothing is easy to the unwilling but when you have a good attitude the work goes much faster. Have you learned the trick that a positive attitude about a task makes the work go faster? Yes__ No__ And the opposite is also true that a bad attitude about a task makes that task longer.

Concentration is the secret of strength in politics, in war, in trade, in short in all management of human affairs. RALPH WALDO EMERSON

1. Super heroes generally have a secret strength that others do not know about. Most successful people have a secret strength that others do not know about. The ability to concentrate is a secret strength that is available to all who work on it. Are you willing to work on and develop the secret strength of concentrating?
2. Do you feel that you will ever pass math class without concentrating?
3. Who was Ralph Waldo Emerson?

Thinking is like loving and dying—each of us must do it for himself. JOSIAH ROYCE

1. It takes a whole lifetime to understand and fully develop our brains. It is a job that has no holidays or time off. Brain development is a task 24/7. Have you ever thought about the fact that you have a brain that will remain small and underdeveloped if you do not exercise it?
2. Are you thinking for yourself about your future or are you depending on teachers and parents to do it for you?

We only think when we are confronted with a problem. JOHN DEWEY

1. If you want to get ahead in life, you must think about more than what has been assigned to you. You must go beyond what you are required to do today and think about your dreams for the future. How much time do you spend thinking about (working out) your future plans?
2. Name some of the times when you concentrate other than in school.
3. Some people sit in front of the idiot box (TV) and never read in their spare time. Do you ever read (develop your brain) in your spare time?

If a man sits down to think, he is immediately asked if he has the headache.
RALPH WALDO EMERSON

1. There is a famous statute of a man sitting with his head in his hand. It is said that this man is thinking. Do you ever sit with your head in your hand while thinking or are you always moving when you think?
2. Does thinking give you a headache?
3. In your opinion, do people expect you to think?
4. Thinking is not daydreaming. Thinking is working very hard to solve a problem. How often do you think?

Compose a quote and write it here:_____

_____

Note to the mentor/teacher: As a result of this lesson, are there any needs that these young men have that can be met by networking with parents, other teachers, social agencies or religious institutions?

I wanted to know the name of every stone and flower and insect and bird and beast. I wanted to know where it got its color, where it got its life-but there was no one to tell me.

GEORGE WASHINGTON CARVER

Chapter 26

Three Kinds of Dumb

Definition of dumb: Lacking normal intelligence, sense or wisdom.

Connecting With and Learning From Your Rich, Personal, Painful, Productive Past. It is very painful for me to look back and see the areas in my life where I have lacked wisdom. I was a very bright kid but very dumb in certain areas. Because of how each of us are raised, we have areas where we are not exposed to wisdom. I was dumb when it came to being streetwise, I was slow to understand where babies come from and for many years I could not understand where the gasoline that I put in the lawn mower went.

What about you? Where were you dumb as a kid? Call up some memories that you can share with the boys. Have fun going down memory lane. Also share with them how you grew in those areas to overcome your dumbness.

CAUTION: Be sensitive to any of the boys who already feel dumb in all areas. Explain to them that this is a discovery session where we seek to identify those areas where we need to grow so that we can begin the process of becoming stronger in our dumb areas.

CHARGE: Charge the boys to always remember that growth is one of the greatest privileges that we have. Let them know that there will come a day when they will be able to look back at their weak areas and laugh at them, just as you can now laugh at yours.

ACTIVITY: Have the boys identify one or more areas where they want to grow. Challenge the boys to begin working to eliminate the unacceptable behavior from their life and set a future date to re-examine the matter.

Lesson 26

Three Kinds of Dumb

When I was a kid, there was a boy in my fifth grade class named Alexander. Alexander was a good kid and we were sorta friends. Alexander was bigger than I was, and I always wanted him to be on my team when we played dodge ball. One thing that always made me sad about Alexander was that he was dumb. What I have learned in life is that there are many ways to be dumb. I know people with Ph.D. degrees who are still dumb in certain ways. My friend Alexander was dumb in three ways.

First of all, he was dumb because nobody could tell him anything. When nobody can tell you anything, you have a problem. If you walked up to Alexander and said: "The bell rang, recess is over and it is time to go inside," he would get mad. I never could understand why he would get mad when you told him something. I think that he just didn't want anybody telling him anything. There are some people who are like that. They just don't want anybody telling them anything at all. Now, to me, that is dumb.

Because of this habit of his, many kids wouldn't talk to Alexander because they did not want him going off on them. When we are dumb in a certain area, we need to work on that area so that we can get better. As we got older, Alexander never did learn to take advice from others and listen to other people. I can look back and see how that really hurt him.

Another way that Alexander was dumb was that he played all of the time. Alexander would throw spit balls across the room while we were taking a test. This was dumb! I was a normal kid and I liked to play, but there are certain times when you really need to be serious. Alexander never knew when that time was because he played all of the time. It was like he was stuck at three years old in this area. I could not get it through his head to stop doing dumb things at the wrong time. Now, I don't want you to think that Alexander was dumb all over. His grades were great, in fact, they were better than mine. This is why I could not understand why he was so dumb in certain areas.

Alexander was dumb in a third way, and that was he did not care about the future. Alexander would goof off when we were facing deadlines. The teacher would tell us that our reports were due on Wednesday and Alexander would wait until Tuesday evening to begin working on his. The future would always catch him unprepared. The future for every kid is adulthood. Smart kids know that unless they die early in a car accident or something, they will grow up. Think about this. Every adult that you see today was once a kid. Time caught up with them and made them adults, and it will happen to you too if you keep living.

Alexander was a normal kid in many ways, but as his friend I remember the three dumb areas that he had. I was always worried about him in his dumb areas because one major mistake while acting dumb can really get you in trouble. I remember when the teacher caught him throwing spit balls during a test. She took him to the principal's office and he was suspended from school for two days. His parents really got on his case and took away many privileges. Even after all of that, guess what? He came back to school and still threw spit balls. I never could understand Alexander in his dumb areas.

Well, the real deal is that you and I have dumb areas also. I want to advise you never to feel bad about being dumb in a certain area. As long as you work on it, you can get better and soon be strong in that area. If you were to ask your mentor, he would probably tell you that he has some dumb areas too. My dumb area has always been talking too much. My friends have told me about this, and it has gotten me into trouble on many occasions. Once in junior high school, the coach said something to me and I smarted off to him when I should have kept my mouth shut. This was dumb. I have been working on that one dumb area for many years, and I am getting better at it. I am learning to open my mouth and talk when I have something good to say and otherwise keep my mouth shut.

What are your dumb areas? Are you honest with yourself about your dumb areas, or are you the person who says: "There is nothing wrong with me." All human beings have faults and areas where we need to grow. Listen to your friends and adults who care about you, and they will show you your dumb areas. Once you have identified them, you can begin to work on growing in those areas. I am happy to report that Alexander did grow up and become an adult, and he did learn how to listen to others. He stopped playing all of the time but he still goofs off a little bit.

Questions
(to discuss and think about or to serve as a written assignment)

1. In my opinion, the word dumb seems very unkind. Do you agree with that?

2. What words or terms would you use to describe people rather than dumb?

3. Do you have any dumb friends? Yes__ No__

4. According to the author, Alexander was dumb in how many ways?_____

5. What was the first way that he was dumb?_____

6. Do you have a problem with people telling you stuff? Yes__ No__

7. Complete this sentence found in the first paragraph of this lesson: "I know people who have _____ "

8. When you are told to do something, does it burn you up? Yes__ No__

9. Do you know people like Alexander who simply will not listen to you no matter how reasonable you are? Yes__ No__

10. Find and complete this sentence: "Because of this habit of his, many_____ "

11. Are there any kids that you stay away from because they are hard to talk to? Yes__ No__

12. Find and complete this sentence: "As we got older, Alexander never did_____ "

13. It is OK to be dumb in certain areas while you are young, but it is not OK to be dumb all of your life. As you read this chapter, did you see any characteristics in Alexander's life that are present in your life?

14. What was the second way that the author said Alexander was dumb?_____

15. Tell the truth and not a lie: Do you play too much? Yes__ No__ Do you play at the wrong time? Yes__ No__ Do you play in the wrong places? Yes__ No__

16. The author said that Alexander did dumb things like threw spit balls across the room. (If you do not answer this next question truthfully, your nose will grow three inches.) When was the last time you did something dumb like that in class?

17. Find and complete this sentence: "I was a normal kid and I liked_____"

18. Do you consider yourself a normal kid? Yes__ No__

19. According to the author, what did Alexander do all of the time?_____

20. The author said that it was like Alexander was stuck at three years old IN THIS AREA. We all have our dumb areas. According to your mother, teachers and friends, in what area are you dumb?

21. Was Alexander dumb in all areas? Yes__ No__   If no, in what areas was he smart?

22. When the author of this book would do something dumb when he was young, his father would say to him: "Son . . . you sure are dumb to be so smart." For many years he did not understand what his father was saying. When he grew up he understood that his father was saying that you are a very smart person but you do dumb things. Can it be said that you are a smart person who does dumb things? Yes__ No__ Sometimes__

23. The author says that Alexander was dumb in a third way. What was it?_____

24. How do you handle the deadlines that you are faced with in school? Do you have your work done on time? . . Do you finish it early? . . Do you wait to the last minute before you get your work done?

25. According to the author, what is the future for every kid?

26. Find and complete this sentence: "Smart kids know that unless they die_____"

27. Is it difficult for you to realize that your parents, principal, teacher, auntie, the President of The United States were all your age once? Is this difficult for you to comprehend?

28. How many major mistakes does it take to get you in trouble?_____

29. What did the author say the real deal was about you and I?_____

30. The author confessed and admitted that he used to run his mouth too much. After working on that dumb area for many years, what did he say he is now learning to do?

31. Are you mature enough to be honest about your dumb areas or do you deny that you have any dumb areas?

Wisdom From The Elders

Read the quotes and explain them to the boys. Use the questions to begin the discussion. Be sure to work with the boys to compose your own quote that relates to this chapter.

Everybody is ignorant, only on different subjects. WILL ROGERS
1. All people are equal because they are ignorant in different areas. The guy who is good at computers usually can't fix his flat tire. The guy who is good at football generally can't sing. Are you ever intimidated by people who seem to be smart in all areas?
2. Once you get to know people, you learn that they are not as good in all areas as you thought they were. Have you ever thought someone was good in every area only to get to know them better and find out that they had their ignorant subjects also?
3. What areas are you most ignorant in?
4. What areas are you the smartest in?
5. What area would you like to see the most improvement this year?

To be ignorant of one's ignorance is the malady of the ignorant. AMOS BRONSON ALCOTT
1. What does malady mean? (look it up)
2. Are you working to discover where your dumb areas are so you can develop them?

There is nothing more frightening than ignorance in action. GOETHE
1. It is a real challenge not to do some of the dumb things that we think of doing. When those thoughts come to our mind, it is very important to challenge them. When you know that you are thinking something dumb, do you challenge the dumb thought or do you accept it?
2. Wise people challenge ignorance when they sense it because they realize how dangerous it is. Have you developed the habit of challenging your personal ignorance?

Your mind is what makes everything else work. KAREEM ABDUL-JABBAR
1. Do you ever think of your mind as the strongest muscle in your body?
2. The mind is the central command center that regulates your whole world. In your opinion, how important is it to develop and strengthen your mind?
3. Who is Kareem Abul-Jabbar?

All of us are born in a state of ignorance, and many of us never change residence. EFFI BARRY
1. Can you remember the dumbest thing that you did when you were young? . . Have you done it recently or have you stopped?
2. We are all born not knowing things. There is nothing wrong with that, but the problem comes when we do not learn. Are you decreasing your ignorance in math by doing your classroom assignments and homework?
3. Are you satisfied with your dumb areas or are you going to challenge them with wisdom?

Some people dream of great accomplishments, while others stay awake and do them. CONSTANCE NEWMAN

1. Be careful of people who always speak of doing something in the future. Always observe them to see what they are doing right now. . . What are you doing right now?

2. Dreams should inspire action. Dreams should never inspire more dreams. It is important to work on your dreams to see if there is any possibility of making them a reality. The author of this book dreamed of it first. Then he worked for over a year, sometimes all night long to make it a reality. . . What dream are you currently working to make a reality?

3. The greatest accomplishment that I can think of is self-improvement. Are you dreaming of improving yourself, or are you awake and working on it?

The mind is like the stomach. It is not how much you put into it that counts, but how much it digests. ALBERT JAY NOCK

1. Do you soak in life or does life just pass you by?

2. We live in an information driven society. It is not possible to retain all that we are exposed to, but have you learned how to remember the things that will help you and ignore the other stuff?

3. In order to digest the information that comes into your brain you must take time to think about it. Do you regularly take time to think about the important things?

4. What have you learned today that you keep thinking about?

When I was a boy of fourteen, my father was so ignorant I could hardly stand to have the old man around. But when I got to be twenty-one, I was astonished at how much the old man had learned in seven years. MARK TWAIN

1. Why do you think the fourteen year old saw his father as ignorant?

2. Do you ever view your father, mother or other adult as ignorant?

3. Something interesting happened between fourteen and twenty one. Mark Twain said that the old man learned a lot in seven years. Do you think that is what really happened?

4. Do you think that as you get older, you will be able to appreciate the wisdom of older people more than you do now?

5. Tell the truth and not a lie: Do you view older people as sources of wisdom, or can you hardly stand to have them around?

Compose a quote and write it here: _____

_____

Note to the mentor/teacher: As a result of this lesson, are there any needs that these young men have that can be met by networking with parents, other teachers, social agencies or religious institutions?

The only discipline that lasts is self-discipline.

BUM PHILLIPS

Chapter 27

What I'm Gonna Be When I Grow Up

Definition of grown up: Grown up is that point in life when you must support yourself. Occupation or what you want to be is the method that you will use to support yourself.

Connecting With and Learning From Your Rich, Personal, Painful, Productive Past. As a child I wanted to be a bus driver. I was very impressed with the bus driver who would sit at the bottom of the hill that we lived on. Each time I got on the bus I would marvel at the knobs, handles and buttons that were at the disposal of the driver. Since I have grown up, my aspirations have changed and I have actually had several professions.

Share with the boys your childhood dreams and how they have developed over the years. Share how time and wisdom affect your career choices. Talk about how the work force has changed over the last few years.

CAUTION: Be careful not to dampen the dreams of the boys. Most young boys want to be in the NBA. We know that this is a far-fetched dream but who knows, one of the boys that you mentor may actually play for the NBA at some point in the future. Encourage their dreams, but also encourage them to prepare for a non-spectacular career like teaching, carpentry, sales, etc.

CHARGE: Charge the boys to start preparing now for the career of their choice. It is possible to know at an early age what you want to spend the rest of your life doing. Charge the boys not to take the easy way out by not giving any thought to their choice, but to give some serious thought to their choice.

ACTIVITY: Ask each boy to make three choices for their career. List the choices in order of priority. Ask each boy to do research on what is necessary to accomplish the goal of becoming what he wants to be. Have them report to the group next session.

Lesson 27

What I'm Gonna Be When I Grow Up

When I was a kid we lived on the top of a hill, and in order to get downtown we had to walk one mile and catch the bus. As a little boy, I was extremely impressed with the big red bus that would take us downtown. There were several things about the bus which impressed me. First of all, the doors in the back opened and closed by magic (or so I thought). The driver had this BIG steering wheel that clicked when he would turn the bus, and the air brakes made this hissing sound. To me, that bus driver was the coolest man alive and he had the best job in the world.

Most kids choose what they want to be based on what impresses them while they are young. When you are five years old, a big bus, truck, race car or airplane will impress you. When you turn ten years old there are other things that impress you, and by the time you are eighteen years old you have a whole different set of things that impress you. So, when a 5-year-old boy is asked what he wants to be, he will usually choose something that impresses a five-year-old.

What I want you to consider is not what impresses you but what are you good at. What skill or talent do you have that you do naturally and like to do? Some kids are born with a love for music, math, athletics, communicating, dancing, healing, competing, designing, building and many other things. I have always had a love for music. I started playing the guitar when I was in the fifth grade and I grew up and played professionally. I also had an interest in auto mechanics and building houses. I ended up getting a degree in music, teaching school and later becoming a minister.

Most kids have more than one talent or gift. This is good because you *never* know what you will end up doing in life. You may plan to do one thing and end up doing another. You may go to college and train to be a nurse and end up with a career selling houses. The world is changing constantly, and there is no telling what will be in demand fifteen years from now.

In the 1930's a man could make good money playing a saxophone because there was no such thing as a record, cassette or CD. All music was live music. Then they invented the record and people started listening to records instead of going to hear live bands play. This has also happened in more recent years in professions like teaching, law, farming and other professions. So when you think about what you want to be, you had better consider how the world will change in the next 20 years.

231

One thing that amazes me is how many young boys want to be in the NBA. It is good to dream and I encourage you to dream, but you also must look at the numbers. Very, very few young men will make it to professional sports. You may be one who does make it, but the odds are very much against that. So don't sit back in your seat, look up at adults and say: "I don't have to study because I'm going to play ball for a living." Adults have read the statistics and they realize that the odds are against you. I am not saying that you should not strive for the NBA, but you should have a back-up plan in case you don't make it.

You see, everybody loves the athlete while he is playing. After his playing days are over, it seems like nobody loves him anymore. That's the way it is when a cute young man plays ball. The bad thing is that the cute young man everybody loved will turn into an adult that nobody wants to pay because he can't play any more.

I suggest that you start now reading everything that you can get your hands on so that you will be prepared to do whatever you choose to do when you become 17 years old. Reading is the key, because if you can read, you can learn anything that you want to learn. If you don't read well, you will be hampered as you seek employment.

What do you do well now? What strength do you have in the classroom? Seek to identify your strengths and start exercising them now so that they will be ready when you grow up. If you are good at organizing things, ask the teacher to let you help her organize the classroom materials. If you have leadership abilities, make sure that you take advantage of every opportunity to lead small groups in class. If you are good at handling and counting money, ask to be the treasurer in your school groups.

Once you figure out what you like and are good at, you should begin to work in that area to prepare you for your future job. If you want to see a miserable adult, find one who has to work at a job that he or she does not like. Your working years can be happy, productive years if you begin to prepare for your future job now.

Questions
(to discuss and think about or to serve as a written assignment)

1. What do you want to be when you grow up?_____

2. The author was impressed with big busses when he was little. What impresses you?

3. To the author, the bus driver was the coolest man alive. Who is the coolest man alive to you?

4. In the second paragraph the author makes the point that what impresses you changes as you get older. Do you think that what impresses you now will impress you in five years?

5. What profession really impresses you right now?_____

6. Do you see someone in the first grade as really immature? Yes__ No__ Do you feel that their decisions are childish? Yes__ No__ When a first grader says that he wants to be a astronaut does that sound silly to you? Yes__ No__ How do you think someone five years older than you are feel when they hear you talk?

7. What can you do well right now?_____

8. What do you do that others feel you do well?_____

9. List five things that you really enjoy doing?_____

10. What did the author begin doing in the 5th grade and continue doing into adulthood?

11. Do you think that you will only do one job in your life or have several?

12. Find and complete this sentence: "What I want you to consider is_____"

13. The author makes the point that some kids are born with a love for certain things. What do you have a love for?_____

14. Have you began working to develop that area that you love? Yes__ No__

15. The author stated that he had a love for music. At what age did he begin playing the guitar?

16. When do you think it is too early to start working to develop yourself in that area that you love?

17. Find and complete this sentence: "So when you think about what you want_____

18. The author states that everybody loves the athlete while he is playing. What did the author say happens after his playing days are over?_____

19. How good do you feel your chances are of becoming a professional athlete?_____

20. Many young men dream of playing in the NBA or NFL. Most of them do not realize that several million other young men have the same dream and there is not room for all of them. Are you going to trust your future to a dream that has very low odds of becoming a reality or are you going to work to develop a plan to provide for yourself and family while you continue to dream?

21. Some young men justify not doing well in school by saying that they are going to be in the NBA so school is not important. Do you believe this? Yes__ No__

22. Find and complete this sentence: "Reading is the key because if you_____"

23. What are you doing to improve your reading ability?_____

24. Find and complete this sentence: "Once you figure out what you like and are good at__"

25. What makes an adult miserable?_____

26. Ask your teacher at what age he/she decided to become a teacher._____

27. Do you think that you want to work with people, or would you rather work with machines?

28. The author said that he started playing the guitar when he was in the fifth grade and grew up to play professionally. What are you doing right now that you could continue into adulthood and make money doing?_____

29. The author mentioned how the job market had changed in several areas. Can you think of any changes in the job market since you have been living? _____

30. Are you a flexible person? Yes__ No__ Will you adapt with the changing job market around you, or will you be left behind as society changes?_____

31. Read or write the last sentence in the chapter again._____

Wisdom From The Elders

Read the quotes and explain them to the boys. Use the questions to begin the discussion. Be sure to work with the boys to compose your own quote that relates to this chapter.

My father taught me how to work; he did not teach me to love it. I never did like to work, and I don't deny it. I'd rather read, tell stories, crack jokes, talk, laugh—anything but work.
ABRAHAM LINCOLN
1. Have you been taught how to work? Yes__ No__ What man has taught you to work?
2. Tell the truth and not a lie: Do you like work? . .   Do you love work? . .
3. In your opinion, how important is it for a young man to know how to work?
4. What would you rather do than work?
5. How can knowing how to work help you in school?

The only place where success comes before work is a dictionary. VIDAL SASSON
1. Do you believe that success in life is going to come to you without working?
2. Are you waiting for success or are you working for success?
3. Some boys never work because their mother gives them everything. Are you expecting your mother to give you everything or are you preparing to work for what you want in life?

I knew I had to make it. I had the determination to go on, and my determination was to be somebody. JAMES BROWN
How determined are you to make it, to grow up and be successful?
Is there a little voice in the back of your head telling you that you've GOT to make it?
Are you a person who has the determination, drive, gusto, force to be successful in life?

We make a living by what we get, but we make a life by what we give. BARBARA HARRIS
1. Many people are rich and miserable. Money can not make you happy. In your opinion, what can make you happy?
2. We should get to give to get to give to get to give. We never get to get more to get more to get more. Between the two, which do you do?
3. Which do you want, a job that will make society better or a job to make you rich?

The best way to develop any career is heart first. MALCOLM-JAMAL WARNER
1. What do you think Malcolm means when he says heart first?
2. Although you are still young, do you know what occupation you have a heart for?
3. How badly do you want to be rich?

No task, rightly done is truly private. It is part of the world's work. WOODROW WILSON
1. Did you realize that the quality of work that you do as an adult will affect many people?
2. Every job affects others. Consider the auto mechanic who fixes the brakes on the car that you ride in or the farmer who grows the food or the printer who printed this book. When one person

does a poor job it impacts many people in society. Are you committed to striving for excellence in what you are doing now and in your future job? Yes__ No__

3. Who was Woodrow Wilson? (look it up)

The best career advice given to the young is, "Find out what you like doing best and get someone to pay you for doing it." KATHARINE WHITEHORN

If you could do what you wanted to do all day, what would you do.

Have you thought about how you could get someone to pay you for doing what you like to do?

How do you think people feel who have to work all day at a job that they do not enjoy?

In your opinion, how can an education help you work the job you want to work?

If a man will not work, he shall not eat. II THESSALONIANS 3:10

Do you feel that people should get free food or should they work for it?

What do you think should happen to a healthy man who refuses to work?

Hunger is a great motivator. Have you ever been hungry?

I am only an average man, but, by George, I work harder at it than the average man. THEODORE ROOSEVELT

1. Are you an average worker or a hard worker?

2. Are you working hard to obtain your current level of success or are you doing just enough to get by?

3. Who was Theodore Roosevelt?

It is only through labor and painful effort, by grim energy and resolute courage, that we move on to better things. THEODORE ROOSEVELT

1. Theodore Roosevelt uses several terms that we need to look at. The first term is painful effort. What does the term painful effort make you think of? . .   In what area of life are you investing painful effort? Home__ School__ Sports__ Other__

2. The second term that Theodore Roosevelt used was grim energy. What do you see in your mind when you hear grim energy? . . Grim energy is the same as grunt work. It is effort that sees no immediate reward. If is very difficult because no one is cheering and there is no encouragement to help you along the way. Is there any task that you are trying to accomplish right now in which you are using grim energy?

3. Roosevelt then uses the term "resolute courage." Resolute means that you have a made up mind that nothing can change. Resolute courage is courage that can not be defeated or turned around. This former President of the United States says that these are the qualities that are necessary for us to move forward in life. ARE YOU PREPARED TO DEVELOP THESE QUALITIES IN YOUR LIFE?

Compose a quote and write it here:_____

_____

What a man thinks of himself, that is what determines, or rather indicates his fate.

HENRY DAVID THOREAU

Chapter 28

The Truth About The Truth

Definition of truth: the actual facts of a case or situation.

Connecting With and Learning From Your Rich, Personal, Painful, Productive Past. We all can remember times in our past when we violated basic, common-sense truth and suffered the consequences. Pick one or two situations from you past that you could share with the boys. Be sure to tell the story with passion.

CAUTION: Caution the boys to test all truth by history. Use history to validate your claims. Call history, science and medicine as witnesses to the truth. Remember that you have lived long enough to see what does and does not work.

Some examples of truth that could be used to make your point are:
● The truth about cigarettes: Although it was a popular fad, the truth is that they kill you.

● The truth about debt: The fact that it is easy to get into but very difficult to get out of.
● The truth about relationships: It takes more than love to make a marriage/relationship work, it takes commitment.

CHARGE: Charge the boys to make truth their friend by obeying it. Remind them that truth is a wonderful friend but a ruthless enemy.

ACTIVITY: Discuss truth as it relates to strangers who approach children and talk to them. In other words, are these people likely to tell you the truth? Mention the following individuals to the boys and ask the boys which persons that they feel would tell them the truth: close friend, teacher, drug pusher, parent, religious leader, someone who wants to have sex with you, mentor, coach, principal, a known liar.

Lesson 28

The Truth About The Truth

I have always been a pretty obedient child. Most of the time, my mother only had to tell me things once. The reason that she only had to tell me once was that I had learned that mom usually knew what she was doing and she would not tell me wrong. My older brother loved to tell me wrong things, so I always had to question anything that he said.

I guess you could say that my mother told the truth. I learned that the truth would always get me in the end if I disobeyed it. My classic memory about disobeying the truth was the time that my mother told me not to touch the lamp in the living room. You see, we had this old lamp that was coming apart at the top. If you were not careful, it would shock you. Well, I did not listen to my mother and I went to turn the lamp on. I touched the raw metal and immediately 110 volts of electricity flowed through my body, causing my bones to jolt and my teeth to rattle. The shock that I received was a shock of truth.

If you ignore the truth about life and specific things, you are bound to get some shocks in life. My friend Terry would always ignore the truth that his mother told him. When I was a kid, we had to walk a long way to school. On the way, there were two busy streets that we had to cross. Terry's mom told him only to cross the street at the corner while the light was green because it was safer than crossing in the middle of the block.

Well, as you might suspect, Terry did not listen to the truth that his mother shared with him. He proceeded to cross the street in the middle of the block. One sunny day after school, he was hit by a little old lady driving a Cadillac. She did not see him because the sun was shining in her face. Terry was not killed in the accident, but his left knee was crushed and today he walks with a limp in his right leg. This limp reminds him of the truth that he ignored.

Truth can be your best friend or it can be a force in your life that constantly corrects you when you disobey it. You see, it works this way. Truth sits in the middle of the road of life. There is no way to go above , below, or around it. Truth will test the choices that you have made and it will reward you with what you deserve, good or bad.

I can remember a boy in my neighborhood named Raymond. Raymond was a bully who would beat us kids up for no reason. He ignored the truth that if you treated people badly, someone will come along and treat you badly. One day Raymond knocked Jamie's front tooth out for no reason at all. It seemed like every day Raymond was causing someone pain. Well, one morning some people found Raymond in the alley behind the recreation center. He was bleeding badly and later died. Nobody knew who did it or what the motive was, but I heard an old person say that if you treat people badly, someone will treat you badly.

Truth was Raymond's enemy, but I decided early in life to make truth my friend. I know that if you treat people with kindness, kindness will come back to you. When I was younger I owned a truck. I helped a lot of people with my truck and rarely was paid for it. A few years later I sold my truck and moved to another state. I found it interesting that on several occasions when I needed a truck, there was always one available "free of charge." There are many, many other stories I could tell about how I did a good deed and later on truth determined that someone should do a good deed for me.

Well, what about you? Are you doing things that will make truth your friend or will truth repay you with negative consequences a few years from now?

Questions
(to discuss and think about or to serve as a written assignment)

1. Everyday you are challenged to filter what you see through the truth that you know. For example. When you see an ad with someone smoking or a teenage smoking you should ask yourself. What does truth say about smoking?_____

2. If you are approached by some young men who ask you to go to the mall with them and steal some stuff, you have two choices: The first choice (which is mindless) would be to go with them. The second choice would be to filter what you have been asked to do through you're the truth that you know about stealing. If you did that, would you go to the mall with them?

3. The author stated that he was a pretty obedient child. Are you an obedient young person?

4. What did the author do to receive what he called a shock of truth?_____

5. Have you ever done something that you were told not to do and as a result suffered pain?

6. Why did the author say that he had to question what his older brother told him?_____

7. Is there anyone that you have to question what they tell you because they have tole you a lot to lies? Yes__ No__

8. What does truth say about running from the police?_____

9. Do your parents(s) tell you the truth? Yes__ No__

10. Find and complete this sentence: If you ignore the truth about life and_____

11. List five adults who share truth with you on a regular basis._____

12. Are you obedient to the truth? Yes__ No__

13. Are you a daredevil who is tempted to defy the truth like my friend Terry did? Yes__ No__

14. What does Terry have in his right leg that reminds him of the truth he ignored?_____

15. Find and complete this sentence: Truth can be your best friend or it_____

16. Do you have any scars on your body that are a result of ignoring truth? Yes__ No__

17. Find and complete this sentence: "Truth will test the choices that you_____"

18. Which truth did Raymond ignore?_____

19. Raymond had an encounter with a Cadillac. Do you think that you could bump heads with a Cadillac and win? Yes__ No__ For Raymond, it was a Cadillac but for other people it may be something different. Do you have any friends who have had a run in with something very powerful as a result of ignoring truth? Yes__ No__ If yes, what did they run in to?

20. Raymond ignored the truth because he got away for many years. If you could get away from the truth for twelve years, would you ignore it? Yes__ No__

21. Truth goes down to the crossroads of time and waits for you. Truth never gets old and dies nor does it ever forget. Based on this fact, what type of person ignores the truth?

22. There was a young man in my town who burglarized homes. The police and everybody in his community knew that he was guilty, but they could not catch him. After several years of illegal activity, truth finally caught him. He was finally caught and sentenced to several years in prison. How do you think he felt when the judge said: "Ten years!"_____

23. Have you decided to make truth your friend? Yes__ No__

24. The author learned a very important truth early in life that he has sought to live by. Find and complete this sentence? I know that if you treat people_____

25. What is the lesson that the author learned about truth from his truck?_____

26. The author used his truck to help others and later found out that others helped him. In what area are you helping others now so that later in life others will help you?

27. The author shared one of his favorite stories about disobeying the truth and getting shocked. What is your favorite story about disobeying the truth?_____

28. Do you have a favorite memory about obeying truth? Yes__ No__ If yes, what is it? If no, you may want to think about it for a while because we have all had incidents that have resulted from ignoring the truth. It is healthy to talk about them and when you can laugh about them. It is not a good sign when you refuse to think about it. As a result of this lesson, do you think you will be alert to make truth your friend and not your enemy? Yes__ No__

Wisdom From The Elders

Read the quotes and explain them to the boys. Use the questions to begin the discussion. Be sure to work with the boys to compose your own quote that relates to this chapter.

Facts do not cease to exist because they are ignored. ALDOUS HUXLEY

1. What is your definition of a fact?
2. We are all tempted to live in our imaginary worlds. Truth and facts always bring us back to reality. Have you ever watched a TV show that was fiction and enjoyed the fantasy while the show was on? When the author was young he used to watch Super Man fly. One day he thought he would try it and jumped off his grandmother's porch. That was a very painful lesson which taught that it is important to distinguish between truth and fantasy. Are you good at distinguishing between truth and fantasy or do you sometimes get it confused?
3. Have you ever tried to ignore a fact hoping that it would go away, a fact like your homework is due tomorrow?

The truth is cruel, but it can be loved and it makes free those who have loved it.
   GEORGE SANTAYANA

1. In your opinion, why do some people think truth is cruel?
2. Do you love the truth or hate it?
3. People who do not like the truth generally fight it. When they fight it they ALWAYS lose. If you could advise these people, what would you tell them?
4. The man or boy who works with the truth and does not fight it is free. Are you free?

I don't give them hell. I just tell the truth and they think it is hell. HARRY S. TRUMAN

1. Have you ever heard the term: "give them hell?" Yes__ No__ It means to give them a hard time. Truman is saying that to many people the truth is painful. Why do you think the truth is so difficult for so many people to bear?
2. Have you ever been around someone who was telling lies on another person? Yes__ No__ If yes, did you interject the truth or did you just stand there and listen?
3. Who was Harry S. Truman?

Pure truth, like pure gold, has been found unfit for circulation because men have discovered that it is far more convenient to adulterate the truth than to refine themselves. CHARLES CALEB COLTON

1. This wisdom is saying that people find it easier to change what truth is than to change and do what is right. Do you know anyone who does something wrong and will say that it is right?
2. To adulterate something is to mix some bad in with the good. The end result being something that is less than it was meant to be. Do you ever try to mix a little bit of lie in with the truth that you tell?
3. When you hear the truth, do you change your behavior to comply with the truth or do you try to change the truth?

There's no free lunch. Don't feel entitled to anything you don't sweat and struggle for.
      MARIAN WRIGHT EDLEMAN

1. The truth is that technology has made life very pleasant for us, but in order to live a successful life you will still have to work very hard. Do you always work hard to do your best or do you sometimes slack off?

2. Many young men live with their mothers and never prepare to take care of themselves. One day, the truth catches up with them and they have to move out, only to learn how difficult it is to make a living with no education.

3. What does it mean to "feel entitled"? (that you deserve something)

4. Do you agree or disagree that you are not entitled to anything that you do not sweat for?

5. Who is Marian Wright Edleman?

Truth is the property of no individual but is the treasure of all men. RALPH WALDO EMERSON

1. Have you ever thought of truth as something that you can own?

2. If it was possible to own truth, how much truth would you want to own?

3. If it were possible to own truth, in your opinion, who in America would own the most truth?

4. If it were possible to own truth, would you sell some of it?

5. You have a mentor who is sharing truth about life with you. Do you view the new truth that you are learning about life as you would view treasure?

6. Do you know of any truth that you feel is yours personally?

7. Emerson says that truth is the treasure of all men. Why do you think he said that?

Some people handle truth carelessly; others never touch it at all. ANONYMOUS

1. Some people can look you right in the face and tell a big lie. Can you do that?

2. In your opinion, what do you think it means to handle the truth carelessly?

3. It is reported that George Washington cut down the cherry tree and because he was a truthful person, he told his father what he had done. What is your attitude about the truth?

4. Have you ever met someone who told lies all of the time? Yes__ No__ If yes, what do you think was wrong with that person?

Get the facts at any price, and hold on tightly to all the good sense you can get.
      PROVERBS 23:23

1. Everybody makes decisions about life based on the information that they have. What type of decisions do you think will be made when a person has the wrong facts about life?

2. Have you ever known what was right but did not do it because of pressure from other young people your age?

Compose a quote and write it here:_____

_____

He that seeks trouble
always finds it.

ENGLISH PROVERB

Chapter 29

Peer Pressure

Definition of peer pressure: A peer is a person who is your equal chronologically. Association with peers causes pressure when we allow their lives or words to pressure us to modify our lives.

Connecting With and Learning From Your Rich, Personal, Painful, Productive Past. Unfortunately, most people struggle with peer pressure at some point in life, although a large percentage of those who struggle in this area would never tell anyone about it. A very healthy approach to peer pressure is to share it with someone who can give you perspective on your strengths and abilities and help you again focus on personal development.

Share with the boys some of your struggles in this area. It will impress them when you show them that you have struggled, just as they may be struggling now. Use a particular situation that you overcame to show them that peer pressure is one of life's passing annoyances. Tell them how you use positive peer pressure to motivate you and how you ignore negative peer pressure.

CAUTION: As always, we focus on the positive potential that is available in each of us. Do not let the lesson degenerate into the bashing of those who have it together. Peer pressure is a roommate of jealousy, and we must guard against hating those who cause pressure in our lives.

CHARGE: Charge the boys to make positive peer pressure their friend. Teach them to let it serve as a motivator and not an intimidator. Remind them that every situation of pressure is an opportunity for them to rise to a new level of excellence in their own lives.

ACTIVITY: Share with the boys a situation in your life where you were under pressure because of the excellence of another. Also share with them how you came out of that situation a better man. Next, ask the boys to share a situation where they struggle with the excellence of another person. Remind them that it is OK to be transparent and share because you shared with them. After they identify the person or situation where they struggle, together seek to devise a system to benefit from the pressure of the situation.

Lesson 29

Peer Pressure

Peer pressure is something that parents have always worried about. When I was a kid, my parents worried about me being affected by peer pressure. Now that I am grown and have kids of my own, I worry about them being exposed to the wrong kind of peer pressure. My kids go to school with many other kids. Some of these kids have not been taught right from wrong. Kids who have not been taught right from wrong may do bad things like have sex at an early age, sell drugs, cuss the teachers and many other bad things.

Now that I am grown, I understand things about peer pressure that I did not understand when I was a kid. One thing that I know now is that not all peer pressure is bad. There are some kids who put positive pressure on others they hang around with. I can remember a kid like this when I was growing up. His name was Charles. Charles was a good kid and everybody liked him. He made good grades and was very confident about who he was and where he wanted to go.

I always admired Charles because he did not let the negative pressure get to him. I never told him that I admired him, I just watched him. I wished that I could walk away from peer pressure and not let it affect me like Charles did. Charles had learned something very important. He had learned how to be peer pressure and not give in to peer pressure. This is the key to success with peer pressure. Learn to be positive peer pressure to the other kids and don't let them be negative peer pressure to you.

You can be positive peer pressure to other kids when you do the following things:
1. Have confidence in who you are and what you want to do in life.
2. Don't be impressed when other people have things that you don't have, such as clothes, fancy hair, good grades, a big house or anything like that.
3. Don't be impressed when other people do things that you don't do such as smoke cigarettes, use foul language, stay out later than they should, experiment with drugs, steal things or anything like that.
4. Don't compare yourself to others but compare yourself to the best person that you can possibly be.
5. Strive for perfection in everything that you do.

Learning to be positive peer pressure is one key to becoming a successful person. In order to be positive peer pressure in someone's life, you must have some positive things happening in your life. Nobody is going to be motivated by you when you are not doing your best. It is easy to do wrong, but it is a challenge to do the right thing when others are doing wrong things. Wrong is wrong even if everybody does it and right is right even if nobody does it. Choose to do the right thing even if everybody chooses to do the wrong thing.

Peer pressure can be used as a positive force in your life. It can be used to motivate you to do better. If there is someone in your class who makes better grades than you do, you should try to find out why they are making better grades and use them as positive peer pressure to help you do better. Positive peer pressure is actually someone setting a good example for you. When you observe the good examples around you, do not ignore them. Allow them to motivate you to do better. It is important to resolve to be good peer pressure rather than giving in to bad peer pressure. Kids give in to bad peer pressure for many reasons. Here are a few:

1. They have no plans for their life. If you have not decided where you want to go in life, you can just follow anybody who gets in front of you. If you have plans for your future, then you know whom you should follow to help you get to where you should be.

2. They feel inferior. Many, many young people feel like they are worth less than those around them. It takes very little for some young people to feel inferior. When people feel inferior, they want to feel better about themselves. Hanging out with someone who seems to have his life together usually makes a person who feels inferior feel better. The only problem is that the inferior person begins to act like the person who seems like he has it all together. Often times inferior people imitate people who only have it together on the outside but are falling apart on the inside.

3. They do not have positive friends. Positive friends are very, very important for people who want to do well in life. The reason is that everybody begins to look like and act like the people that they hang around with.

4. They don't have parental support. Because of divorce, absent dads, drugs and many other problems, some boys do not have parents to lead them like they should. When this happens, the young man must decide to do the right thing even if his parents do not help him.

Good peer pressure and bad peer pressure will always be around to hound you. The question is which one you will choose to follow, the good pressure or the bad pressure.

Questions
(to discuss and think about or to serve as a written assignment)

1. In your own words, tell me what peer pressure is._____

2. Do your parents worry about you being affected by the wrong kind of peer pressure? Yes__ No__

3. Do you feel that your parents have any reason to be concerned about peer pressure?

4. Are there some boys in your school that could possibly be a bad influence on you?

5. Are there some boys in your neighborhood that could possibly be a bad influence on you?

6. What are you currently doing to avoid the young men who could be a bad influence on you?

7. In your opinion, are your parents and teachers better at identifying bad influences than you are?

8. Is all peer pressure bad? Yes__ No__

9. Who can give an example of good peer pressure?_____

10. Do you think that adults have to deal with peer pressures? Yes__ No__

11. The author talks about kids who have not been taught right from wrong. Are there any young people in your school who act like they have not been taught right from wrong? Yes__ No__ If yes, do you ever let them influence you?

12. Find and complete this sentence: There are some kids who put positive_____

13. The author stated that Charles was very confident about who he was and where he wanted to go. Can you say the same thing for yourself?

14. The author says that he admired Charles but what is it that he never told him:_____

15. Is there anybody who is really positive that you admire in your school? Yes__ No__

16. Have you ever told them? Yes__ No__

17. Find and complete this sentence. Charles had learned something very important. He had learned how_____

18. Tell the truth and not a lie: Which most describes you, a person who is positive peer pressure to others or a person who responds to negative peer pressure from others.

19. Find and complete the following sentence: Learn to be positive peer_____

20. The author lists five things that will help you become good peer pressure with other kids. Which one thing do you need to work the hardest at?_____

21. Are you impressed with some of the negative things that other kids seem to do and get away with? Yes__ No__

22. What is one key to becoming a successful person?_____

23. What does this statement mean to you. "Wrong is wrong even if everybody does it and right is right even if nobody does it?_____

24. In your opinion, is that any way that wrong can ever be right and right can be wrong?

25. Give an example of how to use good peer pressure to help you do better in life._____

26. Find and complete this sentence: It is important to resolve to be_____

27. The author gives four reasons many young people give in to peer pressure. In your opinion which of the four reasons affects the most kids?_____

28. Tell the truth and not a lie: Which of the four reasons affect you the most?_____

29. Do you have plans for your life? Yes__ No__

30. Do you feel inferior in any of these ways: sports, smarts, looks, money? Yes__ No__

31. Do you have positive friends? Yes__ No__ If yes, name them_____

32. Do you have parental support? Yes__ No__ If not, what are you doing about it?____

33. The choice is yours. Which type of peer pressure do you choose to follow, good or bad?

Wisdom From The Elders

Read the quotes and explain them to the boys. Use the questions to begin the discussion.
Be sure to work with the boys to compose your own quote that relates to this chapter.

I don't know the key to success, but the key to failure is trying to please everybody.
   BILL COSBY
1. Do you plan to be successful?
2. What will be the key to your success?
3. How many kids in your school do you try to please?
4. How do you think that trying to please everybody will make you a failure?
5. Do you agree or disagree that peer pressure makes you want to please everybody?

Learn to see, listen, and think for yourself. MALCOLM X
1. It takes a lot of courage to think and act for yourself. Do you have that kind of courage?
2. Tell the truth and not a lie: Are you a leader of your peers or a follower?
3. Do you figure things out for yourself or do you believe what people tell you?
4. Are you good at telling when people are lying to you?
5. One of the benefits of getting older is that you do not care what other people think about your clothes, hair, appearance and stuff like that. Do you wear certain clothes, talk a certain way because other people wear them?

A river can't rise beyond its source. What's in the seed determines the fruit. T.M. ALXANDER
1. Understanding your source is very important. The way you think, the things you do are all determined by the source you feel is important. That source may be your friends, parents, teachers or others. What source most determines how you act?
2. Many young people use their friends at school as the source of their behavior. Have you ever thought about how much your parent(s) influence you compared to how much your peers influence you?

Always strive to be more than that which you are, if you wish to obtain that which you are not.   S. B. FULLER
1. Have you learned how to make peer pressure a positive thing? For example, choose to be pressured by the excellent students in the school and not by those who are the most popular.)

If there is no struggle, there is no progress. FREDERICK DOUGLASS
1. Living life is like being in a moving river. If you just sit there you will be swept down stream. In order to get anywhere you must swim against the stream. Are you swimming against the stream or are you allowing life to sweep you away.
2. Some days the struggle is to do what you should do instead of what the other boys want you to do. Do you generally win the struggle against negative peer pressure?

If you expect somebody else to guide you, you'll be lost. JAMES EARL JONES

1. Tell the truth and not a lie: Do you have a direction (dream) of your own, or are you following the dream of some famous athlete, musician or actor?

2. To initiate means to start something. To respond means to do something because someone else has done something. Are you an initiator or a responder?

If a man is called to be a street sweeper, he should sweep streets even as Michelangelo painted, or as Beethoven composed music, or as Shakespeare wrote poetry. He should sweep streets so well that all the host of heaven and earth will pause to say, there lived a great street sweeper who did his job well. MARTIN LUTHER KING, JR.

1. Would you have a problem sweeping streets?

2. In a sense, all jobs are the same because all jobs should be done well. This is a discipline that should be learned while you are young. You can develop this discipline now by keeping your room clean, your desk straight, and being on time with assignments in school. If you are doing these things now, it is highly likely that you will be a very successful person. Are you doing these things now?

3. Who was Beethoven?

4. Does it make any sense to you when you are asked to do your school work the same way Beethoven composed music?

5. Who was Shakespeare?

6. Do you understand what we mean when we say do your math homework with the same determination that Shakespeare wrote his great works?

7. Tell the truth and not a lie: Can you do anything with the same degree of skill as Michelangelo used when he painted? Yes__ No__   Is there anything that you are working on doing that well?

8. Are you determined to work hard to be the best at what you do instead of trying to be what other kids want you to do?

I had heard all kinds of rumors about MIT. They used to say that even the janitors at MIT had master's degrees. At first I wasn't going, but then I couldn't run away from a challenge. I had to compete with the best. RONALD MCNAIR

1. Are you afraid of an academic challenge?

2. Who is Ronald McNair?

3. Does it scare you when a boy says that math in the 6th grade is hard?

4. Do you run away from challenges or do you attack them?

5. It takes years to learn how to be calm in the face of things that used to scare you. Do you feel that you are making progress in that area? Yes__ No__ If yes, name one academic challenge that used to scare you that you are now comfortable with.

Compose a quote and write it here:_____

_____

Student Application

Student's Name _____

Address _____

Phone _____ Birthday ____/____/____ Medical Problems? _____

Mother's Name _____ Phone _____

Address _____

Father's Name _____

Address _____

Phone _____ Student's age _____ Grade _____

School _____

Home Room Teacher _____

Briefly describe yourself _____

Hobbies _____

Favorite Sport _____ Are you good at it? Good__ average__ poor__

Best friend's name _____

Address _____

Comments: _____

_____

_____

_____

_____

Mentor Application

Name_____

Home address_____

Employer_____

Work address_____

Work phone_____Home phone_____

E-mail address_____

Social Security Number ____/____/____ (required for background check)

Your age_____ Marital status_____ Number of children_____

Race_____ Date of birth___/___/___

Have you ever been convicted of a felony? Yes__ No__

Preferred age of students: Elementary_____ Middle School_____ High School_____

Preferred day and time to mentor_____

How soon can you begin mentoring?_____

Do you commit to at least one academic year? Yes__ No__

Please list three character references with telephone numbers:

_____

_____

_____

How did you find out about the TALKS Mentoring Program?_____

Signature_____

Student's Contract

(To Be Completed And Given To The Mentor)

I_____

make this contract with my mentor,

_____

to participate in the program with good intentions.

I will read the chapters and participate in the weekly sessions.

I will genuinely and respectfully consider what my mentor shares with me but will also feel free to express my opinions.

I will not share other people's private information outside of our cell group.

I also understand that my mentor has a busy schedule just like mine and there may be times when it will be necessary to reschedule. I will be understanding when this happens.

I will view this interaction as an opportunity to gain wisdom which will benefit me for years to come.

How much better is wisdom than gold, and understanding than silver!
KING SOLOMON

_____
Student's Signature

_____
Mentor's Signature

_____
Witness

_____
Date

Mentor's Contract
(To Be Completed And Given To The Student)

I_____

make this contract with my student

_____

to participate in this program with good intentions.

I will read the chapters and participate in the weekly sessions.

I will genuinely and respectfully consider what my student shares with me but will also feel free to express my opinions.

I will not share other people's private information outside of our cell group.

I also understand that my student has a busy schedule just like mine and there may be times when it will be necessary to reschedule. I will be understanding when this happens.

I will view this interaction as an opportunity to share wisdom which will benefit my student for years to come.

How much better is wisdom than gold, and understanding than silver!
KING SOLOMON

_____
Student's Signature

_____
Mentor's Signature

_____
Witness

_____
Date

Certificate of Completion

This certifies that

_____

*has completed*_____*weeks of instruction with his mentor.*

All the chapters of the book and related assignments were
successfully completed.

Let it be resolved that your instructor has high expectations of you and
trusts that you will become the leader that you are destined to be.

We believe that if you apply the principles we have studied, you will be an
asset to any community in which you choose to live and we further believe
that those who interact with you will find you a fair and just person.

Inasmuch as wisdom contributes to a successful life, you are strongly
encouraged to maintain a close relationship with wise men who can guide
you as you face the challenges of life.

Remember what we have shared and put the wisdom that
you have learned into practice.

Sincerely

_____

Mentor

_____

Administrator

_____

Witness

Signed this_____day of_____

Notes:_____

Notes:_____

Notes:_____

Notes:_____

_____

_____

_____

_____

_____

_____

_____

_____

_____

_____

_____

_____

_____

_____

_____

_____

_____

_____

_____

_____

Notes:_____

_____

_____

_____

_____

_____

_____

_____

_____

_____

_____

_____

_____

_____

_____

_____

_____

_____

Notes:_____

Notes:_____
_____
_____
_____
_____
_____
_____
_____
_____
_____
_____
_____
_____
_____
_____
_____
_____
_____
_____